Only two seats left!

www.onlytwoseatsleft.com

A CIP catalogue of this book is available from the National Library of Australia.

ISBN: 978-0-646-51588-5

Published by The Great Gathering Company (Pty) Ltd
Front cover photo by Loungepark/Taxi/Getty Images
Designed and Typeset by Sharyn Raggett
Project managed by Messenger Publishing

messenger

www.messengerpublishing.com.au

Enjoy the ride!

THE INCREDIBLE Contiki STORY

Only two seats left!

JOHN ANDERSON

DEDICATION

To my wonderful wife Ali, our amazing children Susie, Peter, James and Sarah, and to those dedicated people who created a unique product and an iconic brand, which to date has had a profound effect on the lives of over two million young people.

– John Anderson

TABLE OF CONTENTS

BEFORE WE START

This is a story that has to be told.

Only Two Seats Left is a story about a group of young people who believed in an idea, believed in themselves and took on the world. Together they created a unique product and the iconic international brand name – 'Contiki'.

As the founder of Contiki, I want to take you on a journey through this incredible story. I hope you will be entertained, learn from our successes and failures but, above all, be inspired!

When I first arrived in London back in 1962 at the age of 23 I had no idea what lay ahead. Now, some 49 years later, I can look back on my life and reflect. It is only now I really understand and realise what was achieved.

My motivation for writing this book was to record the story for the benefit of those pioneering staff and passengers so they could know what the company went on to achieve, for those who have subsequently been involved in Contiki, both staff and passengers, and for those in the future. Above all I have written it for those who are already in business or are contemplating taking that first brave step into the unknown, and starting their own.

I have endeavoured to be as factually correct as possible. However, on occasions, I had to resort to a little poetic licence to get me through the odd situation or period. I began by wanting to acknowledge the key names of everyone involved but, since there turned out to be so many, I reluctantly decided only a few could be included. For the most part, those included are not acknowledged in reference to their relative 'importance', merely at junctions where the story required a name. I'm sure those not named will know who they are.

Finally, I would like to thank all those who have contributed to this book and the patience of Ali, my wife. It's been a long journey for me to complete this story but I believe all the effort will be worthwhile. Hopefully when you get to the last page, you will say to yourself, 'Wow! What a story, what an incredible story – I'm so inspired!'

Enjoy the ride …

1. 'MUMMY'S BOY'

I was born a Scorpio in Wellington, New Zealand on 18 November 1938. My father was a dentist, my mother was a housewife. So begins my story.

When I arrived my mother became completely besotted. All mothers do, perhaps, with their first-born, but mine transferred all her love to me. My father stayed just five short years before he left. He went on to marry his dental nurse, an English lady who had already been married twice and had two daughters, one from each marriage. I inherited two stepsisters.

My father left Wellington and set up a new dental practice in Newmarket, Auckland. Fortunately my parents maintained a good relationship and I was able to visit him and his new-found family a couple of times a year. When I was about 14, he sold his Auckland practice, moved to London and started up a new dental practice in Kensington High Street.

I wrote regularly but my father responded intermittently. Like many fathers he wasn't a good letter writer. However, I still have in my possession a couple of letters he did write which I treasure to this day. In one, he sent me a pencilled portrait a patient had drawn of him. It still sits on a shelf beside my desk where he watches over me every day.

My mother remarried a few years later. My new stepfather was a shirt salesman. Together they adopted a daughter, so I now had two stepsisters and a half sister. A few years later, greener pastures beckoned, and my stepfather left my mother. He married a woman from the next street. My mother didn't venture into another marriage after the second one failed.

Throughout my life I've deeply regretted not having my father with me during my childhood. Yes, I visited him during the school holidays, but it wasn't the same. My mother continued to heap all her love on me, making most of my decisions on my behalf. This carried on until I was a young adult. When I left school to start work, she laid out the clothes I was to wear the next day, even to the point of selecting my tie!

I never had a hands-on dad, and missed out on that special relationship a son can have with his father. It was always my mother on the sidelines of the rugby match, standing alongside all the other kids' dads. I also missed the important opportunity to learn from him about how to be a father. When I eventually had my own children I didn't have an example to draw on. Children need a father to grow with them to learn these things. When that time came for me, I made them up as I went along.

My letters to my father in England didn't boast of great marks, unless a prize for 'most improved boy in the class' qualifies! I attended Scots College in Wellington, a private boys school. At the age of 16, a burst appendix, perforated bowel and further complications landed me in hospital for six months. I missed a year of school, which didn't help my marks when I finally returned.

To obtain a leaving School Certificate we were examined in five subjects (English was compulsory). I chose geography, general science, maths and commercial practice. The total possible score was 400. The pass mark was 200. I scraped through with 206! My best subject was commercial practice – I loved it.

My academic achievements at school were always modest, to say the least. I was in the B class and always very conscious that the boys in the A class looked down on us. Looking back, I think there were benefits to being a B student because my classmates and I had to try that much harder. Throughout my business career I have met lots of extremely successful people, many of whom, like me, started life in the B and lower streams.

I didn't shine on the sporting front either. I'm sure I was considered a 'wet' by the other boys as I always had a note from 'mummy' excusing me from anything too demanding because I was a mild asthmatic. Anything more than the 75-yard dash and I'd end up in a wheezing heap on the ground! Cross-country runs were out and I never mastered the ability to jump a hurdle without getting tangled up in it. I was a hopeless swimmer, managing only widths at a time. I did, however, enjoy gymnastics and since I had the advantage of being very light for my age, I did a little boxing. I also had a turn at rugby and later, hockey.

I know now that to succeed in life you don't necessarily have to be a brain box or an outstanding sportsman at school. It's all about attitude, setting objectives, and believing you can achieve them. Throughout my personal and business life I have proved this time and time and time again. More on that later …

Outside school I led an active social life, centred on church and school dances. I was a cub and became a patrol leader in the Scouts. I belonged to the local tennis club and sailed with a mate, a 12.5 foot *Idle Along* (A1) centreboard yacht on Wellington Harbour. I was a very dedicated and active member of the local Presbyterian church passing through bible class, youth fellowship and, on two occasions, giving the sermon to the Sunday morning congregation during the minister's absence.

My wholesome and safe image definitely worked in my favour with the local girls' mothers when the debutante balls rolled around at the end of the school year! I attended several as a 'Deb's Delight' partner, occasions where the girls drank Pimms and the boys drank beer. The social groups I moved in were quite innocent and conservative with little alcohol and not even a whiff or sniff of drugs.

And then there was my love of growing plants. I planned to become a horticulturist when I left school. I had my own glasshouse in the backyard where I grew vegetable and flower plant seedlings which I sold to the local stores to help bolster my pocket money. This became an extremely lucrative business. I also had a flock of hens in the backyard and sold the eggs to the neighbours. The first signs of a budding entrepreneur perhaps?

My first job was with the City Council Parks and Reserves department. I worked in their plant nursery and planned to go to Massey College to obtain my horticultural degree. Then came winter and after several months working outside in the freezing temperatures I started to rethink pursuing this avenue as a career.

Uncle Arthur, my godfather, who was a successful businessman operating a wholesale hardware business, stepped in and suggested I consider a career in commerce. 'Learn the basics of business,' he said. 'Then in later years you can use the knowledge to your own advantage.' I really admired Uncle Arthur and I still value his wisdom to this day.

A few months later, after taking Uncle Arthur's advice, I had changed my career path, left my council job and was working as an office junior, darting around collecting and posting mail, doing the banking and replenishing each of the director's cigarette boxes every morning in the head office of the Wellington-based cigarette manufacturer WD & HO Wills.

A short while later, I was selected as a junior management trainee. Over the next couple of years, after spending time in departments such as sales and marketing, I took a role in accounts as the head office cashier. This was soon followed by a position that exposed me to the manufacturing side of the business. I loved it all and I learnt fast.

During lunch breaks, I'd stroll down to Wellington Harbour. Sometimes, a passenger liner would be departing, packed full of excited young people heading to the United Kingdom for a great overseas adventure. This was known in New Zealand as the 'overseas experience', or the OE. I started to meet the odd person who'd already been there and back, and I'd listen to their amazing tales. I began to realise there was a whole new world out there.

But sailing off was still pie-in-the-sky for me because I was still studying. When I joined Wills I had also enrolled, part-time, at the local technical college to obtain a Diploma of Commerce. I passed the required exams in just two years – a year ahead of schedule. An accounting degree at Victoria University was to follow. I used to sit in the back row with my friend, Malcolm Brown, a trainee stockbroker, both of us trying to understand what was being taught at the front. It was all too hard, although we did sit some exams at the end of the first year. To pass 'Accounting 1' two papers were required, with an average pass mark of 50 out of 100. I scored 53 in one paper and 47 in the other. No unnecessary effort had been expended there. I never completed the course, but what I learnt would help me down the line.

Around this time, Malcolm introduced me to another world – the local sharemarket. I found it riveting; studying and learning about the various companies, many of them household names. With my savings I started to make a few small investments. It was exciting making the decision to take a calculated risk to invest in a company and watch its progress. I checked the share prices virtually every day. It gave me such a buzz.

However, the images of the passenger liners continued to tug at me and I started to think seriously about going overseas to London. Like many young people, I was looking for adventure and excitement, yes, but there were also deeper reasons.

I wanted to see my father again and I wanted freedom from my smothering mother. I was still living at home as was the norm in those days. One didn't move out until you married. My mother prepared all my meals and watched over every mouthful I took. (To this day I still have an aversion to anyone watching me eat!) She would come to the church dances and secretly watch my activities through a side window.

Once again, Uncle Arthur prodded me in the right direction. He thought my reasons for going overseas were great, the time was right and he encouraged me to do so. He also gave me some advice that I've never forgotten. It went something like this:

'The time you've spent at Wills has been of enormous benefit to you because through that experience you've decided you want to make commerce your career. But I've watched you over the years and have to tell you I don't think you're going to make it to the top of a large established company. You're too much of an individual and will find it hard to fit into the culture of a big organisation.'

Uncle Arthur went on. 'Of course, you could still work for a big corporate, have job security and, provided you are conscientious, slowly climb the ladder of promotion. The ladder is like a pyramid. You start at the bottom with everyone else and over time you climb towards the top. The object of an ambitious person is to make it to the top. People drop off throughout the climb as the number of positions available reduces. Eventually only one can make it, and I don't think you will be that one. All those years of effort would have been lost.'

And finally. 'With your individual flair, attitude, special attributes and the freedom to choose your own course,' said Uncle Arthur, 'I recommend, when the time is right, that you start your own business, just as I did.'

This was a pivotal moment.

The decision was made. My time at Wills had taught me so much about how a business is run and studying at tech and uni had been equally beneficial. But I was getting restless and wanted to go overseas. As soon as I had sufficient funds I decided to take off on my big OE!

I set about looking for ways to make more money as quickly as I could. I immediately boosted my plant production and sold them to stores in neighbouring suburbs as well. I also increased the hen population to produce more eggs and started a side business selling small bags of chicken poo to the keen gardeners in the area. I took on part-time evening work at the post office, sorting mail. I collected empty bottles and used newspapers from the houses in my suburb, selling them for cash. Finally, I turned to my hobby share portfolio. Virtually all my savings were invested in publicly listed companies. Over the years I'd had a few winners and a few losers, but loved following the companies I had a financial interest in. Now, I wanted to make some real money out of it.

One day, in between raking chicken poo and sorting mail, I received a call from Malcolm, my stockbroking friend. He reckoned he had a sure-fire winner that was well worth a serious punt. He reckoned a listed company which was due to announce its year end results in a week or two could be quite spectacular, even better than the market was anticipating, and if so the share price could rise dramatically.

'Would I put you wrong?' he asked. He gave me some researched information about the company, which I studied and it all seemed to stack up. The downsides seemed to be very limited. If it came off I could be off overseas far sooner than currently planned. Yes, I thought, it's worth the risk.

I sold everything that could be legitimately sold including my bicycle and radiogram. I sold most of my other shares and plunged almost everything into this one company.

Bingo! Within a month it all came together like a dream. The company made a number of very positive announcements, and the share price rocketed skywards, as did the value of my share portfolio. My punt had paid off!

I sold the shares and now had enough cash to plan my imminent departure to Europe. I told my mother I was planning to go for a year but in reality I had no idea how long it would be. Little did I know that this was just the beginning of the most incredible journey!

Over the years, I was to take many similar risks. I was to learn that to succeed in life, both personally and in business, you must be prepared to take risks, in other words 'give things a go'. Unless you try something you'll never know the outcome. Welcome to my story.

2. THE BIG WIDE WORLD

It's hard to imagine now, but in the mid 1950s and 1960s many young Australians and New Zealanders called the United Kingdom 'home'. During this period many of them started to leave their shores and head over to England, Scotland, Ireland and Wales. Wherever their ultimate destination was, their first real stop was invariably the same: London.

Their reasons for going were as numerous as the types travelling. Some were going to reunite with relations, some were escaping a difficult home situation, some wanted to find freedom and independence, and some simply wanted a big adventure. Few of them really knew what lay ahead.

The majority travelled to the United Kingdom by sea on a passenger liner. These typically carried between 700 and 1500 passengers. They took up to five weeks to make the journey, some longer, depending on how many times the ships broke down. Most passenger liners went through the Suez Canal in Egypt and a few went through the Panama Canal (which joins the Caribbean Sea and the Pacific Ocean). All would anchor for a day or so at around four or five ports along the way. On discovering this, I decided four or five stops weren't enough for me. I wanted to see more on the way over.

The alternative was to go by air. In those days, the majority of the world's established airlines belonged to the International Airlines

Transport Association (IATA). IATA airlines worked in cooperation with each other. For example, you could buy an air ticket from Wellington to London for a set amount from an IATA carrier and subsequently travel on any of the other member's routes if it suited. Furthermore, as long as you were always travelling in a forward direction you could stopover in as many cities on the route as you liked for no extra cost. Surprisingly the airfare was only marginally more expensive than the boat fare. The enormous choice of stopovers on offer finally clinched it for me. Flying had to be the way to go.

However, I soon discovered a major downside. Flying would turn out to be an extremely expensive way to travel. I realised that every time I stopped over in a city, it would cost me an arm and a leg. I'd have to accommodate, feed and water myself and also find a way to see over, whichever new and strange city I'd landed in. I simply didn't have this kind of money, even with my stock market windfall.

I figured I could probably manage to buy the air ticket and have enough spending money to stop a maximum of six or seven times. I was going around in circles because that would mean I'd not see much more than those travelling by boat. What's more, all the accommodation, food, and even entertainment was covered in the boat fare. I considered asking my father for a loan but couldn't bring myself to write the letter. I think I probably wanted to show him I could do things alone, without his help.

Having taken geography at school, I knew where most of the countries on my chosen route through the east were situated. I had pinned a map on my bedroom wall and the more I studied it and saw all the exotic place names between New Zealand and the United Kingdom, the more I wanted to see them. The names of countries like the Philippines, India and Egypt held such a power over me. I had never met anyone from any of these places, let alone imagined I'd go there. I had lived a fairly sheltered life and there was no TV, let alone internet to bring images of foreign places on demand. (Limited black and white TV arrived in Auckland in 1960 and the South Island two years later.)

The more I looked at the map, the more determined I became to experience places and cultures that weren't on the standard tourist route. But how? My money dilemma felt like a huge immovable force.

Then one day I had an idea. At the time I was an active member of the Junior Chamber of Commerce. Members were known as 'Jaycees'. It was an international organisation with chapters all around the world. Its activities were not dissimilar to the Chamber of Commerce but membership was restricted to those aged between 18 and 40 years old. Members represented a wide cross-section of the community although the majority were involved in commerce.

I obtained the details of the main city Chambers in Australia, Philippines, Indonesia, Hong Kong, Singapore, Thailand, India, Nepal, Pakistan, Iran, Iraq, Jordan, Israel, Egypt, Turkey, Greece and some European countries. I wrote a letter to the president of each one (as long as they had an airport serving their city) and told them I was heading to London and hoped to visit their fine city sometime in February/March 1962. I told them a little about myself and said I'd love to meet them and some of their fellow members. I added that I could only stay a short time as I had extremely limited funds. I posted the letters.

Not long after, I received a telephone call at my mother's place. It was the president of the Sydney Junior Chamber of Commerce.

'I would be delighted to meet you, John,' he said. I barely knew what to say in response. 'Of course, you will be my guest for however long you wish to stay,' he continued.

I was over the moon. During the next few months I received responses to virtually all the letters I had sent with requests of a similar nature. I had around a 90 per cent hit rate! I assumed most of them had not met a New Zealander and supposed I was a novelty and they were just as curious about me as I was about them. Most said they'd be honoured to have me as their guest, insisting I stay as long as I wanted, and offered to meet and show me around their cities. I had learnt that it costs nothing to ask a favour. If you don't ask you'll never know the outcome.

With great excitement I finalised my itinerary from Wellington to London with most of the stopovers planned in the cities I knew I could stay in for free, thanks to the generosity of my fellow Jaycees. I handed in my resignation at the cigarette manufacturer and booked my airline ticket with New Zealand's Tasman Empire Airway Limited (TEAL). I was ready to start my big OE. And what an adventure it would turn out to be!

Mum and a few friends came to see me off as I boarded the Lockheed Electra turboprop-bound flight to Sydney. I had not even been to the South Island of New Zealand, let alone overseas. On departure my eyes watered as I waved goodbye. On the way to Australia I sat alone and contemplated my situation. There was a feeling of enormous elation at what I had done. I was now very much on my own. I had a mixture of emotions from being anxious, nervous, even a little terrified, to an almost overwhelming degree of excitement, but at the same time I felt pensive at what lay ahead of me. The only truly comforting thought I had was that on arrival in London, my father would be waiting for me.

Having crossed the Tasman Sea, I looked out the window to see the spectacular Sydney Harbour with its iconic bridge. I felt exhilarated but with a tingle of apprehension. I had arrived at my first stop. When I disembarked in Sydney, in all the excitement I left my first packet of duty-free cigarettes behind. I was just 23, and a very young and naïve one at that.

I was duly met by my host, accommodated (at his cost) in an upmarket hotel and over the next couple of days he entertained and showed me his city, which to this day is still one of my favourites, with its vibrancy and magnificent harbour. And so the journey progressed.

In Manila, I stumbled upon my first red light district. In Bangkok I saw my first sex show. I've never forgotten, amongst other acts, a girl smoking a cigarette out of her vagina. You can imagine my shock. I was still a virgin at 23!

In a similar vein, when I arrived at my hotel in Hong Kong, The Shamrock on Nathan's Road, I checked into my room to discover a girl already there, in my bed. I flew back to the lift to speak with the Amah on my floor (each floor had a lady sitting by the lift responsible for the guests on that level).

'That's not my room!' I spluttered, only to be assured with a knowing grin that indeed it was. It slowly dawned on me that the girl's presence had been arranged by my host to keep me company during the night. I promptly had her removed. I was growing up fast.

My trip to London took just under seven weeks. I stopped in Sydney, Melbourne, Manila, Hong Kong, Bangkok, Calcutta, Kathmandu, New Delhi, Agra, Karachi, Tehran, Beirut, Baghdad, Jerusalem, Cairo, Athens and Istanbul – 17 stopovers!

My hosts blew me away with their genuine friendship and generosity in ensuring my stay in their city was enjoyable and memorable. My hosts, often in a chauffeur-driven limousine, met me on arrival at each destination. In most cities I was accommodated in comfortable hotels at their expense and occasionally, as a guest in their own home. I was wined, dined and entertained. A couple of times my hosts invited groups of young people to cocktails or dinner to meet me. I recall it was quite overwhelming, but I loved every minute of it.

Every time I arrived in a new city I'd dutifully traipse down to the local post office to send off a telegram to my mother. I'd fill in a form with a message like, 'Arrived Jerusalem. Love John.' Many times during the journey I felt very alone in a big new world that was so different to my own country. Often I would lie in bed at night in a strange city feeling quite homesick. Fortunately, I was rarely scared as I was too naïve to realise that the world was full of people who want to take advantage of you or harm you. This naïvety was a blessing in disguise as it made me more adventurous and ignorantly fearless.

Often I would walk around areas of a city during the day and night oblivious to the dangers that were probably lurking around me. I wanted to see how people lived in the back street slums and to see the streets where the erotic night life was in full swing. On return to my hotel, staff would often comment in amazement that I had been so brave to venture into such areas.

Along the way I met amazing people, often teaming up with one or two fellow travellers for parts of the journey. I travelled through Lebanon, Jordan and Egypt with two German Canadians. They were seasoned travellers whom I learnt so much from, but they also led me astray to an unbelievable degree – I was growing up fast, very fast.

These first impressions of that trip have remained as vivid memories ever since. Hailing from sparsely populated New Zealand, the sheer volume of people in the cities simply astounded me, as did the enormous gap between rich and poor, especially in countries like Pakistan and in India where there were two million people living on the streets in Calcutta (almost the total population of New Zealand at the time). You could hardly walk down the footpaths late at night without stepping on someone asleep. I'll never forget the terribly deformed children being used by their parents to beg. The food was also an incredible change for me. I wasn't fussy and felt constantly challenged to try exotic new titbits.

I was amazed by the dominating importance of religion in people's lives. With so many different faiths such as Buddhism, Sikhism, Hinduism, Jainism and Islam to mention a few, with the constant praying, the myriad of temples, robed monks, the rituals and ceremonies and even the sacred cows. I was quite religious myself at the time and it had a deep impact on me. Christianity was my religion, yet all these other people had their own different beliefs. I was left a little confused, as I still am to this day.

I saw the Taj Mahal by moonlight in Agra, gawked at the floating markets in Bangkok, visited Kathmandu where just over ten years before, fellow New Zealander Sir Edmund Hillary had set out to climb and conquer Mount Everest, climbed the pyramids and travelled down to Luxor to see the Valley of the Kings south of Cairo. I visited old Jerusalem, saw the Dome on the Rock, Bethlehem and the Dead Sea. I was impressed by the sheer beauty of Beirut, then the Paris of the East. I skied through the Cedars of Lebanon in the morning and swam at the beach under the hot Mediterranean sun on the same afternoon. So many sights, so many experiences, so many memories.

Above all I lapped up the opportunity to meet such a diverse array of people and learn about their traditions, beliefs and views of the world. I loved every moment of that journey. I developed a very inquisitive mind and constantly asked questions. People like to talk about themselves and their lives and tell you their thoughts and opinions. I learnt never to be afraid to ask questions, no matter how stupid they may seem at the time, and to be a good listener. By doing this I learnt so much – still do.

On arrival in Istanbul, where the Bosphorus separates Asia from Europe I stood in awe at the sight of the Blue Mosque (both inside and out), and the covered Grand Bazaar with its 4000 shops, however, my journey was about to come to a sudden end. With my funds running very low I had no option but to fly straight to London. In those seven incredible weeks I'd really grown up. I had been well and truly bitten by the travel bug and had developed an intense love for seeing the world, which was to become my life for the next 48 years.

On arrival at London's Heathrow Airport, there was my father waiting for me. It was an extremely emotional moment. He was beaming and with tears streaming down our cheeks, he put his arm around my shoulder, then we hugged and held each other. After nine years, we were again reunited.

Over the next few days we got to know each other again as he showed me around London. I was bowled over by the size and history of the city. Piccadilly Circus, The Strand, Mayfair, Waterloo Station. I was spellbound by the familiar names and places that I knew only from the Monopoly board game I had played at home.

My father's dental practice had become well established. Soon after his arrival in London he had bought a house in Putney Hill – originally the home of the English poet Algernon Charles Swinburne. My father and his family had lived there for a number of years, but just prior to my arrival, they had all moved to Jersey in the Channel Islands. He had also taken on a South African dentist as a partner in the London practice and initially commuted weekly to London. During this period, for the fourth time, he started another practice from scratch in Jersey. Besides being an outstanding dental surgeon, he was clearly an entrepreneur with business flair because each one of the practices he started became extremely successful. His achievements impressed and inspired me.

Many wealthy people lived in the Channel Islands. The top personal tax rate in the United Kingdom was an incredulous 90 per cent in the 1960s, while in the Channel Islands it was just 20 per cent, which I suspect led to my father's relocation. I remember him telling me he had 27 millionaires on his books. (And in the 1960s, millionaires weren't quite so common!) He also had a number of French peasants as patients who he only charged a nominal amount or what they could afford. He balanced this with charging his wealthier patients with the full price, plus a little bit more! On reflection that's where I learned the philosophy of charging what the market will bear – which I was to use time and time again.

But I'll try not to get ahead of myself. When I arrived in London, I only had around £100 to my name!

3. ONLY TWO SEATS LEFT!

In 1962, unprecedented political, cultural, technological and astronomical developments were forming worldwide. The United States launched Ranger 3 to study the moon and the Cuban Missile Crisis threatened the world with nuclear war. Meanwhile, the *Sunday Times* in the United Kingdom became the first paper to publish a colour supplement and the First Lady Jacqueline Kennedy took television viewers on a tour of the White House. The Rolling Stones made their debut at London's Marquee Club, Ringo Starr joined the Beatles and the first James Bond film, *Dr No*, premiered in UK movie theatres. The United Nations General Assembly passed a resolution condemning South Africa's racist apartheid policies and the US military involvement in the Vietnam War was escalating.

As one of the global hubs for much of this cultural and political activity, London in 1962 was an incredibly alive and exciting place to be. I had, of course, grown up in Wellington, a village town by comparison.

A week after my arrival my father returned to Jersey. I booked a room in a cheap bed and breakfast at the Austin Hotel in Lexham Gardens, which was close to the British Museum and Earls Court. It cost 12 shillings and six pence a night. It was a tiny room with paper-thin walls through which I could hear couples enjoying each other's company throughout the night. The hotel manager was looking for staff to assist in the basement breakfast room, so within a few days I negotiated a deal with him to rise at 5.30 am each morning to set up the tables and serve breakfast in return for a free room. It seemed like a pretty good deal to me.

My seven-week epic journey from Wellington had depleted my funds greatly. So I figured I'd work in London while I saved to see Europe. I was about to start looking for a job and a flat when I saw an advertisement offering a cheap weekend excursion to Paris. I booked the trip, which was departing the following day.

When I boarded the coach it was packed with other newly arrived tourists just like me, the majority of whom were around my age. We crossed the English Channel and disembarked at the port of Calais in France. I had arrived on the continent of Europe. When I saw Paris for the first time, dressed in its night-lights – it was love at first sight!

Like most tourists, we drove down the Champs Elysées from the Arc de Triomphe, passing The Louvre, crossed the Seine river to the Eiffel Tower, along the left bank to see Notre Dame Cathedral, through Pigalle, up to Montmartre and back to our hotel.

I didn't tire of the sights for a second. My eyes were hanging out like organ stops! I was impressed by the wide boulevards, the architecture, the grand monuments and the street side cafés. The French language sounded so beautiful and the immaculately coiffured and well-dressed French women appeared so feminine. They appealed to me greatly!

On Saturday night we went to the famous Folies Bergère, drinking champagne as we watched the long-legged women dance the Can Can. When we left later that night, briefly visiting a few other nightclubs, the city was ablaze with lights. After some of the cities I had just passed through on my way to the United Kingdom – Paris was a knock-out. This weekend trip turned out to be the start of the most amazing love affair – between me and Europe!

I returned to the Austin Hotel late on Sunday night, exhausted but exhilarated. My mind was in a whirl as I set the breakfast tables the next morning. Images of Paris kept popping into my head. I simply couldn't wait to return to France and see more of Europe. But I had a major problem: I now had only £25 pounds left to my name.

*

In the early 1960s, Earls Court in London was synonymous with the Australian, South African and New Zealand expat crowd. The region was literally swarming with 'colonials', as we were called. The majority of newcomers to London joined the Overseas Visitors Club (OVC) in Earls Court Road. Members could stay overnight in the club's accommodation, have their mail from home sent there for collection and a travel desk, employment and accommodation bureau provided further assistance.

The social hub was in the OVC basement. The bar, dance area and small restaurant were bursting with existing members and new arrivals every night of the week. Entertainment varied from pianists to small bands, but there was always something happening. Not knowing anyone in London, I was there most nights. I met lots of people who had just returned from touring Europe and their animated tales further fuelled my desire to go. In the mornings I'd set tables and help serve breakfast – all the while plotting my escape. My obstacle remained purely one of funds.

I bought a map of Europe and studied all the countries and place names. An idea began to take shape. The majority of OVC members were always talking about how they were going to see Europe. The most common way was three or four people chipping in to buy a second hand VW Kombi or Bedford van. Some hired or bought clapped-out old cars or even retired black London taxis. They would tour Europe staying at camp grounds and share costs. There were also a few outfits arranging groups to travel together and you could also buy a Eurail pass to travel independently by train. But my lack of money meant I couldn't even contemplate any of these options.

My idea, however, was gathering momentum. I decided to make it a reality. One night I jumped out of bed, turned on the light, grabbed my map of Europe and wrote down an itinerary of all the places I wanted to see. I excitedly worked through the night, my imagination running riot with all the exotic place names. Over the next few hours I plotted a route, using a ruler to calculate the mileage between towns and countries. My itinerary departed from London to Paris through France to Spain, along the French Riviera down through Italy and over to Greece. Up to Turkey, through Yugoslavia, Austria, Switzerland, Germany and around the Scandinavian countries of Denmark, Sweden and Norway. Then it looped back down again to Holland and Belgium and back across the English Channel to London. I allowed an extra few days in each of the towns and cities I thought I'd perhaps like to stay a little longer. The completed itinerary would take a staggering 12 weeks! I eventually drifted off to sleep. When I woke that morning I knew how I was going to see Europe. What's more, I was going to see it for free!

As I reflected on the weekend spent in Paris, I realised one of the things that I'd enjoyed most was sharing the experience with a group of other young people. My trip from Wellington to London had been amazing, but apart from meeting my fellow Jaycees (different ones every few days), I'd often felt very alone. But my time travelling with my new-found Canadian friends in the Middle East and the people on the Paris excursion had been a real highlight.

If I could gather a small group of other people around my age, we could camp to save on accommodation costs, cook our own meals to save on restaurants and see the Continent together quite cheaply. If our group was larger than the average three or four, our overall costs would be cheaper per person. For my initiative in putting it all together I decided I shouldn't pay. Thus my free European trip.

I had total belief in myself that I could do it. After all I had negotiated my way through the East, with all the different languages, currencies and cultures, so surely Europe couldn't be any harder? But where to start?

I hit the London streets to research for a suitable vehicle. Eventually I found myself looking at a red Commer van parked out the back of the Rootes Group vehicle showroom in Earls Court, awaiting delivery to a customer. It had been fitted with 12 bench-type leather seats and, as I jumped into the driver's seat, I could clearly imagine my 11 passengers sitting behind me as I drove around Europe. It just felt right.

The salesman informed me a new vehicle fitted with 12 seats would cost a whopping £480 pounds. Responding to my shocked reaction he said I could pay an initial deposit of £100 and on collection of the vehicle a further £140, bringing it to a total down payment of 50 per cent. The balance could then be paid in monthly instalments over the next 12 months. That seemed like a good option.

But where could I put all the passengers' luggage and the camping and cooking equipment? The only places available were under the seats and in the gap between the last row and the back door. But still, this would not be nearly enough room for the mountain of gear we would need to carry. Pulling a trailer was not an option I fancied. Frowning at the bus, the solution slowly came to me. Could a full-length roof rack be made to fit?

'I know a company that makes roof racks,' the salesman immediately volunteered. I marched over there straight away and they assured me they could make one to suit my requirements. Once the measurements were agreed upon, I then found a canvas manufacturer who could make a cover for the rack.

I roared around sourcing and obtaining costs of suitable tents, airbeds and started a list of cooking equipment and other essential items. I'd had very little camping experience, apart from my scout days and bible class camps, but I stuck at it. The list seemed never-ending.

I went to the Royal Automobile Club to join up. They helped me fine-tune the itinerary and potential costs such as ferry fares, petrol, camping fees, local taxes, and so on. A third party vehicle insurance (green card) was compulsory to travel through Europe. I also discovered I needed a vehicle 'carnet' (which was stamped on entering and exiting countries to ensure you didn't sell the vehicle in Europe). Finally, I bought a Europa book of road maps and a Fodor's guide to Europe. This book was to become known as 'the bible'!

I spent a considerable amount of time, helped by a girl who I was friendly with at the time, attempting to work out what it might cost to feed a group of 12 people three meals a day during the tour. The amount of food we figured the group would be consuming was mind-boggling. We visited local grocery stores and butchers countless times and roughly costed some typical menus. We also obtained input from folk who had already toured Europe. We assumed the food costs around the route would, on average, to be similar to England.

Gathering all this information took less than a week. I wrote out a detailed budget, listing all the known costs and then added 15 per cent to cover unexpected costs. I totalled everything and to get the cost per head I divided by 12. Smiling, I re-divided by 11. I had my tour!

Now I had to find 11 people to join me.

The huge noticeboard at the OVC sprang to mind. It was in the basement and ran the length of an entire wall, advertising anything and everything. People searching for lost friends, others to share a flat, looking for a job, selling unwanted gear or to fill the last seat in a six-seater Kombi van bound for Europe.

I sat down to think. I knew this notice was important, but needed to be worded simply. After a number of false starts I came up with the one that I instinctively knew could work. The notice read as follows:

SMALL GROUP OF YOUNG AUSTRALIANS AND
NEW ZEALANDERS TOURING EUROPE (CAMPING)
12 WEEKS, 15 COUNTRIES, TOUR COST £100,
FOOD KITTY 25/- A WEEK EXTRA,
DEPARTING 29 APRIL –
'ONLY TWO SEATS LEFT!'
PHONE JOHN AT FRO2418

The manager at the Austin Hotel agreed I could use the hotel's telephone number and said he'd be happy to take messages for me. First I put the notice up in New Zealand House in Haymarket, just off Piccadilly Circus. The ground floor reception and mezzanine area was permanently buzzing with visiting New Zealanders reading newspapers from home, collecting mail, and mingling. With the receptionist's permission I pinned my sign on the noticeboard. I then went on my way to Australia House on The Strand where I did the same.

That evening I went to the OVC, heading straight for the noticeboard. Showing an imagined degree of authority, I moved a few of the other notices around so that I could place my notice in a prime, eye-level position. As I was admiring it, an attractive young Australian girl tapped me on the shoulder.

'Are you John?' she asked.

'I am,' I replied, a little hesitantly.

'I've just read your notice and I'm interested in talking to you about the trip,' she said.

Next to the noticeboard was the club bar. I invited her to join me for a drink, which she gladly accepted. We chatted about ourselves and talked about our dreams of a European trip. I then showed her a copy of my typed-up itinerary. It detailed where we would be travelling and camping each night. I talked about the amazing places we'd see and the activities I had planned. I told her I'd been to Europe before (well, I figured I *had* been to Paris, Athens and Istanbul). I was also thinking that 'This could be my first customer!' I glossed over who the other passengers were, just saying they were young Australians and New Zealanders just like her. 'I don't know any of them very well yet,' I hedged, and to avoid the topic rearing its head again, I bought her another drink. I could see that she was dead keen to join the trip.

From previous experience, I knew that the harder it is to get something you really want, the more you want it. So I told her a little white lie.

'If you want to join the trip you'll have to make up your mind very quickly,' I said. 'There are a few others who've already talked to me about the last two seats, however, I'm prepared to hold one for you until lunchtime tomorrow, if you like.'

'Yes please', she responded. 'I'll call Mum and Dad in Australia tonight and talk it over with them to see what they think.'

I added, 'If you decide to book the trip you'll have to pay me cash,' I replied, (because I sure didn't have any). We parted company and planned to meet the next day at the OVC for lunch.

*

When she arrived the next day she looked happy and my heart jumped.

'I rang home last night and Mum and Dad think it's a good idea to go with someone who has been to Europe before and in the safety of a group. I'd love to come if you'll have me!' she said.

'You'll fit in perfectly with the others,' I told her somewhat cheekily.

It was excruciatingly hard, but I didn't rush her. We talked things through to confirm she'd made the right decision. She counted out 115 crisp pound notes, which was the total cost including the food kitty. I gave her a handwritten receipt acknowledging her payment, adding my hotel address and that of my father's London surgery for added credibility and reassurance. I had booked my very first customer!

That afternoon I returned to the Rootes showroom and paid a deposit of £100 on a brand-new red Commer van. I asked them to fit it out with four rows of three seats each for an extra £80. It was agreed I would pay the balance up to 50 per cent of the total when I collected the vehicle in a week or so and the remainder in instalments over a year. The same day I ordered the roof rack and cover.

Over the next ten days I interviewed those responding to my notices. Every night I went down to the OVC bar and socialised, meeting people, the majority were girls, many of whom had just arrived in London. Most were looking for a way to see Europe. As each new person booked it became easier to convince others to do the same. I even had a group of three nurses and a couple who were close friends book. One passenger was so excited she convinced another complete stranger to join her on the trip. I soon had 11 fully paid-up passengers – my bus was full! However, there were still another two very attractive girls who wanted to book on the tour, but there were now no seats left.

I didn't want to refuse them as they were so keen to join and I didn't want to let them down. 'There's still a possibility,' I told them. 'Two passengers haven't yet paid in full so I'll waitlist you.'

The budding businessman in me had responded, intuitively. I wanted to stop them making alternative arrangements until I worked out what to do. Lying in bed that night I decided that when I returned from the trip, never doubting for a moment that I wouldn't, I'd take the bus around again on a second trip.

The next morning I put down a plan. My first tour was due to return to London on 21 July. I'd allow three days to get the vehicle serviced and for me to get my breath back, making 25 July seem like a suitable date to schedule the start of the second tour.

I hot-footed it back to the OVC, New Zealand House and Australia House, took down the original notices and pinned new ones up for round two. I changed two things: the departure date and the tour price, which I increased to £115, as I felt the strong demand could justify it. I kept the food kitty at the same making a total cost £130. I had just implemented what I had learned from my father which was to 'charge what the market will bear', a theory I used from that day on.

I met with the two 'waitlisted' girls.

'I'm terribly sorry, but the other two paid up,' I said.

The girls were extremely disappointed as they had set their hearts on joining the tour, particularly as they had met a couple of others who had been lucky enough to book a seat. 'Could you get a bigger bus to squeeze us on?' they asked.

It was time to tell them the good news. 'On return from the first tour I've decided I'll take the bus around again,' I said. 'If you want a place you can pay me half the original tour fare as a deposit. We'll leave in three months.'

They agreed!

'I've put up a new notice, but if you could convince some others to see Europe with us too, that would be great!'

In just ten days I had filled the second trip. Most passengers paid half the new tour fare as a deposit, with the promise to pay the remainder in three months; two even paid me the full amount. I had both my tours full – I was ecstatic. From just £25 in my pocket and no way of seeing Europe, I'd convinced 22 people to pay me to see Europe not once, but twice!

While I'd been selling the tour seats I had constantly been researching everything I possibly could about running the first tour. My biggest source was sitting down and talking with others that had already travelled around Europe. I fired non-stop questions at them to find out what pitfalls they had encountered and tips that would assist me with the running of my tour. I visited the various tourist offices, constantly gathering information to help me plan the trip. It was a hectic period, hardly ever stopping for a breath as I now had a commitment to the passengers who had put their faith and trust in me. I now had to deliver the promise.

*

I now had the funds to buy the minibus outright, so I did. I started to buy the gear required to take 12 people on a 12 week camping tour of Europe. Tents, airbeds, mallets, gas burners for cooking, pots, pans, plates, cutlery, folding tables, tea towels, cleaning materials, a fire extinguisher, first aid kit, tools, buckets and of course, bottle and tin openers. The list seemed endless.

I arranged a meeting with the first group to talk through our forthcoming adventure. There were 10 girls, just one other guy and me. There were eight Australians and four New Zealanders. We all got along brilliantly as everyone was committed to making our trip a success. I knew the girls were disappointed there were only two males but it reflected the ratio of males to females arriving in London at that time. Men were tied to their careers in those days and it was difficult for them to get the time off; it was a huge time commitment that many men couldn't spare. For a start, it took nine to ten weeks to make the trip to London and back by boat.

I delegated responsibilities to each of the passengers to help with the preparation. After all it was their trip; I was just the guy who put the idea together. The mountain of gear grew and grew. I began to seriously fret over how we could carry it all.

Over the next ten days I coordinated all the paperwork, such as the customs carnet, green card insurance for the vehicle, Italian petrol coupons, traveller's cheques, cross channel ferry tickets and so forth. I made sure we had all our required visas in order, provided copies of the itinerary, the addresses of Thomas Cook travel agency offices around Europe for personal mail to be sent and a list of things they needed to pack.

On one of the last days, we all traipsed out to Hyde Park to practise putting the tents up. It didn't take long for officialdom to appear and pounce and we were told if we were thinking of pitching camp for the night, we had better think again. With my charming ladies at my side, all was explained and the officious park caretakers changed their attitude and proceeded to assist us with erecting the tents.

Several of the girls were given some of the food kitty money to buy the basic staples such as sugar, salt, pepper, tea and coffee and food supplies for the first night's dinner. A mountain of food arrived, increasing my anxiety about space. We all worked until well after midnight before the day of departure. Friday, 29 April 1962 had dawned.

One by one my passengers arrived at the starting point, around the corner of Notting Hill Gate tube station. By 7 am all had arrived, looking a little tentative, nervous but very excited. My horror increased as the pile of luggage got bigger and bigger. All my fellow travellers had enormous suitcases plus sleeping bags and day bags. I'd completely miscalculated just how much gear and luggage there would be.

I clambered onto the roof rack where I had already packed the tents, airbeds, cooking gear and tables. There was no way there was enough room for all their gear. There seemed to be enough to fill the entire interior of the vehicle as well. There would be no room for the passengers. It was a nightmare.

I emptied the roof rack, placed two-thirds of the suitcases flat, then another whole layer of suitcases and gear as a second layer. The tarpaulin that was to cover everything was now too small, but there was nothing to be done about it. There were still sleeping bags, day bags and all the food without a home. We rolled up our sleeves and stuffed gear under the seats and behind the back seat. They laughed; I could have cried. So much for my meticulous planning!

Eventually, with time slipping away to catch the cross channel ferry, everyone climbed onboard. I proceeded to pile the remaining bits and pieces on my passengers' laps, on the floor and around their feet. I slammed the door shut and we were off. We made it to Dover to catch the ferry to Calais, France, with just 20 minutes to spare. Dad's Army was about to take on the Continent!

4. THE BLIND LEADING THE BLIND

It was late in the evening and I was standing outside the Casino Palais Méditerranée situated on the Promenade des Anglais on the Nice foreshore of the French Riviera. I was looking up at the impressive white marble steps that led into the building and steeling myself to enter. I took a deep breath, marched in, presented my passport at the registration desk and headed straight for the roulette table. I took a wad of French francs – my passengers' money – from my right-hand pocket and placed it on the table in exchange for chips.

'Faites vos jeux,' said the croupier. 'Place your bets.'

But how did it all come to this?

*

Driving to Paris on 29 April 1962, I was on a high. We all were. I drove on, happily glancing in the rear-view mirror, seeing my passengers jammed in behind me. Then the reality of what I'd done and the enormous responsibility ahead started to set in. I shook the excitement off a little, focusing on the task at hand.

Anyone who has had the dubious honour of driving in a country that situates vehicles on the opposite side of the road will know it's a genuine challenge the first time round. I'd been to France, sure, but I'd never driven there before. A group of 11 complete strangers had not only paid me good money, they had put total faith in me and were patiently waiting for me to introduce them to the delights of Europe. Memories of some of my boisterous conversations in the OVC bar started to return. I had, after all, boasted that I'd been here before and my passengers had obviously assumed I knew my way around. Well, I didn't. What's more, dismal D-grade schoolboy French was about my limit, let alone any other European tongues.

Luckily the first day I had two major wins. First, I found my way to Paris and second, I found the camp ground. It turned out to be quite easy as all I did was nonchalantly follow the road signs. I did take out some insurance by having one of the passengers sitting beside me with the Europa map book following the route with me. Still, my charges were impressed and my confidence was given a much-needed boost.

The problem I had on that first day was still worrying. The centre of gravity of the van had changed dramatically with all the gear piled so high on the roof, making it difficult to control the vehicle. Every time we went around a corner the vehicle would lurch dangerously and the wheels on one side seemed to lift slightly off the road. The other problem was the vehicle's weight. It was outrageously overloaded making it difficult to stop within a prescribed distance. Despite this, we made it to Paris unscathed.

On arrival at Camping du Bois de Boulogne we erected our tents with surprising ease and the girls started to prepare our inaugural meal of a hot soup starter, spaghetti Bolognaise and a pre-prepared trifle for dessert. I confidently promised to take the passengers later that evening on a night 'recce' of Paris – after all I'd been there before.

While dinner was cooking I disappeared to the loo and locked myself into one of the cubicles and sat down with a map of Paris in one hand and a guidebook in the other. I hastily memorised the route to the centre of the city. Out the gate, first left, then second right, through the Bois de Boulogne (an enormous park), three roundabouts and the Arc de Triomphe should appear right in front of us. From there it would be a matter of cruising down the Champs Elysées to the Place de la Concorde and turning right over the River Seine to the Eiffel Tower and so on. I convinced myself it was a piece of cake. Adding to the facts I'd learnt on my previous trip, I read up the Fodor's guidebook and memorised a few more, even the number of rivets in the Eiffel Tower (2.5 million) and the number of bridges over the Seine, within the city limits (37). I was as ready as I'd ever be.

With my very excited passengers, we left the camp gates and I duly turned left, then I started to turn second right. Disaster! It was a one-way street with a flood of traffic coming towards us. I was forced to continue along the original road but from that moment on I was completely lost. I drove around for a while pretending I knew where I was going. I figured my bluff was working since none of my passengers had ever been to Paris before. Using luck and my innate sense of direction, I aimed the vehicle where I reasoned the city was and drove. Sure enough, I eventually hit the jackpot – the Champs Elysées, the main boulevard of the city.

At night, the Parisian monuments and landmarks are floodlit to wonderful effect. Suddenly there it was, the Arc de Triomphe in all its glory with the tricolour flag fluttering in the breeze as if acknowledging my triumph. I acted nonchalant but I was so excited I'd found it that I forgot all the directions I'd memorised in the loo. From that point on I just pointed the vehicle at any sights that appeared on the horizon. If I recognised one I told my spellbound passengers what it was and asked the passenger in the front seat to read the description from the guidebook. Any major site I didn't recognise, I would make up something suitable. Any large building that was lit up became either a university, or the Ministry of Defence, a military or police academy. I possibly called Musée du Louvre the Elysée Palace but thankfully I don't remember! My commentary was confident enough to match anything we came across. The recce was hugely successful and, miraculously, I found the way back to the safety of the camp.

The next morning I decided discretion was the better part of valour. I had enough sense to know I couldn't rely on last night's beginner's luck in every city. So after breakfast I levelled with my young charges.

'I was lost last night,' I blurted out. 'Sure, I've been to Paris before but I've never been around the rest of Europe.'

Nobody said anything, they just looked at me. After a while, they looked at each other, then back to me and smiled and started nudging each other.

'John, we suspected that was the case, and knew you were hopelessly lost last night,' one brave girl said. 'But we all loved the recce anyway!'

It turned out they were all so grateful and relieved to be on the Continent with a group that seemed to have some sense of organisation and purpose (albeit a leader who had, at this stage, dubious ability) that all was forgiven. They thanked me for putting the trip together. We agreed from then on to run the tour as a team effort and were determined to have a ball. From that moment there was a special bond between us.

Over the next few days we put together some basic rules. Any important decisions would be made by majority rule, with me having an extra casting vote if required. Cooking and vehicle cleaning rosters were set up. We would have a daily seat rotation system so everyone would have a turn in the front seats with the best view and help with the navigation. Finally, it was agreed that although I would do the majority of the driving, some of the passengers would also have a go to give me a break if I became tired. As the leader I would be responsible for the overall organisation of the tour, planning, bookings, finances, the vehicle and equipment. I encouraged the passengers to make suggestions to enhance the tour as we travelled along the route, but was to be the adjudicator in case of any disputes. Each day a different passenger would read from the guidebook to ensure we all received our daily dose of background information and culture.

Apart from transport and accommodation our other basic need was food. The food kitty was to cover three meals a day for each passenger, although we agreed that in each country we would eat out to sample the national dish, which would be an extra cost. I had paid into the food kitty as well, so the total amount was divided by the 12 weeks, resulting in the same amount budgeted for each week, with two people taking a turn each week to buy and prepare the food. Shopping in the local markets turned out to one of the highlights of the trip. Language was a barrier, with some of the antics employed to make the stall-holders understand, often proving to be hilarious. None of us had seen markets anything like them with the sheer size and choice of food on offer. We decided to eat out at a local restaurant in each country to savour their national dish on average once a week. These evenings were equally as memorable with the discovery of dishes such as paella, moussaka, fondue, goulash and a *rijsttafel* (a Dutch meal that consists of many side dishes, all accompanied by different rice dishes). These were the start of many of the traditional experiences passengers on future tours would come to enjoy.

The trip was not without mishaps. A terrifying incident occurred going over the beautiful Arlberg Pass travelling through to Austria on our way to Innsbruck. Our little red minibus that we had nicknamed 'Tiki' (a Maori good luck charm) had an enormous load to carry. It was really struggling to reach the Arlberg summit, so the passengers had to get out on the way up to reduce the weight to allow the vehicle to continue moving. They walked behind in case it also needed an added push. Eventually it made the top of the summit, everyone piled back in and we proceeded down the other side. It was very steep and I had to continually pump the brakes. Halfway down I realised the brakes weren't holding the vehicle. Although they were helping to keep the Tiki in check, they had overheated and I couldn't stop the vehicle.

The passengers were happily snapping photos of the magnificent scenery, totally oblivious to the drama unfolding in the driver's seat. Several requests were made for a photo stop. I convinced them we were running late and should keep going. Little did they know we had no choice. With the vehicle gathering speed I calmly told everyone we had a major problem and to prepare for a crash landing. I carefully pulled the wheel to the right taking the Tiki off the road and gently, ever so gently, ran it alongside the bank beside us until we came to a stop. Everyone clambered out a little shaken. Fortunately the only damage was the panel work, now sporting long scratches down the side. The intrepid passengers hitch-hiked down the mountain and I joined them later in the now not-so-pristine Tiki bus.

The tour was a journey of discovery, new experiences and a fast learning curve for me. We spent many hours driving around cities hopelessly lost, often ending up on the road we had just come in on and blindly heading back towards our morning departure point. Finding the camp grounds turned out to be a constant challenge. Often, we would arrive late at night, exhausted, pitch the tents in the dark only to be woken hours later with torrential rain that needed trenches to be dug around the tents. There were also sudden storms to deal with as the tents took off in the strong winds. We all seemed to have a fixation about the quality of the loos everywhere. The girls on checking them out would yell, 'squat jobs again' – and the bidets were a constant fascination to all. The fresh food raids often done in broad daylight on hapless farmer's properties for melons, corncobs and fruit, were fun at the time, but an embarrassment to me when I think about our antics today.

We completed the extensive itinerary and arrived back in London on the planned date. We'd had the odd misunderstanding and frustration, but we had so much fun experiencing together what Europe had to offer, just like a family. As we farewelled each other, there was not a dry eye. We had become close friends. For me it had been a huge sense of achievement, perhaps even a relief that I'd pulled it all off. I had delivered the promise.

*

Before I knew it, I was back at Hyde Park undertaking the 'practice tent erection' with 11 more passengers. At the pre-departure meeting I told them there was a restriction on the size of their suitcases, which could be no larger than 24-inches (60 centimetres) in length, plus a small day bag and a sleeping bag. I had also reversed the itinerary to make the most of the weather. This time we were to cross the English Channel from Dover to Ostend in Belgium, instead of Calais. The plan was to head north to Holland while the weather was still hot. This way we'd be at the southern end of our trip as autumn approached.

Having just successfully completed the inaugural tour I was excited and confident at the prospect of showing the new passengers 'my Europe'. I had fallen totally in love with it. It was not just the sights, sounds and scenery but the extraordinary diversity, the people and their traditions, the food, the festivals, the history, the culture, the activities and the entertainment. My enthusiasm was limitless. It was a privilege to be showing them, living off their excitement, I was determined they too would experience the same magic I felt.

Again, they were a great bunch of people. This time, the ratio of males to females had dramatically improved by 20 per cent because I had one extra male. He was a very welcome asset as situations would arise where the girls appreciated help in deterring lecherous young men. The extra male turned out to be a godsend.

Once again our Tiki bus accounted for its fair share of 'incidents'. It took a real beating as it bumped and crashed its way around Europe. The accidents always seemed to occur when I was driving – although I'm not prepared to take the blame for all of them!

The most common problem was running into the back of other vehicles. When the Tiki was loaded up it weighed several tons. Once moving at speed it had an incredible self-imposed forward momentum. It was a little like getting an ocean liner to slow down, let alone to stop. Standing on the brakes very early on was necessary, but sometimes it was not soon enough. We met a number of locals we had not planned on meeting this way, as we hit the back of their vehicle! Sometimes we stopped a little too quickly and ended up with having an unexpected meeting with yet a few more locals from behind. Fortunately nothing too serious occurred; although it did help having the Commer minibus engine situated a fair way back from the vulnerable front, under the first row of seats.

The pièce de résistance occurred in Switzerland on the second trip. We were staying in Lausanne and took a day excursion down to Geneva. On our return, while travelling along the picturesque shores of Lake Geneva, it started to rain lightly. It looked quite dark ahead with heavy rain imminent. The passengers were concerned that their washing would get wet back at camp so asked if I could go faster, which I did. I came to a corner at speed, and rounded it only to find there had been an accident ahead and the vehicles in my lane were stationary having almost banked up to the corner. In the other lane cars were coming in the opposite direction. I had nowhere to go, so I yanked the wheel to the right taking us through a fence into a cow paddock. We travelled a few metres, stopped, then in slow motion the vehicle rolled gently onto its side. Fortunately everyone was able to clamber out with only a few minor bruises and scratches. We righted the vehicle ourselves which, although slightly damaged with the windscreen popping out, was still drivable. We limped back to the camp – where the washing was indeed very wet! We had temporary repairs made to the vehicle next day, and continued the trip with the Tiki on a permanent slight lean to the right.

One night, after our visit to the infamous Hofbrauhaus Beer Hall in Munich, I lost the vehicle altogether. I had dropped the gang at the hall and found a park some distance away. Over the evening it became obligatory for everyone to drink a minimum of two steins (two litres) of German beer. However, over a period of four hours with plenty of bratwurst and *bockwurst mit brod*, most of us managed the feat. With that much liquid being consumed everyone was constantly going to the loo. During the evening one of the girls stood on the table in an inebriated state to announce she was off to have a 'twinkle'. We all laughed and after that, a 'twinkle stop' became the accepted name for a toilet stop. Another tradition also began, which lasted about 15 years. If you drank your two compulsory steins you received a Twinkler's Badge as proof of your achievement. The badge was a miniature beer stein and was worn proudly.

That particular evening we came staggering out of the beer hall very pleased with ourselves. Admittedly there were a few exceptions who, during the latter part of the evening, had ejected their *bockwurst mit brod*. As leader I should have been setting a good example, but I had also drunk the obligatory steins and was not in good shape. Unbelievably and stupidly in those days we did drink and drive. I went to fetch the vehicle but couldn't remember where I had parked it.

Twelve super sleuths set out to find the Tiki bus, with no luck. In the process, most of the passengers got lost too, so I spent the next hour trying to find them as well. Eventually everyone was accounted for and sent back to Camping Thalkerkin on the tram. I continued my search with the help of the local *polizei* who not only found the vehicle but insisted on driving me, and it, back to camp. I can't imagine why!

With just a couple of weeks to go before the end of our tour, I was sitting in the warm Mediterranean sun, beer in hand, thinking life was pretty good. We were staying on the outskirts of Nice on the French Riviera at Camping Du Pylon in Antibes. In between sips of beer, I was mapping out the last two weeks of our trip. The plan was to continue along the French Riviera, down through Perpignan and into Spain, passing through Barcelona to Madrid, then up through Biarritz to Paris and back across the Channel and up to London. Slowly it began to dawn on me that I wouldn't have sufficient funds to complete the full itinerary.

All day long I agonised over the situation. The passengers were oblivious to my predicament, which was about to become their predicament. My pride stopped me from telling them. I lay on my airbed that night, sleepless, wondering how I was going to resolve the situation. A daring idea was starting to take shape.

The previous day we had passed through the Principality of Monaco. After visiting the Royal Palace, hoping to catch a glimpse of Princess Grace and experience a drive around the Grand Prix circuit, we had all trooped into the magnificent Monte Carlo Casino. We were all in awe at the opulence of its interior with the grand chandeliers, the luxurious furnishings and enormous paintings and tapestries adorning the walls.

The roulette table beckoned us to have a flutter. After watching what the other punters did, it all appeared quite easy to make money. So we all gave it a go. Some won, some lost. I was totally hooked, and after trying all sorts of bets, came out well ahead. I would like to have stayed longer, but we had to move on.

The next day I estimated how far the remaining funds would take us. It was clear we had enough funds to reach Barcelona for the bullfight, Flamenco and paella night I had planned at the famous Las Caracoles restaurant, which had been recommended to me. At a pinch we could probably make it to Madrid, where on arrival the tour would come to a complete halt through of lack of funds. I loved the idea of seeing Spain again, but hadn't planned on living there!

I calculated how much money would be required to take us directly back to London from Nice, missing Spain completely. The route would take us directly through Lyon and Paris to London. In Thomas Cook's travel agency I changed all the remaining traveller's cheques into French francs. I kept aside the estimated amount required to return us directly to London. I put this amount carefully into my left trouser pocket. The remaining cash I placed in my right pocket.

The night before we were supposed to leave for Spain, when everyone had gone to bed, I got up, dressed and drove into Nice with two pockets of money and my passport.

*

'Faites vos jeux,' said the croupier. 'Place your bets.'

With a heightened sense of the moment I boldly placed some of the passenger's chips on red as that was the colour of our little Tiki bus. I put some on several numbers, some on the splits, corners, odds and some on passé (the high numbers) as this was all a rather high risk strategy. I finally threw a chip on zero for good measure.

'Rien ne va plus,' said the croupier. 'No more bets.'

The wheel spun one way and the ball the other. I looked up at the glittering chandelier, shining down on my tentative but optimistic face, and felt very alone. The fate of my passengers was trapped in that little white ball careering around the wheel. I heard the ball clank as it dropped into the channel of the number. I couldn't look so I awaited the croupier's call.

'Vingt-cinq rouge impair passe,' he said. 'Twenty-five, red odd, high.' I not only had a chip on 25 but also a couple on the relevant splits adjacent. What's more it was odd, and it was red. We had won! I was almost numb with disbelief. I smiled to myself, then nodded smugly to my fellow punters, collected up the winning chips, cashed them in and placed the money in my left trouser pocket along with the remaining funds. My pocket bulged!

I had taken an enormous risk but now there was more than sufficient funds to continue the trip as planned. The following morning, with my passengers unaware of the drama that had taken place a few hours before, we left for Spain and all its pleasures. I suspect if I had lost that night I would have told my passengers and we would all have chipped in and still seen Spain. We completed the tour arriving back into London on the exact day we were due back. It had been an incredible trip. Many tears were shed as we parted.

Those first two tours were the start of creating and establishing a recipe that would take the soon-to-be-formed company to great heights, with the added traditions of the national meals, Twinklers Badges, dressing up in Dutch National Costumes, the trip song (later the morning song), dress-up nights, traditional entertainment evenings and the famed trip diary to mention but a few. But perhaps the most important ingredient to success was to restrict the age, at that point, to those between 19 and 29.

*

A month after my return I arranged for my two groups to meet up. Most of the ex-passengers were staying in London for the winter and had kept in touch with each other, and welcomed an opportunity for a reunion. We knew the experiences we'd had were very special. We relived the trips day by day through the colour slides projected on a basement flat wall. We laughed, we cried, and there was a rekindling of the remarkable feeling of closeness between us all. Memories that would last a lifetime.

After the reunion, when everyone had left, I had a moment alone to reflect. I felt happy and confident, and knew I had learned a lot about myself. I had also learnt a lot about people, their different personalities and their often-complex feelings and emotions. That first morning in Paris, when I told the passengers I had been lost, I realised the value of telling the truth.

Through the casino experience I had learnt to take calculated risks. I'd been very lucky and it had paid off. However, I'd also had the sense to put in place a fall-back position (the money I set aside to get us back to London, skipping Spain) in case it didn't come off. I called it insurance. I was to use this philosophy many times in the future when I took even greater risks, although I must admit my 'insurance' didn't always save me. But at least I usually put it in place, which helped lessen the odds.

I had also learnt how to budget and run a small business, take responsibility and make decisions. I still didn't have much money, but I wasn't broke, as I had gained something very special. I'd learnt to have belief in myself and had gained confidence in my ability to make things happen. Above all, I had learnt how to get along with people. And that's what life's all about. Isn't it?

At the end of the first year I had:

- seen Europe twice
- taken 22 passengers around Europe
- had a turnover of £2725 (including food kitty)
- owned a beat up minibus and all the gear, but
- still had very little money.

5. A BUSINESS AND A BRAND IS BORN

On return to London I tried to sell the minibus, but since we'd hit a few things (and a few things had hit us!) and I'd rolled it on its side, it wasn't in too great a shape. No one wanted it. I did have a few offers but they were always less than I needed for the airfare back to New Zealand so regrettably had to turn them down. As a result I had no option but to stay in London.

Once more I had very little money to my name, so my little Tiki bus became my home. It was becoming very cold in London and I hadn't experienced anything like the cold the United Kingdom had to offer. In addition, the winter of 1962–63 (known also as The Big Freeze of '63) was one of the coldest winters on record in the United Kingdom. After a couple of weeks, I negotiated the same deal as before at the Austin Hotel, involving a free room in return for providing the breakfast service.

I soon found a job in the Continental rail-ticketing department of a business house travel company in the 'city' end of London. I even bought a bowler hat and wore it to work just like all the other male staff in the early 1960s. I moved into an Earls Court flat and shared it platonically (her decision not mine) with an attractive, fun-loving Canadian girl. The flat was very cheap because it overlooked a busy railway line. Every time a train passed by our simple abode, everything in it shook.

The evenings would usually see me at the OVC or socialising at someone else's flat. I didn't seem to know anyone who had a flat at street level or above. They all seemed to be basement flats, politely known as garden flats. I was too embarrassed to invite anyone back to mine due to the noise, although it was at least above street level. The main talking point was the European trip someone had just done, complete with the obligatory slide show, or the European trip people were planning for the following summer.

Gradually, two things became increasingly clear. First, I wasn't going to save enough money for my airfare home. Second, I wanted to go back to my much-loved Europe. What was I to do? The decision was relatively easy. The following summer I would take my Tiki bus around Europe again. People had been asking about my previous tours and I needed very little convincing.

I put down a plan and improved the itinerary based on what I'd learnt the previous year. I also increased the price again. I had realised how important it was to give outstanding value for money so included a few entrance fees to museums and activities in the price. I had the embellished itinerary gestetnered (a 1960s printing method) off with an information sheet explaining I'd already successfully been around the route a couple of times. Two more tours with 22 seats were again for sale.

The majority of my ex-passengers were still in London spreading the word about the fantastic trip they'd taken. Many had written home to their friends who were planning to come over and follow in their footsteps. A number had already enquired if I was doing another tour, indicating they would book for the next one. Some of my friends at home had also heard about my exploits and enquired about the tours. I soon realised the power of word of mouth advertising. There is no more powerful or cheaper means of advertising.

I put my notice up again at the OVC, New Zealand and Australia House. I also walked over to Canada House and South Africa House to pin up the sign there too. People soon started to book, again mostly females, and as the money came in I had the vehicle panel beaten back to its original pristine state, fully serviced, and the camping equipment repaired and replaced as required.

I strategically parked my now near-new Tiki bus in areas where potential passengers would see it, with advertising signs in the windows. Several evenings a week I would take people on a free pub crawl around the East End of London so they would not only experience this scene but also enjoy the fun with a group. Naturally, I did a fair bit of talking about my tours whilst we were drinking pints. In what appeared to be no time at all, both trips were fully booked.

In April 1963, I was back on the European circuit I loved so passionately. It gave me enormous pleasure to show my new recruits all the wonderful places my previous passengers and I had enjoyed. I constantly searched out new places to see and new experiences to work into the itinerary. I wanted to experience things that were different, which I thought my passengers would also enjoy, such as visiting the Volkswagen car factory in Wolfsburg, Germany, and no one had been to a brewery so Heineken in Holland started to receive regular visits. We frequently wandered off the itinerary discovering places such as the spectacular Amalfi Drive in Italy and, on one trip driving into the hills behind Nice found Grasse, where we visited Picasso's home and a perfume factory. Staying in Interlaken, on that first trip I took a drive up a valley road, where I discovered the breath taking village of Lauterbrunnen, still one of my favourite places in Europe. All were to become regular inclusions on the future tours. I befriended other tourists so they'd tell me the gems they had discovered. As I became friendly with some of the camp owners, I badgered them to tell me about the non-touristy places with a local flavour.

As I drove my passengers around the sights I'd often look through my rear-view mirror to see a couple of Kombi vans packed full of Australasian guys following behind, assuming I knew my way around. They certainly didn't. But there was another more pressing reason for their close attention – they were after my busload of girls.

On my third and fourth time around, many suppliers recognised me from the previous year. They started offering me all sorts of deals. I thought I'd done well with the group prices I'd negotiated with the camp proprietors, ferry operators, and attraction operators the previous year but, when they saw me again, they offered even better prices. Shop owners began sweet-talking me with tantalising commission offers. I soon realised my groups, small though they were, had purchasing power. Over the years I would constantly use this to my advantage.

At the end of the second year I had:

- seen Europe four times
- taken a total of 44 passengers around Europe
- (and still) owned the minibus and gear, and
- had some money in the bank!

Again I reflected on my situation. The last two years, without a doubt, had been the most amazing of my entire life. Almost every day had brought new challenges or new experiences. I had found an incredible new confidence in myself and was so proud of what I had achieved single-handedly. It felt almost surreal. I had fallen in love with Europe and loved showing and sharing it with others. I wanted to go again … and again …

At the back of my mind, however, was the thought that, 'I must go home, I must go home'. I could feel the pull. One day I told a girl I fancied at the time, I was planning to return to New Zealand.

'Why?' she asked.

'Well, New Zealand is home,' I replied, a bit lost for words. 'I guess I feel as though I have a responsibility to my mother to return.'

'But are you enjoying your time over here?' she persisted.

'Yes!'

'Do you really want to go home?'

'I'm actually not sure.'

'Are you happy living over here and doing what you are?

'Yes, very much so.'

'Well, why go home?'

Then she said something I've never forgotten: 'John, home is where you are happiest!'

It was a turning point and from that moment, Europe became my home. I knew I had the makings of a successful business. Others had confirmed my suspicions. Through my original need to see Europe I had created a product other people wanted to buy. Why not take advantage of the situation and give more people an opportunity to experience Europe in this way? The words of my much-respected Uncle Arthur echoed in my mind.

'With your individual flair, attitude, special attributes and the freedom to choose your own course, I recommend, when the time is right, that you start your own business, just as I did.'

I decided to run the tours again the following year and add another vehicle to the fleet. I named the tours 'Tiki Tours'. A business was born.

I put down a plan for the following year. I would run a 12-week tour including Scandinavia starting in April and on return, a 12-week tour including Greece, the latter with two buses. Chasing the sun at the end of the year I added a three-and-a-half week tour staying at the Casa Compello in Alicante on the Costa Blanca, Spain. I produced my first ever brochure and included a four-week trip of Scandinavia (just to test the interest, but not operate). It was a small four-sided card with blue print on shiny white-coated cardboard. It detailed the tours, prices and departure dates. I put the address and telephone number of my father's dental surgery in Kensington High Street on the back. My step-sister, his partner's dental nurse, agreed to attend to any enquiries.

With the decision made to settle in Europe, I flew home to Wellington for Christmas. It was wonderful to see my mother again – she had kept all my old letters and telegrams. I was able to relive and reminisce over the experiences with her. Everyone was so interested in my adventures. I met old friends and an increasing number of other young people who were considering going to Europe. I encouraged them to make the journey and proudly showed my colour slides to anybody who dared show even the slightest bit of interest. I was interviewed by the local newspaper and naturally took the opportunity to tell the world about my fledging tour operation, which produced another flood of interest.

I encouraged my life-long school friend John Tingey (Jet) to join me in Europe. I had kept him informed of my activities through the odd letter. He was a little reluctant as he had a good job and hadn't really thought about travelling overseas. In the sixties we were very loyal to an employer and did not move from job to job as often as many of the young people appear to do these days.

'You could drive the second bus I'm going to buy,' I said.

'Sounds like a good idea, but I'm not really sure,' he replied. I kept telling him what a fantastic opportunity it would be for him and the huge range of new experiences that lay ahead. But he was still hesitant.

'The ratio of girls to guys is usually around seven to one, right?' I told him enthusiastically. That did it. Once he'd made the decision, Jet agreed to fly over and join me as a passenger on the first trip and then complete a second trip as a driver. At that time, travelling over by boat was the conventional way to go. Can't think what convinced him to take the fast track!

*

I returned to the United Kingdom ahead of Jet by purchasing a berth for £120 on one of the P&O passenger liners, SS *Arcadia*. It was packed full of young people heading in the same direction. I was booked in a four-berth cabin way down in the bowels of the ship. There was one other guy my age and two older men, no doubt placed there to keep an eye on us. It was the shipping company's policy to mix up the ages to ensure there was no scandalous activity in the cabins. It was the same policy for the girl's cabins, with older women interspersed with the younger ones.

Boat life was a dream. All we did for the whole journey of four weeks was eat, drink, party and enjoy each other's company. The ratio of girls to boys was pleasantly high. Whenever any of us guys needed the privacy of the cabin we would put an unobtrusive sign on the door so the others would know not to enter. We stopped at a number of exotic ports along the way and passed through the Suez Canal to the Mediterranean. A couple of us took an excursion to Cairo and, having been there before, I became the instant expert. The boat eventually docked at Tilbury in East London.

While onboard I offered advice about life in London, Europe and, of course, about my tours. I distributed my little brochure to everyone under 30 and surreptitiously took the odd booking!

On arrival in London, I ramped up the free pub crawls and with my notices everywhere, the vehicle strategically parked and my ex-passengers and newbies spreading the word, the bookings again started to roll in. One day my step-sister called me in despair at the number of people fronting up to the surgery. 'John, sometimes there's no room for the patients!' she told me.

During this period, I let prospective passengers know that I needed to personally interview them to ensure they were suitable for the tour. After all, I'd vetted the others. Normally I would invite them for a pub lunch or a drink in the evening. I had used the same ploy the previous year telling people there were limited seats available and I wanted to be certain they would fit in. The more difficult it appeared I made it for them, the keener they were to be considered. I even asked them to tell me why they thought they were suitable! Thankfully no one ever turned the tables on me, and asked if I was suitable. As soon as I had them totally convinced the tour was right for them, I'd play God and tell them they were accepted. However, acceptance was conditional on full payment within three days.

This served a number of purposes. First, I would have their money in my bank account. Second, once I had their money it would stop them changing their minds or considering other alternatives. Third, it would give me another committed 'word of mouth' salesperson. Eventually I had both trips full – including the second trip planned for two buses.

Jet joined me on the first trip as my trainee. During the tour he took in the sights and the culture plus a very large serving of fraternising with the female passengers! On return to London we picked up the new minibus and, after a hectic turnaround, set off again, this time with 22 passengers.

We travelled in tandem with me driving Tiki One and Jet driving Tiki Two. I had put second-hand two way radios in each van so I could direct my new staff member. The radios were constantly interrupted by the foreign babble of authorities trying to track down the unlicensed interloper on their airways – us! We never got caught and the system worked a treat.

On the second tour we had a passenger from Rhodesia (Zimbabwe). Peter Blake was a very personable guy who fitted in brilliantly. When we returned to London he joined Jet and me in a well-worn top-floor flat in Clanricarde Gardens, Bayswater. We had only been in residence a couple of days when Peter met a very friendly Australian girl who lived on the floor below, Margaret Wellman (remember her name).

At the end of the third year I had:

- seen Europe six times
- taken a total of 77 people around Europe
- owned two minibuses and all the gear, and
- had even more money in the bank!

By this time Jet had convinced his brother to join him in London. They were both avid skiers and wanted to ski in Europe over the winter. One night Jet and I discussed the possibility of running ski tours.

Austria would be the most suitable, we decided, as it had a large number of easily accessible, established resorts and, at the time, it was the cheapest European country to ski. Jet and his brother did a 'recce' and chose St Johann in Tirol, a ski resort in the beautiful Tyrolean mountain area. They found a quaint old guesthouse named Gasthof Dampfl, situated right in the town square. They booked 12 beds and the first ski tour departed, filled primarily with ex-passengers. We were now in the ski business and called the operation 'Tiki Ski Tours'.

By November 1964 I'd finalised the itineraries for the year ahead. I stayed with the proven 12-week itineraries, with just a little fine-tuning to improve them. I added a four-week tour of Scandinavia and a four-week tour at the end of the season to Spain, Portugal, and Morocco, the latter to make better use of the vehicles with a longer season. I decided to add another vehicle to the fleet, bringing the total to four.

I produced a similar brochure to the current one, formed a company and named it Tiki Tours Limited. A couple of copycat competitors had already started to appear, run mainly by South Africans. With the object of appealing to people's nationalism I stated that Tiki Tours was Australian and New Zealand owned and operated. In addition I put in the age restriction of 19 to 29 years. Why? I had proved young people liked to travel and experience things together. A lot of my future business plans were based on projecting my own desires and preferences, assuming it'd work for others too. It turned out to be a sound formula.

*

I had also been busy on another little venture. Not relishing the idea of another cold winter in London, I had planned to return to the New Zealand summer sun again at the end of December 1964 to start running tours around New Zealand, thus working back to back summer seasons.

During my previous year's trip home, I had already looked at the possibility. I had spoken to a successful business friend (Alf Taplin) who generously offered to help me set it up. With his assistance we put a couple of tours together. A 12-seater Commer minibus with a custom-built roof rack was hired, camping equipment purchased and the inter-island ferry booked. Advertisements in a few local newspapers had already been placed and I spread the word among my returning Australian and New Zealand passengers. We called the operation Haere Mai Tours (*Maori* for Welcome).

I ran a couple of three-week tours covering both the North and South Islands. I had previously never seen much of the country and what I experienced made me appreciate and realise what a beautiful and unique country New Zealand is, with so much on offer to see and do. Touring through the country was a doddle compared to Europe. I had a few mishaps around the route but generally all went smoothly. I looked forward to showing a whole lot more people my country in the future.

I returned to the United Kingdom on the Sitmar liner, SS *Fairsky* on another selling mission. Little did I know that some fifteen years later I would be running cruises around the South Pacific on her sister ship, SS *Fairstar*.

Jet, Peter and I had taken a new basement flat in Portland Road, Notting Hill. Here we processed the tour bookings and conducted the tour pre-departure meetings. It became a hub of activity and I suppose the company's very first office. After a successful ski season Jet retired from the road, agreeing to man the London base part-time during the summer. Peter and I drove and another couple of drivers joined us.

During the touring season Jet came out to Europe to deliver some mail. However, he had another reason. He wanted to check on one of my female passengers whom he'd previously met and really fancied, Mary Law (remember her name).

Season number four went fantastically well. At the end of 1965 several of the drivers ran a few ski tours during the winter. Peter and I were exhausted so took off to spend Christmas at his parent's beautiful home in Bulawayo in stunning Rhodesia. Peter had become my business partner, taking a 30 per cent interest in the company, and over many a Lion and Castle beer by the pool, we plotted the future of

Tiki Tours. We decided to double the size of the company, not an insignificant decision for an afternoon's work by the pool.

It was a memorable holiday, especially our visit to magnificent Victoria Falls. I recall staring in awe at the sheer power of all that cascading water. Our days travelling through the Wankie Game reserve with all the fascinating sights of the wild life were such a highlight. I remember making a fool of myself one evening, asking why we hadn't seen any tigers (there are no tigers in Africa!). I loved Rhodesia and its lifestyle so much, that I promised myself I would one day return. But Europe was calling again.

On our return to London we immediately started implementing the expansion plan. It was a hectic couple of months. We had improved the existing tour itineraries, added a nine-week European and a six-week tour to the Middle East (Syria, Lebanon, Jordan and Israel). I wanted people to see and experience what I had on my original journey. Most of the tours were to be run with two buses on each departure. We proceeded to order more buses and equipment.

A new eight-page brochure was produced with the decision to really go upmarket with full colour on the front cover! We produced 2500 brochures in two colours (red and blue) with 'Tiki Tours' printed across the top of the front cover, still using the dental practice as the contact address. We then looked at the promotional brochures displayed in several of the European tourist offices around London. A Swiss one had a beautiful full colour picture of Lake Lucerne with snow-capped mountains in the background. What's more it could be cut to suit the size of our brochure's cover. We somehow persuaded the Swiss National Tourist office to give us 2500 copies of their brochure for publicity purposes. With a team of helpers we cut the pictures out, trimming them to the exact size, and stuck them onto the front cover of our brochures. Our first full colour brochures were distributed everywhere, even to Australia and New Zealand. Almost immediately the bookings started to roll in.

I led the first of the season's double vehicle 12-week tours. When we arrived in Nice, with just 12 days to go, I had a call from London imploring me to return to base urgently. The business was growing so rapidly help was needed. With no spare drivers available, I asked the driver of the second bus, Ian Johnson, to take over the lead, with a trainee onboard, John Lindsay, driving the second vehicle. I returned to London. It was the beginning of a new role for me – John Anderson had retired from the road.

The call had not exaggerated the situation. There were passengers and prospective passengers turning up daily at the dental practice on Kensington High Street. My father's South African dental partner, who was running the London practice, was not at all amused with the situation (although he did admit he was winning a few new patients). The telephone at the Portland Road flat rang continuously. Although Jet had been holding things together, he couldn't cope anymore. It was bedlam. Tiki Tours had taken off!

I decided then and there to set up a real business office – quickly. All my competitors were in the Earls Court area so I decided to be completely different and set up in the heart of London's West End. So in the latter half of 1966, I found a small one-room office situated on the second floor of 62 Oxford Street. I hired an extremely capable girl to answer the phone and deal with the ever-increasing human traffic we were desperately diverting to the new premises. Before the end of the season Pete came back from the road to assist and we sadly bid farewell to Jet. He had decided to return home to New Zealand overland through India to continue his career in paint and wallpaper.

At the end of the season I'd arranged to store four of the Tiki buses in a farmer's barn just south of London over the winter. Early one evening we lined them up and headed south. I was the lead vehicle, like a proud mother duckling with her three baby ducklings following close behind. It was raining and a storm was looming, so I sped up a little. I was really happy, reflecting on the past year and singing along to the radio on full bore. Suddenly a dog ran out onto the road in front of me. I jammed on the brakes, abruptly stopped, and immediately felt a massive thump in the rear of my vehicle. At the same time I heard Bang! Bang! Bang! All three vehicles concertinaed into the back of each other. I thought I'd just written off half of my entire fleet – well almost! Luckily, the engines were so far back in the vans that there was only extensive damage to the bodyworks.

Towards the end of the year I received a very official looking envelope from Her Majesty's Government of New Zealand. 'Surely not a knighthood already?' we quipped in the office.

The letter inside was no such thing. The directors (Pete and I) of Tiki Tours had been served with an injunction to 'forthwith, without delay, desist from using the name 'Tiki Tours' in New Zealand and overseas. Unbeknown to us the name was owned by the New Zealand Government Tourist Bureau. End of story. We now had a tour operation – with no name.

I was mortified. The name was becoming so well known but we had to give an undertaking not to distribute any more branded publicity material. We even had to cover up the Tiki Tour name on our remaining brochures. I loved Tiki Tours as a name as it had given me so much good luck which I didn't want to lose. One night, a group of us sat around in our Portland Road flat, drinking a few Double Diamond beers in an effort to resolve the crisis. It turned out to be easier than we'd expected.

We were running tours of the Continent, right? We all loved the name Tiki, right? We came up with the idea to put Con (for Continent) in front of the Tiki. Thus 'Contiki' the international brand name was born! We added the word Travel to describe Contiki. A logo was designed with a C and an arrowed T on its side, depicting 'going forward'.

With all of this activity going on I received some devastating news. My father had dropped dead. With his two o'clock patient in the chair, he'd had a sudden massive brain haemorrhage and fallen to the ground. The year was 1966 and my dad was only 56 years old. I loved him so much and he was gone. I've always felt terribly sad that he never met my wife or saw what I went on to achieve. But tragically that's life.

Some 30 years later I was interviewed for a magazine article.

'John, what drove you to pursue success in those early years?' the reporter asked. I dug deep, very deep, and with tears welling in my eyes, I replied:

'I've never really thought about it, but I think I now know the reason. I wanted to prove to my father I could be successful like him and do something worthwhile with my life.'

My father had encouraged me, seen what I'd achieved in those first few years before his untimely death and knowing how proud he was inspired me greatly. Everyone needs a reason to achieve and succeed in life. Some parents give their children every material thing they desire and shower them with money. I believe young people have to earn and learn the value of money. Give it all to them and you've taken away their incentive. Give them love and encouragement and they will achieve, often way above their (and your) wildest dreams.

6. HOLD ONTO YOUR SEATS AND ENJOY THE RIDE

It was the beginning of 1967 and time for me to take stock of my situation. At this point I'd been operating for five years. What had started as a simple idea, based largely around my own desire to see Europe cheaply, had developed into a business based around other young people's desire to do the same. What's more, I'd enjoyed every minute of it. I was ready to take the business to the next level.

Up until this point I'd been shooting from the hip, operating like a typical early-stage entrepreneur. I had no plan, in fact, I was pretty disorganised. Virtually everything I did was on 'gut feel'. If it felt right I'd say 'Let's do it!' Many of the decisions I was to make in later years were still based on this instinctive response. I have learnt that not only does researching an idea or project in too much detail delay the decision, but all the 'what ifs' can kill it. I'm a great believer in assembling the facts, bouncing ideas off others, and if the idea feels right, just to go ahead and do it while the competition is still contemplating.

I needed a basic plan to take me over the next couple of years. Up until now I'd just concentrated on each year at a time with little thought given to the following one. Towards the end of each year I would only then turn my attention to the next. I needed a 'blueprint' that could be updated by adding another year, each year.

I took five pieces of paper and laid them out on the desk in front of me. I had decided to write down my first personal plan and my first business plan. I know there were just five pages because I kept those original plans for many years. On the first page I listed my overall long-term objectives. On the second, my personal objectives for the current year. On the third, my business objectives for the current year. On the fourth, my personal and business objectives for the following year. And on the fifth, a rough income and expenditure budget for the next two years. I looked at them with satisfaction. For the first time I had written down my dreams, turning them into objectives I believed I could achieve. These were to change my life dramatically.

On the personal plan I listed my priorities. The most important priority to me all those years ago is still one of the most crucial to me today – my health. After spending such a long time in hospital in my younger years I learnt very early on that unless you keep good health you may be restricted in achieving your ultimate objectives. I listed a number of other goals such as 'live life to the full' and 'make lots of money'. Yes, money, as it gives you freedom of choice and security. And my business plan? I was going to Contiki-ise the world!

To this day I still start off every New Year with my five pieces of paper. I like to keep things simple. Once you *write* something down that you want to achieve, something goes click in your brain and the next stage turns into how can you make it happen.

We began with my ambitious business plan in mind. Under the new Contiki banner we produced a new three-colour brochure with a few black and white photographs for the forthcoming season, kicking off in April 1967. Six different tour options were introduced, including our first tour to Russia, via Finland, Poland and passing through the East German corridor. We purchased another couple of buses, and took on a second office adjoining the original at 62 Oxford Street. This one, however, was three times larger. We would often arrive in the morning to find a queue of people winding down the corridor outside our door, much to the annoyance of the other building tenants.

We continued to finance our expansion each year from the increasing profits we were generating, and a loan from our friendly local bank, The Midland. However, occasionally, we continued to dip into the money passengers had paid for their tours in advance. We were conscious this was risky, but assured ourselves, that as long as the bookings kept rolling in we would be okay. Fortunately they did.

The larger office had a couple of couches where Peter and I continued to interview prospective passengers to assess their suitability. One day in 1967, I interviewed a couple of girls who were close friends from their school days in Christchurch, New Zealand. One was really keen to book on the 12-week European tour, but her friend was not at all interested as there was no way she was going on an organised tour. She was too independent for that, or so she claimed. She was particularly attractive and had a quiet mischievous spark about her. But after a two-pronged attack by her friend and me, she caved in and booked on the tour with her friend. Ironically it would turn out that this reluctant passenger would be the first to give me a major problem.

When their tour arrived in Athens, this particular passenger fell ill. Although it was nothing too serious the Greek doctor recommended she fly back to London to receive specialist medical treatment. This was the first time I'd ever had to repatriate a passenger. Arrangements were made and she was admitted to Middlesex Hospital. I visited her a couple of times to monitor her progress and after ten days she was discharged. She had been enjoying her tour so much, she decided to rejoin it in Rome. Her name was Alison Peate (remember her name).

By now, we not only had offices but a small operations base as well to accommodate a business growing at break-neck speed. Our operations base was established during the year in Hounslow, West London – a series of huge lock-up arches under a railway line, overseen by a very capable ex-driver. Here we stored and mended the ever-growing mountain of camping gear and equipment. It seemed as though every month we co-opted another arch to cope with demand. As the business continued to grow we started to service our vehicles with our own mechanics. We bought a Morris mini minor van to drive around London fetching supplies and running other errands and, always quick to pounce on a free advertising opportunity, erected Contiki placards on top of it and the logo on its side doors.

By now we had appointed the company's first full-time operations manager to take responsibility for running the tour operation. Rick Gesterkamp, a New Zealander, had been one of our most successful drivers. He was a brilliant organiser, very conscientious and took on the role with enthusiasm.

With the increasing number of staff transitioning in and out of London, we rented a flat in Aberdare Gardens, Swiss Cottage, a North London suburb, to house them all. Predictably, there was a huge amount of activity 24/7 in and around the staff flat. There were always at least four red minibuses parked outside and this residence was responsible for many a rowdy party.

While all this was happening I continued to closely monitor my troublesome passenger, Alison Peate. She had surprised herself by enjoying her trip so much she even took a couple more, one to Scandinavia and another to Morocco. Being a radiographer, in between tours she worked in a number of different hospitals, while I ran the company. She reminded me recently that on our very first date I took her to see the award winning film, *A Man for All Seasons*. Romantic? I don't think so. After a wonderful year together, we realised we had fallen in love. I proposed to Ali one evening at a staff and passenger party onboard a ferry on the Thames. I pulled the ring top off a beer can and placed it on her finger in lieu of the diamond ring I faithfully promised to give her later. In November 1968, Ali and I set out to return to New Zealand with plans to get married the following January. However, we didn't go straight back.

I wanted to research America with the possibility of expanding Contiki operations there. Starting in New York, Ali and I took off for a six-week tour around America. We bought a second-hand Plymouth station wagon and drove through America, crossing into Canada at the Niagara Falls. We visited Quebec and then drove right across the country to Vancouver. Canada made a strong impression on us. We met so many friendly Canadians and especially loved our time enjoying the sheer beauty of the Banff/Lake Louise area.

We progressed down the west coast of America, classic road trip country, as far south as San Diego, through Las Vegas, then headed back east through New Orleans, Miami and back up to New York. We slept in the wagon, camped, stayed in motels, cooked most of our meals or ate at a Denny's diner. We enjoyed each other's company so much that we laughed almost the entire way around. We squeezed in as many new experiences as we could, all in the name of business research. Ali kept fastidious notes, which were to prove invaluable later when we were planning the American tours.

On arrival in New York, the plan was to sell the station wagon and fly home to New Zealand. We were a bit nervous about our chances of selling the Plymouth, but as we drove through the outskirts of the Big Smoke, the problem was miraculously solved. A motorbike and our wagon collided. The motorcyclist was shaken, but he was OK, and fortunately there was not much damage to either his bike or our vehicle. We got along very well as I suspect each of us thought it was our mistake. We told him our situation and right there, on the roadside, he bought our wagon and camping gear for cold hard cash! We both drove on to New York, where our buyer took possession of the vehicle. Ali and I took off as planned for our long journey home the next day, stopping over for a final bit of R&R in Hawaii and Fiji, arriving home in early December for Christmas and three very special weddings.

The first wedding was on 14 December when my old friend and ex-tour driver Jet married the girl he had fancied on my tour, Mary Law. The second wedding was on 30 December when my original business partner Peter Blake married the girl he met living in the flat below us, Margaret Wellman. The third wedding was four weeks later on 25 January, 1969, when I married the first passenger to give me a major problem, Alison Peate (remember her name? I certainly do!) We three guys were each other's groomsmen. On 25 January 2010, Ali and I celebrated our 41st wedding anniversary. To this day Ali still reckons I owe her for the 10 days food kitty from her trip that was never refunded to her!

For our honeymoon Ali and I went to Africa, visiting South Africa, Kenya, Tanzania and Rhodesia. Yes, Rhodesia. Four years later I had returned as promised but this time with my wife. Peter and his new wife Margaret joined us there, and we travelled throughout the country. We even went on a shooting safari where I impressed Ali no end by shooting a nob-nosed duck with a single stray pellet from a shotgun. It was even less sporting, however, because I didn't realise you were supposed to shoot the duck in flight. Mine was still innocently sitting on the lake.

After the trio of weddings and the honeymoon, we returned to London where it was all hands on deck. Ali joined us in the office as head receptionist. We leased a couple more offices in the same building to deal with the ever-expanding administration and tour operations. The original small office became the domain for Peter and me to plan new tours, sales and marketing initiatives and to plot the future direction of Contiki. We dubbed it 'The Inner Sanctum'.

Pete was becoming increasingly restless to return to his African homeland, and a few months later, he and Margaret returned to settle in Johannesburg. Their objective was to open a Contiki sales office to promote our European tours to South Africans and to set up an overland tour through Africa from Nairobi to Cape Town.

Around this time I visited Australia and New Zealand to introduce Contiki to the local travel agents. They were extremely enthusiastic about this new product on the market and could clearly see a great opportunity to not only sell a young person a boat berth or airline ticket to England but also book them on a European tour.

Over the next five years new tour routes were constantly introduced to tempt potential passengers. These included European tours ranging in duration from one week (Paris, Brussels, Amsterdam) to nine weeks

(16 countries including Greece). Often time was a factor in a passenger choosing a suitable option, so shorter tours to Russia, Scandinavia, Spain, Portugal and Morocco were also offered. A tour around England, Scotland and Wales was soon in the brochures and Ireland eventually made its début.

The number of departures on each of the tours increased relentlessly to keep up with the growing demand. Contiki was constantly innovating by improving the camping equipment such as the quality of the tents and introducing new ideas, activities and unique experiences. Everyone was always looking for ways to make the tours even better than the previous ones. In fact at the end of each summer season, all the drivers, operations and sales personnel would meet for the annual debrief – a major event. This was always an enlightening session, with no holds barred, where everybody had the opportunity to discuss the past year's activities and offer suggestions for improvement and new ideas to be considered.

The Commer minibus fleet continued to grow at an alarming rate. However, they were underpowered, overladen, and with the roof racks packed high, the elevated point of gravity made them prone to tipping over when rounding a corner too fast. We looked at alternatives and decided around 1970 to start switching to Ford Transits. These had more space inside, a wider wheelbase, a more powerful petrol engine and, above all, an extra three seats to make a total of 15. As the cost penalty was minor, we slowly phased them in over a year replacing all the Commers. Over the ensuing years we added more and more and more Transits with the fleet finally peaking at 38.

In 1972 the Austrian ski programme was expanded with the addition of Lofer and Hopfgarten – two stunningly beautiful village resorts not far from St Johann. The number of pensions and gasthof beds were continually increased to cater for the growing demand. One, Gasthof Shoneck, was to become an exclusive base for Contiki in both winter and summer.

The ever-lengthening queues of passengers made it clear we would have to move to larger office premises, so in 1975 we made the bold decision to take on a retail shop front at 7 Rathbone Place, just round the corner from our Oxford street offices, which we vacated. The premises were huge! As if they weren't big enough, to acquire them we also had to take on the entire basement, which was equally as large, and at the time was of no use to us. The front third of the ground floor was turned into the retail reception area and the remainder was dedicated to administration, operations, sales and accounts.

Next door to our new offices was The Black Horse pub which we commandeered as our local, using it to have our pre-departure tour meetings. This was an opportunity for the passengers to meet their fellow travellers before blast off.

The last five years had been breathtaking. We were no longer talking about hundreds of passengers per year, we were talking thousands.

7. THE BEEHIVE

'You see them here, you see them there, you see them bloody well everywhere!' people would say. Europe was awash with little red minibuses. Thirty-eight separate party units in their own little capsule, in some cases running riot or causing mayhem somewhere in Europe. Not a day or night went by that either the passengers or buses didn't deliver us some manner of headache.

All tours departed and returned to the United Kingdom through the English Channel ports of Dover or Folkestone. For improved efficiency and cost savings, at the end of 1969 we moved our entire London operations base in Hounslow to Folkestone. We commandeered a disused fire station and adapted it to suit our requirements. From here all the servicing of the vehicles and equipment was carried out. We built a mezzanine floor to accommodate large custom-built tables, sewing machines and a seamstress to repair all the tents. We even developed our own custom-designed cooking stoves named after their inventor (Dave Jorgenson's 'Jorgo Burner'). Initially we took over one of the local hotels, The Marine, to accommodate our staff until we leased our own house, affectionately known as 'The Bayle'.

Roving field units were introduced to help drivers with problems that arose on tour. These were VW Kombi service vans packed full of replacement equipment, spare mechanical parts and a 'can do' driver who knew the routes well. If something went awry, instead of the whole tour being derailed, Contiki could provide assistance almost immediately. This was a valuable initiative as it was something our competitors didn't have.

Locating and training new drivers to replenish the ranks and man the ever-increasing fleet was a mammoth task, but it was one we took very seriously. We knew that once trained, the next time drivers were in Europe they would be alone with the responsibility of 14 complete strangers. Not only was this task one that required a responsible person, they also needed a healthy dash of initiative and charisma. Those in their bus were looking to have a great experience and we didn't want some stick-in-the-mud or smart Alec driver to ruin their chances. In those days the tour driver was also the tour leader so they really set the tone for the trip.

None of our trainees had experience in the tourism business. Few could speak any foreign languages, most hadn't previously shouldered much responsibility, and the vast majority had never even been overseas before, let alone to Europe. For some it was their first real job. We took these totally raw recruits aged in their early twenties who were previously plumbers, bank clerks, lawyers, salesmen, builders, accountants, teachers, students, butchers – we got the lot! We had to turn these prospective employees into responsible and hopefully conscientious European tour leaders.

I had run the first dedicated training in 1967 and continued to do so for the next three years. Our top drivers then took over the annual responsibility. Often the new recruits selected couldn't keep the smiles from their faces as they thought they'd been given the opportunity of a lifetime, to not only tour around Europe in the company of other young people but also get paid for the privilege – what a dream job. They were in for a very rude awakening. Most had no idea how tough the training trip would be when they set off. I knew these trips were the only way to sort the strong, capable and conscientious from the weak and lazy.

We completed the entire 12-week tour itinerary in just under four weeks, often driving through the night. The trips were done off-season in February in the midst of the European winter. It was always freezing, so when camping it was extremely unpleasant and character building. There was no time to relax, with all potential drivers taking turns driving and learning their way from city to city, through borders, and around cities. Cities such as Paris and Rome required repeat circuits of up to a dozen times, only moving on when the drivers felt confident. All constantly took turns reading from the guidebook, testing each other. I pushed them hard because I wanted to see how well they coped and how well they could absorb all the necessary information about the countries we passed through. This was crucial because I knew from experience they would be constantly relied on and peppered with questions from their passengers when they led their own tours. They soon realised they needed to know as much as they could because next time they would be on their own with no one to hold their hand or turn to for help.

There were all sorts of subliminal tests as well. I would occasionally allow them to relax. In Istanbul we'd go to the Turkish baths and after bathing, the obligatory massage. In the evening it was onto a nightclub to watch the belly dancers and have the opportunity to experience the close attention of the female hostesses. Most, if not all, the trainees had no experience with this kind of situation. Not only did I need them to gain some experience of the nature of red light districts (passengers were always curious), I also wanted to see how they responded to the offer of prostitutes. It was, in fact, me seeing if they'd take the bait. It was a way for me to test their character again. This was also re-tested in places like Hamburg and Amsterdam.

I'd do a similar test with alcohol. I'd pretend to drink whilst encouraging them to top up all night. I needed to see how they handled their alcohol as this was another crucial indicator of character. Some drinkers change when they get a few drinks under their belt and I couldn't risk unleashing anything unexpected on my passengers. I also keenly observed how they dealt with women, especially when intoxicated. If they hassled them, I assumed they could do the same with the females on their bus.

Lastly, I wanted to see how well they got along with the others on the bus, often with little sleep or under stressful circumstances. All were necessary skills for being a capable Contiki tour leader.

Although the original selection of the trainees was very thorough, at least 20 per cent would on average be put off the training trip along the way. Some didn't even make it past the first couple of nights stop in Paris. Either they or I soon saw their unsuitability.

Those that passed the exhaustive training trip went into the classroom to be addressed by Contiki personnel. Finally they had to pass an extensive test to graduate. Before they went out on the road with their first group of passengers, I would say this to them:

'You have the responsibility to give our passengers an amazing tour. They have saved hard for this and put their faith in Contiki to give them an experience of a lifetime. We are now putting that faith in you. Don't let us down, don't let your passengers down and above all don't let yourself down.'

Before all tours departed the tour leaders were fully briefed. They received a detailed passenger list, with any personal points about individual passengers (such as medical matters or specific requests), ferry tickets, petrol coupons, funds in the form of travellers' cheques and currencies to run the tour. They were informed of every possible detail such as itinerary changes, new places to visit, price changes and potential border problems – everything we thought they might need to know (not unlike an airline crew before take-off). They were reminded to be well attired in their smart Contiki T-shirts and ensure their appearance reflected the professional image of the company – aside from dress-up and special occasion nights.

The Fodor's European guidebook and the Europa book of road maps were the original source documents but over the years we compiled our own additional 'bible'. This vitally important document was the guide to running the entire tour. It was a detailed file that ballooned in size over the years. It contained a brief summary of each country detailing the basic facts such as history, population, religion, politics, customs and currency. There was information on the main sights, excursions and activities plus details on the accommodation, where to shop for souvenirs, food supplies and recommended restaurants. It listed the costs of everything from camp fees, entrance fees, road tolls, ferry fares, taxes, our key contacts and contracts, to the price of a beer in each country. Border procedures in each country were also detailed, plus dealing with emergencies and consulate information. We constantly communicated with our field staff, often through regular newsletters to keep them updated and about new developments, so they were always in the loop.

Looking ahead I forecasted that at the current rate of growth our minibuses tally would more than double over the next two years. I realised we could soon hit 100! The image of 100 red minibuses running loose all over Europe was like envisaging a rash of the measles! What's more, we would require 100 plus trained drivers. We decided to look at introducing coaches.

The economy of scale was the first benefit that became clear. A coach could accommodate three-and-a-half minibus loads with half the number of staff: a driver and a tour leader. Even better, the operating cost to carry each passenger on a full coach would be dramatically cheaper. Coaches would not only make our tours cheaper they would provide considerably more comfort for our passengers and more space for the luggage and gear.

But we knew absolutely nothing about owning or running coaches. Not only were they very expensive beasts to buy, they needed drivers with coach licences and transport licences to operate them in Europe. And what happened if one of the coaches broke down while on tour? We couldn't just run out a replacement like we could with the minibuses. It was a whole new world and fraught with difficulty. Where on earth did we start?

In 1971 an opportunity arose to test a coach. We decided to hire a coach from a Belgium company with a Belgium driver and our own tour leader for a charter group of 45 Californians booked in for a three-week tour of Europe. The experiment turned out to be a huge success. The decision was made to slowly phase out the minibuses and replace them all with coaches.

Our next hired coach embarked on one of Contiki's regular Scandinavian/Russian tours, again very successful. We continued to use the Belgium company, adding a couple more coaches. By the end of the year, however, we had started to run into difficulties as the drivers were often older, had little interest in helping or joining in with the group, often didn't speak good English and disliked camping and the food intensely. Being professional drivers they were accustomed to their own hotel rooms and restaurant meals. They were also very strict about their driving hours, so often we were unable to take our passengers out in the evenings unless we found alternative transport. Some, however, rather liked being among so many young women and often became quite lecherous.

We switched to a couple of Dutch coach companies that were slightly more suitable, with younger drivers. The standard of the coaches, however, left a lot to be desired. In desperation we attempted to rectify the situation by buying our own coaches. We would not only take responsibility for the standard of coach but above all have our own drivers. With an arrangement to buy them over a period of time through our bankers and the coach manufacturers, on paper it looked to be a better option than hiring the Continental ones with their expensive and often unsuitable drivers.

We researched the best option and in 1974 we bought the first of three brand new English Bedford YRQ 'Dominant' coaches, which could seat 48 passengers. We called them Dom One, Two and Three and gradually introduced them into Europe, supplementing our hired coaches. Our drivers had to obtain a Public Service Vehicle (PSV) licence. In addition, to operate coaches with fare-paying passengers around the continent it was necessary for Contiki to have licences to do this, which we didn't yet have. We found that we could operate our coaches around Europe provided we had a UK licence and started and finished our 'closed door' tours in the United Kingdom. We obtained the required UK licence (not without difficulty) with our coaches required to travel both ways on the cross channel ferry, but this was a small price to pay to overcome the situation. The minibuses were phased out with a mix of hired coaches and our own.

Major troubles with the Contiki-owned coaches soon surfaced. The Bedfords were built to take a load of pensioners on a day trip to Brighton or a local rugby team to an away match in the United Kingdom. They were not built to carry our passengers plus their luggage plus the huge amount of camping equipment and food supplies. They didn't have enough locker space so we had to remove eight seats and build a four sided 'pig pen' inside the coach to take the overflow. It was unsatisfactory – déjà vu of my very first trips. What's more we'd lost eight fare-paying passengers instantly, with the removal of the seats. The engines were totally underpowered to cope with the extra weight and the various terrains we travelled. Whether it was climbing a Swiss mountain pass or descending from Andorra, the 'Doms' had no power to climb and the brakes weren't up to a steep descent. On the upside, the engines were fairly reliable and ran on some pretty rough diesel, which was handy, particularly in the communist countries.

Over time, we suffered from constant problems with the clutch, gear change linkage and broken springs and spring shackles. A spare water pump was usually part of the tool kit. Few garages around our routes had seen a Bedford, so we often had difficulty rectifying a problem, often having to fly spare parts out to Europe. When a coach became unserviceable we had no spare as a replacement. We had made a terrible mistake in running our own coaches. We had to think of another way – and fast, to resolve the situation as it was becoming untenable. It was then that the obvious dawned on us. We were not coach operators, we were tour operators!!

I remember telling my management team:

'Let's concentrate on what we know best, selling and running tours, and leave the operation of our coaches to a specialist coach operator. Let's find the best one we possibly can.'

Little did I know that the cavalry would soon arrive …

8. AT YOUR SERVICE

When WWII ended in 1945, Australia introduced the 'populate or perish' policy to address the desperate labour shortage and also assist the millions of Europeans displaced from their homelands. By 1947, a post-war immigration boom was underway. As part of the government-assisted incentive, migrants were offered a berth on a passenger liner for £10. As a result, by 1950 hundreds of thousands of migrants had arrived in Australia and New Zealand. The boats delivering the migrants, on return were packed with primary produce to feed the mother country, but the passenger cabins remained empty. The shipping companies needed to make these trips back to the United Kingdom a lot more profitable and hit on the plan of offering cheap fares to tempt curious Australian and New Zealand travellers to fill these cabins and enjoy an experience that would be the start of their once in a lifetime holiday. Different fare rates were introduced to cater for a range of travelling budgets and many offered entertainment. The idea of the modern-day cruise ship holiday was created. For a one-off fare, accommodation, three meals, organised activities and 24-hours of entertainment and carefree fun were included. The journey to the United Kingdom had the potential to be one long party.

Once these passengers stepped off the ship, they faced new challenges in the next stage of their big overseas adventure. As the competition was growing for tour passengers in and around London, we decided to intercept the new arrivals before they hit London. We placed Contiki salespeople on the train for the journey from dockside to the city of London. Those suitable as potential customers received a personalised voucher for either a tour of London or a pub crawl. Unfortunately our competitors decided to latch onto this idea too. Wanting to be two steps ahead of the competition I decided to intercept the passengers onboard the cruise ships – before they'd even arrived in the country. I flew a few tour leaders back to Australia and New Zealand and they did their undercover work on the journey – it was a highly successful strategy. However, the shipping companies got wind of my cunning plan and made it difficult for our sales people to sell onboard. Not one to throw in the towel, I tried planting staff on the boats at their last port of call before the United Kingdom, such as Lisbon or Genoa. This strategy didn't turn out to be very effective as the Contiki staff didn't have a chance to bond and gain the trust of those travellers onboard. Despite this, the passenger liners were dropping young and adventurous travellers as fast as they could get them across the Indian and Atlantic Oceans.

The opening of our Rathbone Street office in 1975 had coincided with the start of an explosion of young people arriving in London from Australia, New Zealand and South Africa. The passenger liners were running at full steam and landing thousands of passengers each week, with many of the younger ones heading directly to our doorstep.

The prime objective of these fresh-faced tourists was to see and live in London before taking off to see other parts of the United Kingdom and Europe. However, there was another much stronger underlying objective – they wanted to continue to enjoy their freedom and experiences, coupled with that primeval urge to meet other young people, particularly of the opposite sex!

Many of these young travellers had worked hard to save for their big trip, with their parents often making a monetary contribution. Most of the girls arrived in pairs or threesomes but some had just decided to 'up sticks' and take off alone. For most it was the first time they had lived away from home and virtually all had never been outside of their home country. They arrived in London needing advice about London, accommodation, jobs, an address to have their mail sent to, even a place to store their luggage and of course a way to see the United Kingdom and the Continent which we were already providing. We jumped at the opportunity to provide these extra needs! So, over the next few years we set out to provide the services to meet the ever increasing demand.

Initially we staffed our office reception with fellow New Zealanders and Australians who'd been through the experience of living in London and touring with Contiki, so the newly arrived could relate to them. Later we hired Londoners as well, as they had a more intimate knowledge of the city and its surrounds.

The first thing a new London arrival needed was somewhere to stay for those first few nights. We selected a couple of suitable hotels in the Bayswater area in the West End of London, close to Hyde Park and Oxford Street. We took a bed allocation in each, negotiating special discounted rates because of the volume of bookings. We booked our passengers in and when we offered the service to the Australasian travel agents the bookings went to another level. We constantly had to increase our allocations and add new hotels. One hotel, The Plaza, the largest in the area, became virtually exclusive to Contiki, being constantly booked out with our passengers. Within a very short period of time we convinced the hotel owners to turn the basement of the hotel into an exclusive Contiki disco.

Over the years with the popularity of this service, we still needed more beds. We were determined to stay out of Earls Court, where our gowning number of competitors were based, and we wanted to be seen as different and perhaps a little more 'upmarket'. We found a hotel right in the heart of the West End overlooking Piccadilly Circus. The Regent's Palace Hotel had over 1000 rooms. That should see us right, we thought. We became the hotel's biggest customer. As our custom increased the hotel turned away the majority of their regular tour wholesalers to accommodate us. All went fine until the hotel attempted to hike up the room rates to a level we considered unreasonable.

Without any resolution to this pricing change, we pulled out of the hotel. The hotel learnt a huge lesson as they were suddenly left with hundreds of empty rooms. It was a classic case of having all their eggs in the one basket – a big mistake.

A growing number of people wanted more semi-permanent accommodation pre- and post-tour since they had a fairly open mind as to how long they would stay. In the sixties and seventies most young people stayed one to two years. So in typical (rather gung ho) manner, we thought, 'Why not set up an accommodation bureau?' Landlords liked Australasians as tenants and we had a never-ending supply. The property owners would provide us with the details of their respective properties and we would endeavour to make the match. We received payment from the landlord either as a commission or the first week's rent.

Employers also liked Australasians. They'd send us their vacancies and paid us an introduction fee for an appropriate candidate. We considered developing an employment agency but realised it required too much capital to operate so we limited it to charging a fee for introductions.

As our passengers wanted to make other travel bookings, separate from their Contiki tours, we saw an opportunity to offer this service. So we set up our own separate travel agency. As such we were required to be a bonded member of The Association of British Travel Agents (ABTA). Membership necessitated sufficient capital, trained staff, audited accounts and a cash or bank bond posted in case the agency defaulted. We passed all the hurdles and became a member.

To run a full service travel agency, however, we needed to book flights, which required an International Air Transport Association (IATA) agency licence. We thought ABTA membership was hard to wrangle but in comparison an IATA licence was even tougher. With persistence, we gained it and now had a fully licensed travel agency. And the bonus? With an IATA licence the directors and key management could now apply for AD75s (75 per cent discount) for travel on all the member airlines around the world.

We also offered other sideline services free of charge such as allowing passengers to use our office address for their mail sent from home. This started with a trickle of mail delivered by the postman, ending up with the post office van turning up daily with sacks of mail. It almost got out of hand as our office staff had to sort it, pigeon-hole it, and look for the mail when the recipients came in to collect it so we sent the service down to the Plaza hotel in Bayswater.

Our visa service was also growing fast. The faster we added countries to our new travel routes, the more visas our passengers needed to secure. Young people of increasingly diverse nationalities had started to tour with us, which added another complexity to the type and number of visas required. Contiki was already managing all the Russian visas, due to their strict requirements. For a small fee we offered to obtain the required visas for the routes as well. This became a very active service, with two full-time staff on Vespa motor scooters roaring between consulates, waiting in queues and pleading with authorities to urgently issue visas for passengers who had dallied too long. It was a huge responsibility. We ended up buying a separate safe just to store the growing mountain of passports we had in our possession overnight.

All the additional services we provided covered costs and made a small contribution to our retail office overheads. Until we stumbled on, wait for it: luggage storage. Yes, as humble as it sounds, luggage service ended up being a licence to print money!

Bring to mind my nightmarish moment on tour number one in 1962, when my first round of passengers arrived with gargantuan suitcases. You might recall I quickly made a rule that passengers were permitted one suitcase which had to be under 24-inches (60 centimetres). Over the coming years this was troublesome, as few travellers actually showed up with the right sized suitcase. To get around this, early on I started to buy cheap suitcases of regulation size in bulk, and sold them to passengers (plus a sleeping bag if required). Problem solved! Once they'd bought the case, however, they needed somewhere to store their original bag, plus all the other bits and pieces they'd carted over from home. A weekly fee was charged for each item stored. Initially a couple of lock-up garages in the outer suburbs were rented, which quickly grew to five. With passenger numbers increasing we were starting to drown in luggage, but the upside was that fees collected were also increasing.

By 1976, the enormous unused basement at the Rathbone Place office had at last found a use. It was commandeered and racks put in to allow for thousands of items to be stored. When that filled up we took over a warehouse and employed a delivery van and full-time driver. Luggage storage had developed into a truly profitable sideline. Provide a service that people want, run it efficiently and there is a successful business right there in front of you.

Contiki regulation-size suitcase sales continued to boom. By now we'd bypassed the suitcase wholesaler and were dealing direct with the manufacturer. The service made so much money I often thought, 'Forget the tours, why don't we go into the storage business?'

In the early seventies, we created the Contiki Travel Club. The purpose was to continue offering all the current services, but also promote exclusive privileges to members. We produced a regular club newsletter – the *Tiki Times* with helpful travel tips, special deals, forthcoming excursions, events and entrance to the club's lounge and disco in the Plaza hotel.

Every second day we ran free two-hour orientation tours of London. The ulterior motive was to show off our great little buses with clued-up drivers onboard who would expertly explain all the sights as the bus toured around, demonstrating their ability to do the same in Europe. We always made sure the minibuses were the newest ones with the Contiki logo displayed on the side. We made sure the driver was good-looking, smartly dressed and had a charismatic personality, all designed as a subliminal sell – it worked a treat. Many of the publicity ideas came through suggestions from our drivers, who we encouraged to help us promote the tours, as it was also in their interests to fill the buses to be assured of a driving job.

In the evenings we continued to run pub crawls around the unique East End pubs of London. Each pub had a particular type of entertainment. Some, like The Waterman Arms on the Isle of Dogs had a staged music hall sing-along, others had comedy acts, some with drag queen performances. Two of the most popular included Dirty Dicks on the banks of the Thames River – a dark, dingy and claustrophobic pub with dead cats hanging from the ceiling for novelty factor – and the famous Prospect of Whitby, that lays claim that it is the site of the oldest riverside tavern in London dating back to 1520.

We ran excursions to areas outside of London to places such as Oxford and Cambridge and even up to Scotland for the Scottish New Year's tradition of Hogmanay. There were excursions to all the major events such as the Henley Boat Regatta, the famous Grand National horse race, or rugby matches. Rugby was a predictably popular option when the All Blacks, Wallabies or Springboks were playing. Contiki ran all of these short trips at cost so they were outstanding value.

We encouraged those that had already been on tour or booked with Contiki to take these excursions. Those that toured raved about their trips, encouraging others who had not booked to do the same. You simply can't beat that word of mouth advertising. If a passenger had already paid a deposit to tour with a competitor, we would offer to reduce the tour fare by their deposit amount if they jumped ship. We would gain a passenger and the opposition would lose one.

By 1977, with all this activity in London and the tour operation growing at a hectic pace, we took over, one by one, all three floors above the ground floor retail office to house our operations administrative staff, accounting department, and a now very active sales and marketing team producing countless brochures and sales material. The top floor was another inner sanctum where the directors, among other things, planned and plotted the future growth of the company.

Just two years later in 1979 we outgrew the top three floors, vacated them, but kept the ground floor retail reception premises. We moved south of the river Thames into even larger premises, in Brixton Road, just a short stone's throw away from the famous Oval cricket ground near Brixton.

The little venture that started out as a way for me to see Europe was definitely beginning to snowball. The next leg of my journey with Contiki was about to begin – with all the unexpected twists and turns.

9. A KING-HIT INTO ANOTHER LEAGUE

It was 1974, and the cavalry duly arrived in the form of a fleet of exceptional Mercedes-Benz coaches. After searching far and wide, it was a small village in Holland called Hellevoetsluis, south-west of the Dutch city of Rotterdam, that gave us what we needed. Vermaat's Autobedrijf BV was a family-owned company established in 1908 'by Royal appointment' to the Queen of the Netherlands. Vermaat operated many of the local bus services and had a small fleet of luxury touring coaches. It was run by Managing Director, Dick Vermaat, the son of the founder.

Contiki's directors took an immediate liking to Dick. He understood our predicament perfectly. He had a solid knowledge of Contiki as he'd observed us hiring coaches from his competitors. Vermaat was in a different league to the other outfits and we were very impressed with the quality of their bus and coach fleet, their efficient operations base and their staff. We decided Vermaat had to be the answer to so many of our problems and they, in turn, agreed to provide us with what we wanted. To put this simply: a reliable fleet of high-quality coaches at a realistic cost. It would, however, be an expensive exercise but compared with our previous coach hire and ownership debacles, we decided it was well worthwhile.

Running second-rate, cheap coaches had been an unmitigated disaster. We elected to go down the quality route. It may be a cliché, but there is no substitute for quality. On reflection, this single move was one of the most important reasons for Contiki's ultimate success. We progressively sold all our second-rate coaches and dispensed with the other coach hire companies.

We entered into a 'dry hire' agreement with Vermaat. This meant they would lease us Mercedes-Benz coaches and allow us to use our own drivers. We agreed to pay a guilder rate (Dutch currency) per kilometre, with a combined minimum number of kilometres each year. The rate would increase or decrease each year based on Holland's annual inflation rate. Vermaat agreed to shoulder the responsibility of training and employing our drivers and we would reimburse them for the driver wages.

The first coaches were Mercedes 0302s with V6 engines and progressed over the next couple of years to 0303s with V8s. The passengers loved the new coaches because they were comfortable, quiet and above all, reliable. The drivers felt so proud to be driving a Mercedes-Benz, particularly when they flew by one of our competitors in their older, often unreliable buses.

Vermaat had a sensible coach-servicing regime of preventative maintenance. They didn't wait for a part to become unserviceable. Instead, they systematically replaced parts once a certain number of kilometres had been clocked up. If any of the coaches had a difficulty with either a breakdown (almost unheard of) or a major accident that incapacitated the coach, Vermaat guaranteed to provide a replacement coach at no extra cost within 24 hours anywhere in Europe. We were very impressed with this guarantee as it was quite unheard of at the time. If our coach broke down in the middle of Yugoslavia or some other remote area, Vermaat's contacts all around the continent would ensure a replacement. If they could not procure a local vehicle, they would drive one from Holland until they got to the breakdown site. This gave us tremendous, and unprecedented, peace of mind.

The first coaches were painted in a dark Vermaat royal maroon, but with the introduction of the superior 0303 coaches we painted them in a bright Contiki yellow, and to make them appear really different placed a huge winking sun decal on each side. They looked amazing, attracting a huge amount of attention as they toured Europe. The 'big yellows' as they were affectionately known were moving advertisements.

At the end of the 1974, for practical reasons, we once again shifted the entire operations base, this time from Folkestone to Holland. It was a monumental task, but the base crew rolled up their sleeves and got to work filling up a couple of coaches with the gear. The tents, gas cookers, wicker baskets, airbeds and all sorts of other paraphernalia were stacked in the under-floor lockers and piled high within the bus, the coaches crossing the English Channel. At about 3.30 am one wintery morning they lumbered into Zeebrugge, Belgium, and were greeted at the border by an officious customs officer who asked 'And where do you think you're going with that lot?' We had been blissfully unaware that you can't shift such large quantities of goods from one country to another without documentation. The border guard was unwilling to allow a 45-seater coach with no passengers and camping gear stacked to the rafters to enter his country. It was probably only the staff's innocent explanation, coupled with desperate pleas and his own reluctance to unload tons of gear onto a freezing dockside that saw them waved through. They were similarly waved through a very busy Dutch border without a problem.

We initially set up the new operations base in Hellevoetsluis in an old bus garage that Vermaat kindly provided. We bought a house for our extremely capable operations base manager, Peter Webb, to live in. Another house was leased nearby to accommodate drivers on their tour turnarounds.

We kept seeking out new ideas and innovations to improve our tour product, be different and remain the industry leader. The 'supercooks' were the next part of this ongoing process.

The role of supercook was created to shoulder the huge responsibility of providing meals for groups of up to 52 passengers plus crew. The organisation and supplies required were mind-boggling; let alone the buying and preparation of them. This was a huge relief for the passengers, who were still rostered on to assist, but made for a far more superior and efficient operation. The supercooks also stayed at the new operations base on their tour turnarounds. We designed new custom-built cooking units (webco burners) to fit neatly in the coach luggage locker. These could easily be operational within minutes of arrival – a masterpiece of innovation. In the coaches we also installed small refrigerators which created a constant battle between crew members. Were they for the supercook's perishables or for the tour crew's beer supply? The decision was left to the strongest personality on each tour!

A club area was introduced at the back of the coaches where we removed a row of seats, reversed another, and put in a couple of tables. Many a card game of '500' or poker was won or lost there. Video players were introduced later for the overnight ski runs.

Our involvement with the Vermaat team took the company to a whole new level. The close relationship and trust that developed between our two companies over the next 15 years was nothing short of incredible. Successful businesses often revolve around people, their relationships, mutual trust and cooperation. Vermaat and Contiki were in business together as a team. We needed them and they needed us.

Around this time (1975) with me having passed the age of 35, and still feeling I could easily fit in with our younger passengers, we lifted the age restriction which had crept to 18–30 to 18–35! This increased our target market size by nearly 40 per cent.

In 1977 another idea began to germinate. The number of copycat competitors was hovering at around 15 – too much for our liking …

We hatched a plan with the objective to make our product unique – 'the point of difference', so we could move away from the pack once and for all. We reckoned we could not only grow the overall market but also take people away from our competitors. With the increased passenger numbers we would obtain even better economies of scale. And the brilliant plan?

Imagine this. A coach with 50 or so passengers arrives at a campsite in Barcelona late in the evening and it is raining heavily. It's been a long, long drive since leaving Lyon early that morning and everyone is very tired. The coach pulls up at the dimly lit campsite and the passengers pile out only to face the enormous task of unpacking and setting up for the night. Tents need to be erected, airbeds need to be pumped up, the cooking equipment set up and the evening meal has to be prepared. A day or two later, as the tour moves on, everything is dismantled and packed away on the coach. The gear is wet and soggy making it hard to pack up, not to mention being time consuming. At the next site the whole rigmarole is done again … and again … and again.

Our plan was to erect permanent tent villages in the camp grounds, initially on our European routes and eventually throughout our entire network. They would be built at the beginning of the season and taken down at the end. We decided to use French-style frame tents which you could walk into instead of crawling into. The supercooks would be based at the villages instead of on the coaches, which would also give us an extra fare paying seat. In addition we would have a huge custom-made cook tent for catering. All the camping equipment could come off the coaches, saving wear and tear, and therefore allowing more storage space. And the huge bonus – the amount of time saved was incalculable. As we nutted out the finer points, the advantages kept multiplying.

That, in essence, was the plan. How on earth were we going to make it happen? Nothing like this had ever been done before. The thought of convincing the camp owners and local authorities was overwhelming. But we knew that if we could pull it off, we would skyrocket into another league.

We had trialled a tent village for a week in the south of France during the previous season. To ensure secrecy, we pretended we were investigating options for a new product catering to English families on their annual holiday. This enabled us to configure the best use of space, see how it all worked with live passengers and take photographs for the new brochure. However, as we calculated the costs we realised that to make it all viable we would need to increase the number of passengers by a staggering 60 per cent!

Up to this point our occupation of the camp grounds was very patchy. Some nights we could have three or four coach loads of up to 200 passengers, yet on other nights, just one of 50. If we were to build a permanent tent village we would be required to pay for the space or number of passengers (however the camp charged) whether there were groups staying there or not. If we were going to promote 'never having to put up a tent' it would mean all the passengers would expect this. Our cunning plan faced a huge hurdle.

The logistics of dove-tailing all the different itineraries and departure dates to fit into the available village accommodation became complicated, almost impossible. A master chart was created, affectionately known as King John's *Magna Carta*. Many long hours were spent sorting the massive jigsaw puzzle. Every change affected coach numbers, staff, equipment and the eventual selling price of the tours. It was finally decided to build villages that could accommodate four coach loads and the site staff totalling 220 people – huge!

We still faced two major tasks. Could we get permission to build the villages in each city? And once committed to the concept, could we sell the massive number of extra seats required to make the whole idea financially viable? The capital expenditure required for the new tents alone was uncomfortably high. The project was fraught with risk but all those involved agreed that the benefits would outweigh the risk.

The company was becoming increasingly profitable. The directors had a policy of constantly reinvesting the profits back into the business with the aim of building a strong company base for future growth. It was decided to we would go ahead with the idea as its successful implementation would pull us way, way ahead of our competitors

We held off as long as possible before approaching the campsites with our proposal. There was a strategic reason for this. We wanted our competition to have already committed to their brochures for the following season before getting wind of our new plan. This meant we could strike with a brand new product. In the end, we had to commit to our own brochure too early and include the village concept before we had permission from all the campsites. With the pressure on to produce the brochure, we had a fall-back position. Instead of saying 'every night' we said, '*most nights* you will not have to put up a tent'.

The negotiations to build the villages were not easy. Campsite owners had been doing the same thing, the same way for years and it took extreme patience and negotiating skills to make them understand the new concept. By explaining the advantages and benefits long term for them – we did it. We obtained permission from every single campsite we approached. In some of the smaller sites where we could not justify a village, accommodation was arranged in cabins or very reasonably priced hotels.

At this point, it's worth mentioning what I learnt in those early years when it comes to negotiating. Whenever I wanted something either personally or for the company from someone else, the first thing I would do was put myself in the shoes of the other person. It was not just about what I wanted, it was equally important to know or identify what the other person wanted. If you can satisfy, within reason, what the other person wants, you'll more often get what you want. Think about it.

New tents were ordered, manufactured and delivered to the sites, through all the different custom borders (often in the dead of night to minimise customs regulations). It might appear to be straightforward; it wasn't. Prior to the season starting a small operational team was sent out to set up the villages, which turned out to be an overwhelming physical effort. The finishing touches to the first village were added days before the first tour came through.

You can imagine the stress for those involved, particularly with tight time pressures on them. Nevertheless, a dedicated team of people who believed in an almost impossible task set out on a mission and achieved it. I can't express strongly enough what it does to a company or organisation's culture when a team of people set out together, with an almost impossible task, and pull it off. We were on a high!

Our sales force loudly trumpeted our new initiatives. Within a matter of weeks, bookings for the following year went through the roof, and continued to do so. In 1978, Contiki carried over 65 per cent more passengers than the previous year. We had taken a calculated risk, largely based on gut feeling, and delivered a new and unique product to the market. We named the new tour our 'concept tour'.

And the bonus – our competitors were in total disarray. Not only had we pulled market share from them, but one by one, they realised they would have to introduce something similar to keep up. Yet without the passenger numbers, it would be nearly impossible to make it commercially viable.

Many of our prospective passengers wanted to travel with other young people, but disliked the idea of camping and cooking their own meals. They wanted and could afford a little more comfort. After lifting the age restriction to 35 we decided to take Contiki to introduce hotel tours with restaurant meals. Initially we introduced a 20-day and a 33-day tour of Europe. The content of these tours was similar to the concept tours. The response to the hotel programme was just as enthusiastic as for the new concept tours.

In those few short years we had hit the jackpot. With our Mercedes-Benz coaches, concept tours and hotel tours we had moved Contiki up into a whole new league. We'd delivered not just one king-hit but three! Contiki would never look back – the only way was up!

10. NOW FOR SOMETHING COMPLETELY DIFFERENT

I was standing in the driveway of Villa Torre de Gattia and could barely believe what I was seeing. The villa was situated diagonally opposite Piazza Michelangelo where a statue of 'David' stood, overlooking the River Arno and the stunning city of Florence. The villa dated back to the 13th century with its own olive grove and swimming pool set in the most magnificent gardens.

It was late 1977 and I had flown in to nearby Pisa from London that morning to meet Kit Nixon, one of Contiki's field managers. Three months before, Kit had been given a mammoth mission. His brief had been simple:

'Find a villa in Italy, in either Rome, Florence or Venice. It has to be close to town and sleep up to 220 passengers.'

Contiki had decided to take its tours to yet another level. With the successful introduction of the Concept Tours, we were on a roll. We also knew it was only a matter of time before our competitors tried to copy us. And again, we were determined to remain the market leader, never the follower.

An idea started to take shape, which would make the implementation of the villages seem like child's play and totally overwhelm the opposition.

Instead of our concept tour passengers staying in a tent every night, why not put them in a hotel for the odd night? On investigation we found that even though we could accommodate up to four in a room it would still be considerably more expensive than camping, let alone finding enough suitable hotels. Plus, we would not be able to cook our own meals and restaurants would be too expensive. Why not give our passengers the experience of staying in character accommodation typical of the country they were travelling through? Perhaps a villa in Italy, a chateau in France, a castle in Germany, a chalet in Austria or Switzerland, a farmhouse in Ireland. Our imagination knew no bounds.

Who was going to find the properties? What was the cost? What were the risks? How would we run them? Did we have the resources? How did we keep things secret? We were about to enter a whole new territory that would present us with challenges far beyond anything else we had tried before.

We agreed, one property at a time. Each would present a different set of circumstances needing a clear brief and plan. Ideally we didn't want to own any of the properties but if there was no alternative to leasing we would consider buying them. The properties had to be situated in areas where we had high passenger volumes passing through and be able to accommodate a minimum of one coach load – 54 passengers, plus crew. We used the cover that we were looking for accommodation for the English domestic market so we could investigate without alerting the competition.

Enter Kit Nixon, one of our very capable field managers, and his Italian mission. Knowing very little Italian or where to start, he began the search, enlisting the help of several of our Italian suppliers. Several months passed before Kit started to concentrate his efforts in Florence. With the help of one of our key suppliers, leather store-owner Paolo Fortini, Kit investigated numerous properties. Discouragingly, there was always some major impediment ruling the potential places out. But one day I received a phone call from a very excited Kit.

'John, I think I've found it!'

I was on the first plane out to nearby Pisa the next morning.

It didn't take me long to understand Kit's excitement. Villa Torre de Gattia had been the palatial home of the aristocratic Pitti family before they moved down to the Pitti Palace. The villa was situated at Viuzzo di Gattia 9, Firenze, and was a pleasant walk from the centre of Florence. It had most recently been occupied by students learning about the finer things in life at an upper-class American finishing school. The school had vacated the year before and the villa was completely stripped of every stick of furniture. The villa was huge, had enormous rooms and a kitchen with a 3000-litre refrigerator and immense cooking stoves big enough to 'feed the 5000'. We excitedly estimated that the villa could fulfil our requirements.

It was owned by Madame Andina who lived on the shores of picturesque Lake Lugarno in Switzerland. I was given the task of convincing her what an excellent idea it would be to lease the property to us. Accompanied by my wife Ali, we met Madame Andina in her magnificent antique-filled apartment. To our utmost relief she spoke fluent English. I told her our passengers were not unlike her previous finishing school tenants. They too were young people but from the Commonwealth countries of Australia, New Zealand, Canada, etc, and were eager to learn about the history and cultural treasures Florence offered.

'Many have graduated from universities in their home countries with fine arts degrees,' I assured her – anything to convince Madame Andina.

Over afternoon tea, with her 20 year old son by her side, Ali and I successfully negotiated the lease of the villa. I was elated. However, this was just the beginning.

First, we had to satisfy a never-ending series of Italian regulatory requirements for permission to occupy the property. The frustration on occasions was almost intolerable as we seemed to be wantonly blocked at every step. With sheer determination and help from Paolo (who seemed to have many friends in high places) we got through it. We also paid a few million lire to oil the wheels of officialdom. Initially this was something I felt very uncomfortable about, but soon learnt it was often the way business was done – and not just in Italy.

Next was outfitting the cavernous property to sleep and feed 220 people. We divided it into bedrooms, public rooms, a lounge with a bar and an enormous dining room. The list of furniture, bunks, kitchen gear, cleaning gear, light shades, wall prints and so on was endless. The buying spree was a sight to behold. The costs were staggering, inching higher each day.

Early on we found three antique refectory tables in a back street market. These long thin monastery-type tables were massive and also aesthetically in keeping with the property. They would be perfect to fill space in areas such as the hallways and could also be used as dining tables.

'You're very lucky,' the market stallholder assured us. 'These tables are quite rare and a very good investment.'

We were suitably impressed and, after much haggling, we bought all three, asking the vendor to watch out for more that might became available. He assured us he would search relentlessly and let us know. The following week he had miraculously found two more tables, which we promptly snapped up. But we still needed more. A few days later our man had located yet another at which point he asked how many more we required.

'Another five or six would be ideal,' we said.

'I think I can help you as you are such a good customer,' he said with a grin.

He took us down some narrow back streets to a warehouse, far from the tourist area. To our astonishment, there in front of us, were a couple of 'antique' tables similar to our own, being lashed with chains to 'age' the wood. Further along the assembly line we saw others that had just received the 'treatment' being varnished. Lesson learnt!

We did a deal, all was forgiven, and we obtained our full complement of tables at a substantial discount.

We eventually had the villa up and running. It was required to be registered with the authorities, so we chose the name of 'The Art Treasures of the World Cultural Association', a non-profit making organisation. All passengers had to be enrolled as members and given a membership card. We had to be registered (for tax purposes) to receive income for food and accommodation. We had to produce accounts and pay tax, which we did. The bar was run outside the scope of the Association and lavishly stocked with an amazing array of duty-free spirits, which somehow managed to find their way onto the bar shelves!

At the same time we were setting up the villa in 1978, we were also on the hunt for more character accommodation around Europe and turned our attention to France. All our European tours went through Paris and headed south to either Nice or Barcelona in Spain, requiring an overnight stop on the way. Why not a French chateau for this stopover? We gave this responsibility to Dave Hosking who was engaged to research new routes and develop new ideas. There seemed to be dozens of chateaux available but few suited our strict criteria. That was until Dave came across Chateau de Cruix near the small village of Theiz in the heart of the Beaujolais wine-growing area, just north of Lyon. This baroque style chateau had been built around 1876 on the site of an ancient chateau, with an original 16th century private chapel still beside it. A procession of counts, barons and French aristocracy had lived there through centuries. Unfortunately it was not available for lease.

Dave thought it would be ideally suited to our requirements. Sure it was a little rundown, but most of the ones he'd seen were in a similar state of disrepair. The geographical position of this property was perfect and it had the potential, with some imagination, to sleep a coach load of 54 plus accommodate the staff required to run it. The owner was interested in selling – so we bought it.

We set about preparing the property, again with the same hiccups experienced with the villa. Fortunately we found an extremely helpful bi-lingual English lawyer, who lived in Lyon, to guide us through the minefields.

We'd seen a few hot air balloons flying through the region and mused that it would be another unique experience for our passengers. We were unable to find a local operator who would operate and station the balloon at the chateau, so decided to do it ourselves. We located a company in Birmingham, UK, to make us a balloon with our 'winking sun' and logo on the side. They also agreed to take responsibility for operating our balloon experience. Our lawyer dealt with the legal requirements to import the balloon and fly it. We soon learnt about all the complexities of French law relating to flying an aircraft. Balloons are defined as an aircraft. *D'accord, oui*, no problem. The balloon duly arrived with Bruno, a fully licensed pilot. We were ready to ascend!

Originally we took our passengers for flights over the countryside, but on many occasions our retriever vehicle had difficulty trying to keep up. When we finally located the passengers they would often be found merrily traipsing around with some farmer in his vineyard tasting the local drop. The balloon had a mind of its own, often landing in the middle of someone's crop, with the basket cutting a swathe through his valuable maize or vines. Hysterical for those onboard, not so funny for the hapless French farmer.

Our final Waterloo appeared one evening when the balloon came down in a paddock that was home to a prized mare, which had recently won the prestigious *Prix de l'Arc de Triomphe* race at Longchamps near Paris. The horse was in foal, but with the unexpected landing of our balloon it panicked, went berserk, and began galloping wildly around the paddock. A day later it tragically miscarried. Our insurance company dealt with the matter …

We reduced the flights to tethered ones in the grounds of Chateau de Cruix. One day, the local gendarmerie turned up. 'The neighbours have complained, the noise of the burners is too much,' they told us.

We were instructed to take the balloon to the local air force base. Our chateau manager spent the night in custody and our local solicitor was again fully employed. Our hot air balloon experience skidded to a halt.

The area around Chateau de Cruix proved to be wonderful for passenger's activities such as day trips on bicycles around the countryside. A picnic lunch (with the obligatory baguette stuffed with *fromage* and *jambon* and a bottle of Beaujolais vin ordinaire) completed the picture.

Many still remember the nights spent in 'The Cave' basement (the disco, bar and entertainment epicentre), where the staff would often tap into their showbiz alter-egos and perform, such as the rock-group Status Quo. And those dress-up nights were something no one ever forgets!

Meanwhile our local man on the ground in Athens, Spyro Spyromilio, who had become our close friend and business partner, had been very active. Originally he'd been responsible for finding an exclusively leased boat, *MV Contiki*, on which our passengers could stay overnight and cruise around the Aegean Sea visiting the idyllic Greek Islands. Although unique, it had been a very expensive exercise. Spyro also found us tavernas on the islands and hotels on the mainland. He even helped to arrange for a straw hut village to be built on the island of Corfu exclusively for the use of our passengers. Any problems, anywhere in Greece, Spyro or his son Miltos would sort them out.

One day Spyro came to us with a proposal. He had located the hull of a disused Greek mine-sweeper that could be picked up cheaply. It could be converted into a 130-metre, three-masted schooner, 54 berths (a coach load) plus staff accommodation. It would be a great investment, and long-term, it would be cheaper than our current arrangements. The total cost would be in the vicinity of US$1.5 million, which made us cringe. But we decided to spread and limit the risk by going ahead in a three-way partnership between Contiki, Spyro and a Greek investor. Spyro would take responsibility to build, license and operate the boat. We would deliver the passengers.

The SV *Artemis* took a year to build. It was not plain sailing, with constant difficulties, delays and cost overruns. Eventually it was completed and obtained its seaworthiness and operating certificates. With a skipper, a crew of four, plus Contiki's representative, our passengers could again cruise the Greek Islands in their own exclusive schooner.

We operated the boat for four years. However, with the growth in the number of passengers it became too small for us, and with its inability to sail due to inclement weather, it was sold at a considerable loss on the original investment. Ouch! Although our passengers enjoyed their time on board, it had been a mistake to build it in the first place. We were tour operators not boat owners. We went back to using other people's boats for the cruises.

The beautiful village of Lauterbrunnen in Switzerland is one of my favourite places in the world. I had discovered it on my very first tour in 1962. It is situated in a hidden valley surrounded by high, snow-capped mountains including the Eiger but dominated by the mighty 13,642-foot Jungfrau. With small picturesque villages on the green-grassed mountain sides dotted with cows, and the sound of cowbells ringing throughout the valley, it is the ultimate Swiss postcard scene.

When I arrived with my original group we decided to stay there for a couple of nights. There was no camp ground, so I drove down a side road to an old farmhouse and knocked on the door, requesting the owner's permission to camp on one of his paddocks.

That farmhouse door belonged to the Von Allum family. Twenty-five years after that first knock, I was flown from New Zealand as the guest of the Von Allum family and the village to celebrate our long and successful association. From that first meeting in 1962 Hans Von Allum, his family and Contiki developed a wonderful business relationship. After the first Contiki group stayed in his paddock, the Von Allum family began to transform their small farm into the largest camp ground in the area, eventually building a 100-bed purpose-built chalet to exclusively accommodate the Contiki passengers.

We had a similar relationship with the owner of Gasthof (guesthouse) Schoneck in Hopfgarten, Austria. This became our ski season base after our move from St Johann in Tirol. Gasthof Schoneck was run by a delightful Austrian lady, Lorie Pendrick, who could never do enough for us. We all adored Lorie, her Gasthof, the village and its people so much that we decided to bring our summer tours through as well. We entered into an arrangement where we would lease the property year-round and completely take over its operation with our own staff.

In the late 1980s the directors of Contiki received a letter from Lorie.

'You are the only family I have. I love you all dearly. I have instructed my legal advisors to leave Gasthof Schoneck to you in my will.'

Now if that isn't a close business relationship, I don't know what is!

In the seventies the vast majority of passengers would spend the last night of their tour at a camp ground in Brugge, Belgium, before heading back to the United Kingdom. Every night there would be around 200 passengers having their final party night – and I mean partying! A lot of the time it was raining and activities on the night often didn't fit with the other campers, so we decided to find an alternative last night stopover. Our team in Hellevoetsluis discovered a disused WWII hospital on the outskirts of Noordgouwe, a small village just south of their base. I reckon some of the passengers after their tour and last party could have done with a real hospital to recuperate in!

The Groothuis, as it was affectionately known, had four wards, which previously accommodated around 16 beds in each. We slept a coach load of 50 in each by bunking the passengers three high. Can you imagine, at night, all that humanity in one room? Sometimes in the middle of the night someone would rollover on the top bunk and somehow fall over the side landing with a crunching thump on the wooden floorboards below. Sometimes there would be a thump, then another thump off the same bunk – if you know what I mean!

Over the years we gave our passengers the experience of staying in one of the many castles perched high on the hills in the Rhine Valley overlooking the river, on which we had our own exclusive boat for a cruise and an overnight stop. The tours around Britain received the same treatment. These included our country house in Caernarvon, Wales (Glan Gwana Hall), our Scottish castles (Craighall and Dalnaglar) our hotel in Devon and farmhouses in Ireland. Contiki found all of these properties and negotiated their use for our passengers so they could experience something unique, something very special.

Even the hotel tours joined in, with unique properties like Chateau Fontager near Lyon in France and Hotel Bellevue on top of Mount Pilatus overlooking Lake Lucerne in Switzerland (only accessible by the steepest cog railway in the world). Hotel Bellevue was the one featured in the James Bond movie, *On Her Majesty's Secret Service*!

Every one of those special stopovers has its own story. How it was found, set up and enjoyed by the passengers. Many of you reading this book that have travelled or worked with Contiki will have your own very special memories.

With the addition of special stopovers all over Europe and the United Kingdom, we had created another unique product. It took years of determination and hard work to achieve such a strong position in the market place, but we did it!

11. THE COPYCATS

When my first tour bumped its way around Europe, there were a couple of other outfits also running similar camping tours. Once I was successfully operational, I knew it was only a matter of time before the copycats would start to climb on board and start up in opposition, taking market share. I never expected it to come from one of my own trusted drivers.

You will recall when I retired from the road in 1966 that the second driver had taken over from me. Ian Johnson, an Australian, was intelligent, enthusiastic, had a dry sense of humour, and was someone I thought of as a great addition to my team. After another European tour he travelled as a trainee on our first tour to the Middle East. On that tour he met Lynne, an extremely attractive passenger, whom he subsequently married. What I didn't know, when he claimed to be unavailable the following season, was that he was planning to start up as Contiki's first genuine competitor. At the end of what turned out, in hindsight, to be Ian's last trip, he didn't hand in his account books or the trip bible. He told me that he'd lost them. With this information and the practical experience he had gained, Ian was ready to go. He and Lynne teamed up in 1967 to start Transit Travel which grew to become my biggest competitor. Transit Travel even used Ford Transit minibuses identical to ours – except they were blue.

Soon after Ian had jumped ship another of my drivers, Warren Sandral did the same thing. He was also an Australian with heaps of confidence and personality. He named his company NAT Travel and, like Ian, chose Ford Transit minibuses. These minibuses were red – exactly the same as ours.

For the first couple of years Warren didn't paint NAT's company name on the side of his vehicles. As a result some of his drivers regularly passed their tours off as Contiki and were able to benefit from the special deals I'd made over the years with the camp grounds and suppliers. Often when NAT passengers were over the top, unruly or in trouble, Contiki was blamed. Fortunately, NAT changed direction and became a major tour operator catering for the English packaged holiday market to resorts in places like Spain and Greece, ceasing to be close competition.

The defection of two people I'd deeply trusted was a wake-up call. I had naïvely trusted everyone in my fledgling enterprise. I had given people a unique opportunity to see Europe and be paid for the privilege. But Ian and Warren made me realistically aware that I had also trained them and provided them with all the details and information on running a tour; the tricks of my trade. While I felt terribly betrayed, I also knew they were completely within their rights to start their own businesses. They were doing nothing illegal and, like everyone else, Contiki was fair game. My lesson? Trust people to a point, but always watch your back.

On one occasion, I came across one of my ex-passengers in the Rome camp who had seen a similar opportunity. He had put up a few notices in London, bought one of my old Commer minibuses as I replaced them with the Fords and was running his own operation.

From the late sixties onwards, the rise of the copycats was meteoric. Some outfits lasted one trip, some lasted a season and some chugged around for a good couple of years. There were a few real cowboys sporting a fleet of clapped-out old vehicles, which constantly broke down and limped around their chosen itinerary. Their drivers had never been to Europe let alone been trained around the route (sounds familiar). Their camping and cooking equipment was often totally inadequate and in disrepair. Some were disorganised and underfunded to the point where passengers had to pitch in extra cash to keep the tour on the road (yes, that could have been me too). Occasionally through weak leadership, their passengers did not get along too well and fought constantly as the tour disintegrated.

In the early years a few unscrupulous competitors surfaced going out of their way to make life difficult for me. Typical of their underhand tactics was removing the petrol caps from my minibuses while they were parked overnight in a camp ground, and pouring sugar into the petrol tank. Some even left a camp ground without paying the bill and when our tour arrived we were asked to pay as the previous group had a similar type and colour of vehicle.

There were, however, other operators who approached their business ventures in a very professional manner. They had strong entrepreneurial leaders at the helm who had seen the huge potential this new camping tour industry offered. They were determined to take advantage of the opportunity to create a well-run company for their future benefit.

As the industry grew, Contiki, together with the other serious operators, became extremely concerned at some of the cowboy operations. Their vehicles were sub-standard and unsafe, their equipment was in disrepair, and many of their drivers were untrained and often unscrupulous. Many passengers were terribly disillusioned that they had not received what they'd been promised and paid for. They were giving the whole industry a bad reputation so we decided we had to do something about it.

In 1969, Contiki, along with other tour operators, instigated the formation of an association called the Association of Camping Tour Operators (ACTO) and invited all camping tour operators to join. The purpose was to lift the standard of each company's operation. The founding members were Contiki, Transit, Protea, Sundowners, CCT and Atrek. We wrote a constitution with strict rules and regulations that members had to fulfil to become and remain a member. These required minimum standards for tour operation, training, office premises, and the submission of annual accounts to an independent auditor to ensure that the company was viable. It was the beginning of the death knell for the cowboys.

A logo was created that members could display on their brochures. The standard of most operators started to improve dramatically. Prospective passengers and travel agents could differentiate between operators and book with confidence. Likewise, suppliers such as the camp grounds gave ACTO members preferential treatment on factors such as space and price. All operators were encouraged to join, no matter how small, as we reckoned it was better to have them in the fold rather than acting as loose cannons outside. Establishing ACTO can be credited for changing the overall quality of the industry.

All the companies at one stage or another were plagued with rogue drivers and tour leaders. Some were opportunists ripping off their passengers for their own advantage. Some would destroy a tour through total mismanagement, excessive alcohol consumption, personality problems, womanising, negligence at the wheel, dishonesty or even criminal activity. Some even abandoned their passengers halfway through the tour, running off with the girlfriend they'd hitched up with on the trip. Some took off with the tour funds after the first couple of weeks never to be seen again.

Often an offending staff member had to be dismissed. These individuals then applied to other tour operators who hired them with no knowledge of their previous misdemeanours. To rectify the problem, ACTO established a black list of errant staff and circulated it among members.

Over the years the owners and management of the mainstream camping tour operators became well acquainted. We were a mixed bag of individuals. Originally all were Australians, New Zealanders and South Africans but later the English climbed aboard the wagon too. We were all very competitive and, on occasions, quite aggressive in securing passengers. However, once a tour was on the road, most closed ranks and supported each other. It could be anything from a vehicle breakdown, an accident, or lending items (such as a driver).

There were the inevitable business failures with operators going bust, some quite dramatically stranding hundreds of passengers around Europe, not to mention those already booked to travel with no bus to pick them up.

The most spectacular implosion was Ian Johnson's Transit Travel. Transit had become extremely successful; second behind Contiki with regard to quality, innovation and passenger numbers. However, it all came horribly unstuck early in the summer of 1980. A number of factors, including one of their major sales agents defaulting, their brochure being delivered three months late, adverse currency movements, guarantees given to a London hotel that could not be fulfilled, Contiki's new product innovations and an intransigent bank contributed to their downfall.

Contiki banded with the other ACTO members and picked up some of the stranded Transit passengers across Europe wherever seats were available so they could complete their trip. For passengers at home who had already fully paid for their trip and were looking glumly at the prospect of no tour at all, Contiki offered to carry them at a 50 per cent discount on an equivalent tour. It was a huge undertaking but we understood the passengers' predicament and genuinely wanted to help. We also realised we would receive invaluable publicity by being the good guys, even though it would come at considerable financial cost. Many of these passengers were grateful but there were some who expected more than we offered. People are very quick to criticise but slow to compliment.

I had mixed feelings about the competition. I'd worked so hard to get my little company successfully established and the product accepted by the market. I constantly innovated and seeing other outfits jumping onto my ideas and copying them was, at times, very frustrating. If you can't beat 'em, go after them. And Contiki did, in a big way.

Up until this point we'd monitored the competition through their activities on the London market and reports from our field staff and suppliers. We checked their brochures to work out what they were offering, their itineraries, tour fares, and departure numbers. We found out who owned and operated the businesses and their *modus operandi* and, to a degree, where they sourced their passengers.

We decided to go one step further to find out even more about our competitors. We hired English university students in their holidays to visit Europe incognito, pretending to research a thesis on the increasing numbers of antipodeans travelling the continent. We briefed them requesting they interview our competitors' field staff, passengers and suppliers. They were to find out absolutely everything about them. We gave them lists of suggested questions, but told them to use their own curiosity and initiative – no questions were barred. It was the prerogative of the person questioned to decide if and how they responded. While they were at it, we asked them to talk to Contiki's tour staff and passengers as well.

Naturally the burning question the one we *really* wanted answered from our competitor's passengers was: 'Why did they book the tour they were on and why not Contiki?' We thought we knew the reasons but wanted to know if there were other reasons too. We also wanted to know what the competitors' field staff thought about their own company and about Contiki, and also what our suppliers thought about us too.

With some detective work we found out a little more about their financial situation, their policies, training regimes, what they paid their field staff, passenger numbers and even some of their plans for the following year. Fortunately not many had any firm plans!

Our suspicions as to why passengers were travelling with the competition were soon confirmed. We were seen to be too expensive, too big, too organised, too structured and too commercial. On consideration, we were prepared to accept the 'charges' laid down. We knew that these, when viewed with a positive lens, rather than a negative one, were also the attributes that made Contiki truly successful. Too organised? The flipside of this meant few border delays or mechanical breakdowns for example. Too big? Size was what gave us purchasing power, the capital to try new routes and the opportunity to innovate. Too expensive? We had far superior coaches, equipment, exclusive accommodation and more included excursions and entrance fees and so on.

The market research discoveries that did concern us were the false assumptions and rumours that surfaced. Some thought our company and passengers were elitist and that we were ripping off our passengers with our higher prices. They believed we were making too much money. Some of the competition gossiped that we were about to go bust. There was a strong feeling that our passengers were unfriendly, posh, or had been shouted their trip by mummy and daddy and hadn't earned their own money. We were seen to be the ogres that were hell bent on putting our competitors out of business. This last claim was not a rumour.

Our little team of uni students also reported back some disturbing facts about our suppliers. We discovered some were not as loyal as we had believed. Some broke our confidences or were critical of our operations. Their criticism of Contiki was usually to win favour with the competition and feather their own nests. Still, I was surprised. Often a supplier I may have lunched with the week before, would make derogatory comments about the company not knowing they were actually talking to a Contiki employee, who would duly report the conversation back to us.

These days this type of research would be classed anti-competitive or deemed not quite above-board. Back in the 1970s and 1980s it was okay. How times have changed.

Armed with all our new-found information, or should I say intelligence, we strengthened our campaign to weaken our competitors. If there was the option to work together with them, we would. The others, we would pursue. A four-pronged attack was planned.

The first was to ensure that everything we did was far superior in every possible way to our competitors. We looked at all elements of our operation. This covered the quality of our office staff, starting with how the telephone was answered, the receptionists, reservations system, quality of our brochures, right through to the training of our field staff, vehicles, equipment and tour operations.

The second was to identify our competitor's major weaknesses and highlight our major strengths. We put more information in the Contiki brochures, justifying our higher prices. We clearly detailed the extras included in the tour highlighting the fact that the others didn't have these. We included all the points of difference and emphasised our experience with the fact we'd been established since 1962. Although our tours would remain the most expensive, they would always offer the best value.

The third was a long-term strategy to continue to innovate and introduce new and exclusive elements to our business. We were determined to keep differentiating ourselves, creating new and unique elements to the tours.

The fourth was to strengthen and extend our sales and marketing initiatives, firmly establishing the Contiki brand name as one that could be trusted to consistently deliver what it promised.

Following this approach took Contiki to new heights – in due course, it also contributed to the demise of all our competitors, bar one.

Competition is a good thing for business. While it can seem confronting, especially if others appear to be stealing your precious ideas, ultimately it keeps you on your toes and forces you to continually pull ahead of the pack. Complacency is not an option with competition at your heels. With other operators in the market, we looked hard at what made Contiki different, re-enforced these things, and kept innovating. We were forced to reflect our best attributes in our marketing materials and sales efforts. It made us a tighter and a more disciplined operation. If a business is strong enough, competition will not kill it; it will only make it better.

For the historical record I list below the majority of competitors who operated European tours exclusively for the 18 to 35 year old market. The list may not be complete, for which I apologise, but it was a long time ago!

Kangaroo Travel, Autotours, Tan Travel, Protea Tours, Vikings International, Frontier Travel International, Atrek Travel, Transit Travel, NAT, Sundowners, Top Deck Travel, Pacesetter Travel, Adventure International, Playmates European Tours, Trek Europe, Minitrek, Fun Trek, Suntrek and CCT (Continental Coach Tours) who went through a difficult patch, so Contiki bought them out.

Every one of the above companies all contributed to the unique period of camping tours around Europe throughout the sixties, seventies and eighties. By the late nineties an era had come to an end. Top Deck and Contiki were, and still are, the only ones left.

12. TAKING A CUT

I was sitting in the back row of Sotheby's Auction House, Bond Street, London. I watched with something akin to horror as the hammer came down on the sale of a variety of Russian religious icons. In the front row, the entire length of it, sat our Russian tour crews who, as I discovered that afternoon, had been using their roles as our much-trusted tour leaders to smuggle the icons out of Russia. On completion of the auction they enthusiastically congratulated each other. I met them in the aisle on the way out …

What were our tour crews doing selling Russian religious icons for outrageous prices? Well, it all began with shopping.

It hadn't taken me long to discover that passengers simply love to shop. On my first tour in 1962 I was with my group inside a jewellery store called Bucherers in the Swiss town of Lucerne. This shop attracted our attention as it had a large dazzling window display of watches. Some of us bought watches for ourselves or as presents to take home. As we were leaving, the store manager, having sussed I was the tour leader, invited me into his office for a moment. He thanked me for bringing my group into Bucherers, told me how many Swiss francs my group had spent and gave me an envelope full of cash. He shook my hand and said 'See you next time?' Yes, indeed he would, for many, many years to come.

After we'd crammed ourselves back into the little minibus, I excitedly told my passengers about our good fortune. I counted the cash, which turned out to be 10 per cent of the total amount spent. I paid each passenger who had purchased goods in Bucherers his or her share. I'd stumbled on what was a whole new undercover payment system I never knew existed – commission payments. On my next visit to Bucherers I again received the envelope. This time I returned only five per cent to the passengers. The next time I kept the lot! I felt a little guilty doing this, but comforted myself, thinking it did not cost my passengers anything extra.

Most countries have items for which they are well known, and often certain towns and cities within those countries specialise in those goods. It may be leather coats in Barcelona or Istanbul, watches in Lucerne, delftware in Delft, leather handbags in Florence, diamonds in Amsterdam or Antwerp, perfume in Grasse, cameo jewellery in Pompeii or glassware in Venice. The list goes on and on.

In the early 1970s, as our passenger numbers swelled, we were constantly approached by store owners asking us to visit their businesses. At the end of the season we entertained a flood of people visiting our offices proffering presents and inducements. Often it was commission cash, which they felt they owed us, or gifts of appreciation. I remember a retailer from Sorrento arriving with a fold-up musical table for each of Contiki's managers.

It is customary throughout Europe for tour companies to receive payments for providing business to retail shops, restaurants, attractions or entertainment. These commissions can vary enormously from five per cent for a group photo in Dutch national costume in Vollendam, to 10 per cent at a leather factory in Florence, to 40 per cent at a cameo store in Pompeii. Restaurants provide free meals to staff or free entrance to attractions, sometimes with a little *ex gratia* payment on the side. In Contiki's early years such payments were made direct to the minibus driver. With the introduction of coaches in 1974 the crews divvied up the loot between them.

Within a few years the number of commission paying outlets ballooned and the payments being collected by some staff became unacceptable. The passengers were being used as tools for some of the crews to make money. At every opportunity they'd be ferried to outlets and encouraged to buy a bargain they could 'never get anywhere else, trust me'. Field staff began to earn considerable sums on the side but the passengers were starting to wise-up. We had to take control of the situation.

There is a considerable amount of discussion in the tourism industry in countries outside Europe about commission payments being paid to tour operators. I don't think it is unreasonable for a marketing fee to be paid. After all, if they deliver a coach load of passengers to the door of an establishment with a recommendation to buy, why shouldn't they receive some recognition? It cost the retailer nothing to get potential buyers delivered to their shop, so surely a small contribution can be justified.

Our passengers did want guidance as to where they should buy big-ticket items such as jewellery, carpets, watches, leather goods and cameras. They wanted to shop with reliable retailers, who sold the genuine article and offered the best value. Above all, they wanted to know if the goods turned out to be faulty or didn't turn up to their home address if posted, they could have recourse, through us, to the retailer to rectify the situation.

Over the years we selected a whole raft of outlets we felt confident in recommending. We insisted their prices be competitive. We told them our passengers were our police force and would rapidly let us know if they were not offering good value compared to their competitors. If this happened we assured them we would remove them from our list. By doing this Contiki was putting its own reputation on the line.

Smuggling was another problem altogether. There was a considerable amount of smuggling occurring on tours by both passengers and field staff. This could generate huge amounts of cash. For a number of years we tolerated it until we realised how serious it could become if it got out of hand, which of course it eventually did, with the authorities clamping down, big time.

In the early days of the Russian and Scandinavian tours in the sixties and seventies there were many opportunities for the crews to make money 'on the side' for both their passengers and themselves. At the pre-departure meetings in London, passengers were quietly told to buy several pairs of pre-washed Levi jeans and even a few boxes of biro pens because there was a vibrant market in Russia for these goods. At the time jeans were a treasured Western clothing item, which could not be bought in Russia, and could sell for between five and 10 times the original UK purchase price.

There were thriving blackmarkets for currency in Russia and the Eastern bloc countries such as Poland and Czechoslovakia. The popular hard currencies at the time were American dollars and the English pound. In Russia these currencies could be exchanged for roubles at up to five times the official rate. This made touring there very, very cheap, even though many payments for accommodation and the like had to be prepaid with hard currency in the early years. Some of the field crews took advantage of the blackmarket and did very well out of it. It was a very risky business, which for the most part management was powerless to stop.

At the end of the summer season many staff returned home to Australasia. Either they had finished their employment with us or were going home to escape the bitterly cold Northern winter before returning for another season. We were asked to forward any personal mail onto them. One day we received a letter for an ex-staff member for whom we had no forwarding address. We opened it to obtain the address to 'return to sender'. The letter was from Sotheby's Auction House in London informing the staff member that his Russian icons were to be auctioned the following Thursday. You know the rest of that story!

For those passengers travelling on tours that included Scandinavia, it was suggested they buy their full quota of duty-free whisky on the cross channel ferry from Dover to Ostend in Belgium. More often than not the crews – who were more hardened to the practice than the passengers – would buy considerably *more* than their full quota and hide it away amongst the gear on the coach. On arrival in Sweden the whisky was sold for up to five times the original purchase price, which was still 50 per cent cheaper than the local Swedish price.

It was several years before I personally learnt about the extent of this racket. I found out by accident as I was reading a passenger's feedback questionnaire. Ironically, she seemed to have no concern about the smuggling, commenting innocently: 'I had a wonderful trip but was concerned that the cases of whisky stored in the aisle of the coach threatened the safety of the passengers if an emergency occurred.' A stop was put to the whisky practice.

One year, during the minibus days, we were notified on two separate occasions (three months apart) that all the tents had been destroyed by a major storm that had swept through the Istanbul camp ground. A considerable amount of cash was sent out to the driver to cover the cost of replacing the tents. The next year it happened again. We discovered it was the same driver on all three trips. Yes, he had been knocking off our fine French tents every time he passed through Istanbul. They must have fetched huge prices.

Occasionally, during this time some of the food kitty money was siphoned off for the personal use of the staff. It was frustrating to hear drivers boasting about their new leather jacket but the food kitty scam was almost undetectable. Often false receipts were put in for extra fuel or other imagined costs. It was said you often saw the drivers at petrol stations hunting around for discarded petrol receipts to add to the fictitious cost of running the tour.

Again, during in the minibus era, the occasional driver would take off on unauthorised excursions without our knowledge, sometimes charging the passengers extra. On one occasion a driver was on a tour that included Morocco and dipped as far south as Marrakesh. His vehicle broke down and he had to ring in for assistance. When we asked where he was so we could get assistance to him, he had to admit he was way south of the authorised route, on the other side of the Atlas ranges near Meski Oasis.

When the coaches were introduced, there was the odd occasion which we became aware of, when a tour leader's girl friend took a spare seat joining the tour *gratis*, with the other passengers oblivious to the fact she was not a genuine paid up member of the group.

As I was researching this book I talked to many of the ex-staff about these situations. I heard of a number of schemes that were used for some crew members' personal gain. This behaviour disturbed me considerably. Again I realised that not all people can be trusted. That said, Contiki has given so many young men and women the opportunity to work for a very special company. It hurt that some people repaid that privilege dishonestly – they know who they are. Fortunately the vast majority of staff were dedicated, hardworking, honest individuals who did their jobs with total integrity, serving the passengers and company as well as they possibly could.

Over the years Contiki continued to tighten up on all the extra 'bits on the side' and as a result, everything became very tightly controlled and monitored making sure the passengers were protected from these scams and rackets.

In the mid 1980s, at the end of the summer season our European operations manager went to supervise the closure of the Villa Torre de Gattia in Florence. He arrived in the driveway to find two brand new red Ferrari motorcars parked outside the front door. He thought 'Oh it must be a couple of our Italian supplier friends visiting'. He was wrong. The cars belonged to two of our field staff who had just been to Modena to collect their treasured new possessions. They were visiting to bid their final farewells after several years working with the company, before returning to Australia. Both the Ferraris had been purchased with contributions made from taking their cut!

13. IT ALL STARTS FROM THE TOP

Show me an organisation in trouble and I'll go straight to the top – weak leadership! Show me a successful organisation and again, I'll go straight to the top – strong leadership! The success of any organisation all starts at the top. But even the strongest leaders can't achieve exceptional results alone. They need others to help.

In 20 short years we had taken a simple idea and turned it into a major European tour operation with plans to expand further afield. But ideas don't just happen: you have to make them happen. Initially I was the driving force, creating ideas and having confidence in those around me that together we could achieve them. As time passed, I saw the value in delegating challenges to those who were working with me. I wanted them to be able to suggest and implement new ideas, some of which were brilliant successes and others unmitigated disasters. We needed staff who believed in the company, believed in the product, believed in the brand and, above all, believed in themselves.

On the home front, my wife Ali ran our household, looked after our children and was my sounding board for everything. She was always there to support and encourage me. She stood beside me through all those years, through all the tough times we experienced in building the business, and some of them were really tough. There is no way I could have achieved what I did without her. And on the business side, if it wasn't for the amazing team of people I slowly built around me, the company would not have reached the heights it did, and continues to do.

We had a saying in the company: 'hunks of meat'. We would give staff challenges far greater than they thought they were capable of achieving. We threw them into the deep end and waited for the results. Some sank and didn't surface. But that's the cost of delegation, you can't do everything on your own. Others surprised us and themselves, with fantastic results. When they did so, we threw them back in with another challenge. Staff love being given the opportunity to prove they have ability, and when they are successful, love being recognised and rewarded accordingly. That's how we found our leaders. Those that achieved were pulled in to assist with the administration and future development of the company. Several down the line became directors of the company.

Typical was a young New Zealander, Garry Draffin. Garry joined the company as a tour leader in 1971. Very early on he showed exceptional ability, strong leadership attributes and solid organisational skills. He had a positive attitude and always showed his eagerness to progress with the company by taking on more responsibility. After a couple of seasons he was pulled from the road and placed at the operations base in Folkestone, after which he led a few training trips around Europe. He became Operations Manager, followed by his role as Contiki's General Manager. Just seven years after his first tour, Garry joined the Contiki Board as Managing Director of the group. A meteoric rise but his outstanding skills were needed when the company was moving at such a dramatic pace.

Another New Zealander, Wayne Page, started his career with the company in 1972 as a tour leader and coach driver. Aside from being a very personable, capable and down-to-earth sort of guy, he soon demonstrated a practical ability in being able to think outside the square when it came to problem solving. He managed some training trips before taking over from Garry as Operations Manager at a time when we were constantly changing elements of the product we were creating. Six years later, Wayne also joined the Board as Operations Director.

The dramatic growth of the company during the 1970s caused our turnover to approach the tens of millions of dollars, resulting in our financial control getting the wobbles. In the early years any field staff who had financial experience were fast tracked into our accounts department to help out. We hired a number of accountants over the years who grappled with our finances but always ended up way out of their depth. Many were newly graduated with no experience in dealing with international activities. Many cut their teeth learning from their mistakes at our expense.

A solution to these problems came in the form of a young English accountant, Andrew Fleming. Andrew had begun his training at Arthur Andersen (one of the top international accounting firms of the day), and from 1977 onwards, he steered the company through its financial growing pains. It was no mean feat as he had to learn fast, adapt and implement strategies to control a very complicated situation. We had become an international operation with our sales revenue coming from overseas and payments made throughout Europe. The diverse range of currencies the company was dealing in was mind-boggling. Four years after a standing start, Andrew joined the Board as Finance Director.

A design agency had taken over the production of our brochures. Each year the brochures grew in size and became more complicated. They soon became a major production each year which needed an increasing amount of time and attention. By the mid seventies we realised we needed someone with the specialised expertise to take on the overall responsibility, so decided to appoint a Sales and Marketing Manager to take overall responsibility for our publicity. Ali and I had an English friend, Alison Loyd, who created and analysed the passenger feedback forms for us on a part-time basis. She became very interested in Contiki and we, in turn, became interested in her abilities.

Alison was highly intelligent having previously been employed with the global conglomerate, Lever Bros, as a Marketing Manager. She had expertise in developing sales and marketing strategies and, as a bonus, had produced countless brochures: one of our key selling tools.

We persuaded her to join us and immediately our brochures and promotional material entered another league. Alison became an outstanding asset, contributing her specialised marketing insights and initiatives. Three years after joining us she became the Sales and Marketing Director. Although we had just one woman on our board, I've often said we had two. The other woman inconspicuously behind the scenes was Alison Anderson – yes, my wife.

I can't stress enough the importance of having women in top business management roles and as directors. A balance of genders in decision-making roles is critical. We proved the value of this, time and time again, as women bring a whole new logic, female intuition and balance of thoughts to crucial decisions. For Contiki it made particular sense to have women well-represented as we were in the people business with the majority of our customers being women. But aren't we all in the people business? No matter what the service or product, we all sell to people.

With me as Executive Chair, Garry as Managing Director, Wayne as Operations Director, Andrew as Finance Director and Alison Lloyd as Sales and Marketing Director, we had a formidable team – 'the tight five' as it is known in rugby circles. Our various strengths complemented and combined brilliantly. However, as time passed, we knew we needed more specialist expertise so we set out to find it.

Richard Lewis, yet another New Zealander, was previously a management consultant with the highly respected international consultancy firm W. D. Scott. He had recently completed a project for them for the San Miguel brewery in Zaragoza, Spain. What's more he could even speak Spanish. He joined the company in 1979 to take responsibility for personnel, systems and special projects worldwide. A year later he joined the Board – a very quick rise but we needed his expertise.

Dick Vermaat, the Managing Director of our European coach operator, Vermaat, joined the Board taking overall responsibility for all our transportation requirements. This was a relief as he was such an asset. What Dick didn't know about coaches wasn't worth knowing.

All directors at some stage had successfully taken on major challenges successfully, serving their 'hunks of meat' apprenticeship. With the combined expertise of the Board it became a very powerful unit to not only run the company but guide it into the future.

It's all very well having a strong Board that makes the tough decisions but it's equally important to have leaders who can successfully implement those decisions. We found them mainly through our field staff. But first we had to find the raw material.

People applied to work for Contiki from an incredibly diverse range of backgrounds. Certainly, none had worked in the tour business before. In fact, if they had worked for a competitor, we didn't want them, as you can't change a leopard's spots. Personality, interesting CVs and, above all, the right attitude were the main ingredients we were seeking in our applicants.

I remember interviewing a guy applying for a driver position back in the minibus days. He had been a steward on a cargo ship and my first impression of him was very unfavourable. He wasn't particularly well dressed, didn't express himself very well and had a few obvious tattoos, which I felt uncomfortable about. However, he was very keen to get the job and told me over and over again that he would be a great asset to the company.

'Will you give me the opportunity?' he said.

'No, I won't,' I replied.

'Why?' he asked.

'Because you have a beard,' I said, admittedly looking for an excuse. I didn't like beards then, in fact I still don't!

'Do I have to take it off to be considered?' he asked.

'It's up to you,' I said.

He returned the next day with his beard shaved off, asking if I would now change my mind. Again, he insisted how confident and how keen he was etc.

'Sorry,' I said. 'I'm not relenting.'

'Why?' he asked, in utter dismay.

'Because you left your moustache on!' I detested moustaches and still do!

He politely left and returned two hours later with his moustache gone. Only now, to my embarrassment his harelip was now clearly exposed. His facial hair had covered it before, and was obviously the reason why he hadn't been clean-shaven in the first place. I gave him the job on the spot! Why? Because he had revealed a great attitude. He was so determined to get the job he was prepared to persist to achieve his objective. I knew he was the type of person I needed in the company.

He turned out to be one of our best field staff members and after a few years with us, he left to return home to Australia. I met him, by chance, some 10 years later at Los Angeles Airport. He told me, proudly, that he was heading up a major Australian trade delegation to America and Japan.

'John, I want to thank you for giving me that job, it taught me so much,' he told me. 'There is no way I would have achieved what I have without that incredible experience because it gave me real confidence in my own ability,' he said. I told him I had always known his positive attitude would take him a long way; we embraced, and went our separate ways.

By the mid 1980s we had around 100 coaches on the road at any one time, which meant around 5000 people running riot around Europe every day. We had to feed, accommodate and entertain them but, above all, we had to be responsible for them. Problems arose day and night which needed attention, often urgently. We had already introduced area supervisors to monitor operations. We divided Europe into geographical areas of responsibility with our small team in VW Kombi vans and area managers in smaller vehicles touring the routes. Still, we couldn't be everywhere at once so we often enlisted the help of our trusted suppliers. They could not only speak the language but had useful contacts. They also acted as our policemen by keeping an eye on our field staff. In addition, our field staff could always contact company managers directly in London or Holland for advice and assistance.

It was a real team affair. Little did the passengers know what a sophisticated web of operations they were encircled by, or how many people were watching out for their welfare.

There were clear lines of responsibility in our operations department that worked efficiently – until one memorable day I realised otherwise! As a favour, a friend asked me to book a hotel room (at a discounted rate) for him and his wife in Lauterbrunnen. I passed the request on to our Managing Director, he passed it to our Operations Director, who passed it to the Operations Manager, who passed it the Area Supervisor, who passed it to the Site Manager who requested the booking with the hotel. The request had been delegated down the line five times! Alas, it turned out the hotel could not accommodate them on the dates required. So, up the chain it went again – what a saga. With an alternative date, it started back down again, at which point I picked up the phone and spoke directly with the hotel and made the booking – something I should have done in the first place! This process and its clunky chain of command was probably representative of other processes within the company, not just me trying to book a room for a friend. I had learnt that the closer management can get to the coalface, the better.

I really enjoyed getting out into the field and seeing what was going on first hand, but as the years went by I did this less and less, and my enjoyment of the company suffered as a result. Whenever I made an attempt to show up unannounced, the tom-toms would sound after my first stop, telling everyone I was out there, so by the time I arrived at the next one, everybody knew, so everything was pristine perfect on my arrival. At least I had the opportunity to meet the European field staff at the beginning of each season as I would drop by at the end of the training sessions to give the new recruits a pep talk.

It was imperative that I kept in touch with what was going on in the field. To this day none of Contiki's personnel ever knew that I had my own secret department. Sure they may have had their suspicions as occasionally I was aware of things in the field that they were not. But I was extremely careful in the way I used the information in my possession. I achieved this by hiring a number of young people to book on tours in each of our operating regions, for which I personally reimbursed them, to be my informants. In addition I gave them an allowance for day-to-day expenses. Their brief was to enjoy the tour, just like their fellow passengers, but report to me weekly by phone and send regular written reports to a private box number about the tour and others they came into contact with (including our competitors). I only wanted to hear about anything unusual or anything my informants thought I should know about. I also wanted to be sure we were delivering what we promised. Yes, I had my very own 'secret shoppers'.

At first I felt very uncomfortable doing this behind my trusted staff's back and it was perhaps a little underhand. The only knowledge I had of the ground operations was from my odd trip into the field and what my staff told me. I had to be sure I was being told all the negatives not just the positives. And did our key staff know everything? My suspicions turned out to be right – of course they didn't. Fortunately there was nothing too major to worry about, although I did find out a few things about some of the staff and their unacceptable activities. Also, an unexpected incident happened with one of my female 'moles'. She fell for the tour leader which I only suspected because of the rave reports coming in from the tour. We're all only human after all.

The company built close relationships with its many suppliers. These included the camp ground and hotel owners and managers, restaurants, food suppliers, activity operators, retail stores, ferry companies, nightclubs, bars and discos. They all formed part of the team. They were interested in us growing successfully because we in turn would help to grow their business by delivering more passengers. With our sheer volume of passengers we were able to continually negotiate very special rates for the goods and services supplied by them. Often, we requested them to improve the facilities or service they were providing, such as requesting camp grounds to build more amenity blocks to stop overcrowding as a condition of us using their property. Many of our staff became lifelong personal friends with some of the suppliers. To mention just a few of the European characters such as Paolo, Walter, Lorie, Tony, Piero, Spyro, Renato, Hans and Juan. The other regions also had their special suppliers and characters.

Over the years many of our suppliers became multi-millionaires through the regular business they received from Contiki, year in year out. Contiki had become the springboard to take their businesses to a totally new level, often far beyond their wildest dreams.

Then there was the reservations hub based in London. Passengers didn't just happen to be on the correct coach on the correct day. Oh no indeed! We had an extremely efficient team responsible for processing the tour bookings. Originally bookings came in by aerogramme, later by telex, later still by facsimile and finally, through the internet. From the days where we processed bookings manually we progressed to an extremely sophisticated computerised system. Early on we realised the importance of frequent system upgrades to the point where we hired a full-time computer guru.

All reservations centred around a key document known as the 'Sell and Record' which was automatically updated every time a booking was made. This vital document listed all departure dates and up-to-the-minute data, such as passenger numbers booked on a given tour. Critical decisions were based on this document, such as when to close off a tour for sale, whether to add or reduce the seat capacity, and how many hotel beds, ferry tickets, and so forth, to book.

Once a passenger had booked on a tour, the fare had to be collected either directly from the passenger or from their travel agent. This required a credit control team, because no passenger could travel unless Contiki had received full payment. On the odd occasion the passenger had paid, but the travel agent had not yet passed on the payment, meaning the passenger couldn't embark at the departure point. Delaying the boarding of these passengers soon ensured payment was forthcoming! The other major responsibility of the finance department of course was to take care of all the outgoing payments.

Each department was dependent on the other, so they had to dovetail in with each other. With good leadership and communications we managed to keep the ball rolling, although at times I admit we did lose the plot, primarily due to growing too fast and lacking the resources of sufficiently trained personnel to keep up.

And not to forget the passengers, at the end of every tour they were asked to complete a feedback form, telling us about their experience, what they liked and didn't like about their tour, any suggested improvements or new ideas, and comments about their tour crew. In the early years, once completed, these were handed to the tour leader for passing onto operations. We soon found that some of our ever so trusted crews were doctoring them, enhancing them and pulling any detrimental ones. Once that was uncovered, we had the person meeting the returning tour personally collect them from the passengers who also had the option to post them in directly. The passengers were indirectly also part of the team. We needed them – they needed us.

We thrived on input from our suppliers and staff – understanding how others see your business is a way of making sure everyone is treated well and feels included. Contiki was about fun, but it was also about encouraging others and giving people opportunities to grow and rise to challenges, to push the boundaries. Building this teamwork was a big part of the amazing results that Contiki achieved – and a little bit of luck.

The obligatory photo of mother, father and son. Perhaps my first taste of travelling.

Travelling through Cairo with my highly entertaining companions on either side.

The first group (with one taking photograph) Cologne Cathedral in background, 1962.

Helping hands!

Souvenirs from a night out at the Hofbrauhaus beer hall, Munich where the "Twinkler's" badge originated.

Jet (left) and John (right) – Tiki 1 and Tiki 2 – Belgium.

John (middle) with Jet (right) on his first driving trip, 1964.

This is the life, camping beside the Rhine River, Germany.

So much for travelling light.
The notorious overloaded roof racks!

First New Zealand
'Hare Mai' tour, 1964.

John, Ali, Pete, Marg, Jet and Mary, 1969
(from left to right).

First Middle Eastern tour with the locals. Luckily both
camel and bus made it through the shifting sands.

An idyllic setting – eating outdoors was one of the joys of being on the road.

Dinner al fresco.

Woops!

Eight Students From N.Z. In Rome Sensation

ROME, Sept. 24.—An Australian student was under arrest in a Rome gaol tonight on five charges, including injuring a public official.

The student, Michael Godby, 25, of 179 Gipps Street, East Melbourne, was one of 11 students involved in a "Dolce Vita" incident last night.

The group, including eight students from New Zealand, shocked Romans by parading down the city's fashionable Via Veneto in bathing costumes. But first several girls in the group had a swim in Rome's famed Trevi Fountain, police said.

The fountain is sometime used by high-spirited tour ists who follow the exampl of Anita Ekberg in the fil "La Dolce Vita" (The Swee Life).

Police said Godby ha been charged with injurin a public official, resisting public official, acts contrar to public decency, blockin traffic and disturbing th peace.

The students caused a sen sation by parading pas crowded open-air restaur ants with five of their num ber in various stages of u dress.

Police said three gir were in bikini swimmin costumes, two men ha "nude torsos."

Newspaper photograph showed one man with towel round his hips, an another round his shoulder A second man was drape in a striped bath towel.

Challenged

Two policemen patrolli the Via Veneto challeng the students. They ask them what they were d ing, and demanded the identity documents.

Police said the group fl to a mini-bus parked nea

An international affair – we make the headlines!

Runabout mini with original Contiki logo, London. Always looking for an opportunity to promote.

LOW COST
TRAVEL
AROUND
EUROPE

First brochure cover, 1964.

TIKI
TOURS

Cut and paste. Our first colour brochure with the 'additional' Swiss picture!

1. 12 WEEK TRIP OF THE CONTINENT AND SCANDINAVIA, *visiting*:

Holland	Austria	Spain
France	Liechtenstein	Monaco
Belgium	East Germany	Denmark
Bavaria	West Germany	Sweden
Italy	Switzerland	Norway

Departing London, 22nd April, 1964. Total cost £125. Food 30/- a week extra.

2. 12 WEEK TRIP OF THE CONTINENT INCLUDING GREECE, *visiting*:

Holland	Austria	Spain
France	Liechtenstein	Monaco
Belgium	East Germany	Jugoslavia
Bavaria	West Germany	Greece
Italy	Switzerland	

Departing London, 21st July, 1964. Total cost £125. Food 30/- a week extra.

3. 4 WEEK TRIP OF SCANDINAVIA, *visiting*:

Holland	Germany	Sweden
Belgium	Denmark	Norway

Departing London, May, June, July, August, September, 1964. Total cost £39. Food 30/- a week extra.

4. 3½ WEEK TRIP TO SOUTH OF SPAIN STAYING AT COASTAL VILLA

Departing November, 1964, January, February, 1965 Total cost £39. Food 30/- a week extra.

These trips are of an informal nature and designed to let younger people see Europe at a cost they can afford.

Inside details of the first brochure. Inspiring marketing?

EUROPE
on a mini budget

contiki travel limited

The front cover of our first real full colour brochure, 1970. Our happy-go-lucky models were our ever accommodating staff and friends ...

contiki travel limited
Evelyn House, 62 Oxford Street, London W1N 9LD, England
Tel: 636 6416 or 636 1909 Cables: TIKI London W.1.

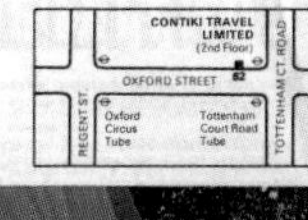

Australia: Contiki Travel (Australia) Pty. Ltd.
20-22 O'Connell Street, Sydney, 2000
Telephone 28-7843

New Zealand: White Heron Travel Ltd.
P.O. Box 2648 192 Queen Street, Auckland
Telephone 31345

Printed in England

or Agent:

And the back cover!

The retail office - 7 Rathbone Place, London – such a hive of activity.

A typical pre-season staff party in Dropkick T-shirts early 1970s.

Meeting the locals.

A section of a tent village. One of our first innovativ ideas, putting us way ahead of the competition.

The end of year staff dinner, 1969 – Top of the Tower London. An annual tradition rewarding our hard working staff.

A staff weekend break-away, Brugge, Belgium - a chance for time out

John (left) and Pete (right) at Nottinghill Gate departure point with an early hired bus.

Dressed for the occasion at the salt mines, Salzburg, Austria.

A European 'Big Yellow' Mercedes-Benz. You couldn't miss us!

The inaugural Contiki staff soccer team v Leonardos/Walters/Red Garter team, Florence 1982.

The legendary Gasthof Schoneck – snowbound, Hopfgarten, Austria.

Field Managers on duty in Europe.

The magnificent Chateau de Cruix, Lyon France.

Villa Torre de Gattia, Florence, Italy. Our special stopover. A table or two?!

The Groothuis – Noordgouwe, Holland. The last nights 'hospital' party stop.

Something completely different – Straw Huts, Corfu, Greece.

Suntan line showoffs.

Our 'super' Supercooks.

14. BE PREPARED FOR THE UNEXPECTED

With operations running 24 hours a day, seven days a week anything can happen at any time. The increasing number of passengers, tours, and kilometres travelled meant it was inevitable that incidents and accidents would also be on the rise – some minor, some extremely serious. Over the years we learnt to be prepared for the unexpected.

A good tour operator has contingency plans in place to deal with emergencies. In the early years we were not at all prepared, but through trial and error with various incidents we soon learned. The field staff were trained and briefed on how to deal with situations, and Contiki head office was always just a phone call away. Of course, incidents often happen when they're least expected, often in remote areas or in the middle of the night. We constantly boosted our 'preparedness' over the years but no matter how experienced we became, 100 per cent preparation for 100 per cent of incidents simply wasn't possible. Something, somewhere will happen someday that you've never faced before.

When a major incident occurred it was crucial for the field staff to have direct access to Contiki head office. However, telephone lines could be engaged or become jammed. To overcome this, we added a special telephone number that was to be used exclusively in cases of absolute emergency. It was manned 24 hours a day by senior staff members and patched through to the on duty staff member's home line after hours. Naturally, in the early days I took regular shifts manning the emergency line. I dreaded any call coming in, particularly in the middle of the night, as I knew when the line rang, it could be something serious that needed an immediate response and action.

Our two biggest concerns stayed constant over the years: serious accidents and drugs. If the Contiki name was ever to be damaged it would more than likely be one of those two. We had a black and white rule with passengers and staff: no drugs, full stop. If drugs were detected onboard a tour there was one warning. If they were discovered again it was off the tour, end of story. We were always watching.

Generally we had great relationships with our field staff but there was always the odd renegade. One year a few of the minibus drivers asked for an increase in pay. We thought their request was unreasonable as we believed they were more than adequately compensated and certainly above the industry norm, so refused their demands. To make their point on their next Scandinavian tour, two drivers waited until they reached the furthermost point in Oslo, Norway and rang in stating that unless we succumbed to their demands they would walk off the tour. We didn't – and they did, leaving 28 passengers stranded. We learnt a real lesson as we had misread how strongly they felt about the matter. We should never have allowed the situation to deteriorate to that point. On another occasion a driver, who was also a lawyer (in real life), tried unsuccessfully to form a driver's union. As if we didn't have enough on our plate!

On the flipside, one driver proved his dedication in a very physical way. He and his tour group had boarded the ferry sailing between Denmark and Sweden. As the boat was leaving the wharf he realised with horror that he had left his satchel with all the trip documents and travellers cheques back on the wharf. Without hesitation he stripped off to his underpants, dived over the stern and swam the short distance back to Denmark to retrieve the documents! He caught the next ferry over to rejoin his passengers.

Over the years we lost a few passengers – mostly temporarily, thank heavens! Often a passenger would meet a local they liked and decide to stay on a little longer in his or her company. Inevitably the passenger would catch up with the tour later, after causing a great deal of worry onboard because we always felt responsible for the passengers in our care.

We also lost a couple of minibuses, fortunately not with passengers inside! One was stolen whilst the group was inside the Blue Mosque in Istanbul. Another was stolen in West Berlin, however with only a few days to go on the trip the group took a train to Amsterdam where a replacement vehicle picked them up. The original bus turned up a few weeks later in East Berlin packed with stolen copper wire. Some passengers ended up in jail for minor offences. One year a group visited a lock-up in Spain, after throwing their cushions into the bullring at a bullfight – an absolute no-no!

One night in 1964 a tour group I was leading threw a Chianti party at the Seven Hills camp ground in Rome to celebrate one of the passenger's 21st birthday. A few bottles later, we dressed up in Roman 'togas' using towels (or anything else we could get our hands on) held together by safety pins. We jumped into the minibus and roared into the city for some further activity.

First we had a paddle in the Trevi Fountain, then headed for one of the posh streets in Rome, the Via Veneto, lined with five star hotels, luxury shops, classy restaurants and pavement cafés. As we proceeded to innocently walk down the footpath, with most of the girls quite scantily dressed, we started to gather a growing number of admiring Italian males. On arrival at Piazza Novona at the end of the street, all hell broke loose when a couple of the admiring Romeos tried to tug the togas off the girls. When in Rome do (not) what the Romans do! One of our male passengers, desperate to protect the girls in the escalating melee, pulled out a tear gas pistol he'd acquired in Germany and fired it at someone who turned out to be a plain-clothes policeman!

With flashing lights and more commotion, the carabinieri arrived. We were all carted off to the local police station and our sharp shooter spent a couple of nights in the local lock-up. At the time we thought it was great fun, until the fall-out the next day. The first telephone call came through to the local New Zealand consulate from the distraught parents of one of our passengers. The incident had been on the radio news and reported in papers throughout New Zealand! The Prime Minister at the time, Keith Holyoake, even made an official comment. We subsequently wrote letters of apology to everyone involved, including the PM, for the embarrassment we had caused his nation. It was certainly a wake-up call for me. I realised I needed to take more responsibility for my actions and those of my passengers.

Late one evening in Barcelona, a group was staying at the Ballena Alegre (laughing whale) camp ground, when a terrible accident occurred. Opposite the camp entrance, across the road, was a local bar. A male passenger came to the door of the bar and seeing his girlfriend across the road at the camp entrance gestured for her to come over and join him. She checked the traffic by looking right instead of left and ran out onto the road. Tragically she was hit by a car coming from the other direction. Her boyfriend impulsively ran over to check on her and, unbelievably, was hit by another car coming from the other direction. Both were seriously injured.

Just outside Minsk, a minibus with a full load of passengers went over the side of a bridge. The vehicle landed on its roof in a shallow riverbed. Everyone managed to escape with minor injuries except one female passenger caught in a back seat corner. A Russian farmer's forklift was commandeered to slowly lift the rear of the vehicle so we could extract her. However, just as she was about to be freed, the ratchets on the forklift slipped and the vehicle fell back down on her. She was seriously injured and ended up in a West Berlin hospital for several months before being repatriated back to Australia.

We also had to deal with accidents involving third parties. When a fully loaded coach is moving at speed it's not always easy to stop suddenly. One of our coaches was travelling on a main highway in the former Yugoslavia, when a car packed with a family of five locals crossed directly in front of its path. Our coach hit it with the inevitable tragic fatalities of those inside the car.

In a case like this the road crew is forced to deal with the most horrendous situation. First, it occurs out in the country, miles from any major town or city, in a place where nobody on either side can speak the other's language. It is raining heavily, with dead and badly injured people on the road and 50 distraught passengers in a bus that has been immobilised by the impact. There wasn't the easy access to help with mobile phones back then. So help didn't come as quickly as it does when emergencies occur today and it also wasn't as tightly coordinated with police and emergency teams taking control of such a tragedy.

In this particular case the driver of the coach was carted off by the police, leaving the tour leader to deal with a smashed coach and 50 stranded passengers to be moved on from the scene as quickly as possible. It is in these situations that you appreciate the value of a truly professional and established coach operator. Vermaat had a temporary local replacement coach on the scene within a matter of hours.

Sadly, during my time at the helm, Contiki suffered a number of serious coach accidents, where passengers were seriously injured or killed. These are tragic, devastating events, which profoundly affect everyone involved. It is a terribly gut-wrenching experience to inform passengers' parents that their loved son or daughter has met with a serious accident.

As a tour operator we are often on the receiving end of sad news from a passenger's home base, which we have to deal with. For example, one of our passenger's parents were involved in a serious car accident back home. The passenger's mother had died and her father was in hospital in a serious condition. The relatives contacted us, requesting us to inform the passenger. On this occasion, rather than leave it to the crew, I flew out to Europe to tell her personally. To see this passenger having so much fun and then having to tell her of the tragedy was a harrowing experience I will never forget.

There was the occasional passenger death, such as the girl who had an asthma attack in a Paris hotel and died. Another prospective passenger – and the brother of a friend of Ali and mine – walked under some scaffolding on his way to our London office. At that moment a piece fell, killing him instantly. We became involved with the sad aftermath of this tragic freak accident.

Over the years, as Contiki spread across the world as a tour operator, major incidents occurred in other countries as well. In New Zealand a married couple on a South Island tour had a terrifying relationship breakdown when the husband suspected his wife was having an affair with another passenger. He confronted her one evening to resolve the matter, disbelieved her explanation, and stabbed her to death in the tent.

The wanton thieving by local gangs, particularly in Southern Europe, was always a problem. The majority of misfortunes occurred in Italy where it seems like a never-ending epidemic. The thefts so often occur in the same popular tourist locations. Why Italian authorities don't put effective plain-clothes police officers in those areas to stem the plague never fails to amaze me.

One day, a minibus parked temporarily in Mestre, Venice, was stripped of all personal gear inside, even the radio. The vehicle had only been left while the driver put the passengers on the ferry. A local Italian minder had been paid to keep a watch: of course he was not there on return.

With all the many dramas we had to deal with, there was one glaring lesson I learnt, which is simply this, 'Be prepared for the unexpected' as you never know what might hit you or your business, often when you least expect it. It can be anything such as a tragic accident, a death, a serious illness, a crime or a financial meltdown. Very few people have contingency plans for themselves personally, for their families or their business. Most think 'it won't happen to me'. Don't for a minute believe it, as every moment of every day something traumatic happens in someone's life. Get those contingency plans in place immediately.

15. THE OVERLANDERS

In the sixties more and more young Australasian passengers were returning back home from the UK overland through to India, Kathmandu and Calcutta. This route had been pioneered in the late fifties by a company named Indiaman. The major tour company operating the route in the sixties was, however, Penn Overland. Other smaller operators existed too, including one run by a small, dapper and personable Italian named Gino Teseo. Gino owned a small 20-seater Mercedes-Benz coach specifically adapted for the route's rough terrain and conditions.

He was well respected and had approached us to become his sales agent in London. We agreed and successfully sold a large number of seats on his tours. As a result, in September 1967 we contracted him to run an overland tour for us, with his vehicle under the Contiki banner. It was a mammoth 75-day tour from London through to Calcutta. It was hugely successful so we ran another one the following year. Then with Gino taking a break from the route, so did we, to concentrate on Europe.

By the mid seventies the popularity of the journey had increased considerably. It had grown into a two-way route with people travelling west to Europe as well. The number of overland operators had mushroomed to cater for the demand and there was a bewildering choice of transport options. Many outfits were simply one-man bands with one vehicle. Others were reasonably organised with a small fleet of vehicles. The transport ranged from modern coaches pulling custom-built accommodation trailers sleeping around 20 passengers, to minibuses, 40 seater buses and even the odd double-decker bus and converted truck.

The list of operators was mind-boggling, not to mention some of the interesting characters that ran them. They included the following: Anglo Australian, Asian Greyhound, Capricorn Overland, Budget Bus, Encounter Overland, Exodus Expeditions, Frontier, Hann Overland, Hughes Overland, Inter Trek, Magic Bus, Penn Overland, Rotel Tours, Sherpa Expeditions, Sundowners, Swagman, The Overlanders, Transit Travel, Top Deck, Tent Trek and Safaris Overland. Every year a couple of them went bust.

In 1976 we decided to return to the route, this time with our own programme. We felt confident that we had the resources to take on the existing competition with our operational experience, reliable coaches and loyal passenger base that trusted the Contiki brand. There was also an added commercial reason relating to the running cost of our coaches. Our coach contract was based on the number of kilometres the coaches travelled each year. The more we clocked up, the cheaper the Dutch guilder kilometre rate. The coaches were under-utilised during the European winter (the overlander season) so an extra 20,000 kilometres for the return journey would bring the overall rate down dramatically.

There was, of course, one more reason, a personal one. I had never forgotten my own eye-opening trip through the region in 1962, when the volume of people, the exotic food, and the incredible diversity of religion, culture and sights had blown me away. I wanted others to be able to have a similar experience. My company was going to give them that very opportunity.

In January 1976 we sent out our Operations Manager, Wayne Page, as a passenger, incognito on a Penn Overland tour to research the route. He sat for most of the journey in the back seat of the coach, writing the 'bible' for our future overland drivers and tour leaders. He gleaned every possible piece of information from the many years of experience Penn had accumulated. Déjà vu.

We approached our brilliant coach operator Vermaat to provide us with a coach suitably adapted for the rigorous route ahead. At first they were reluctant and rather uncomfortable with the request but, after analysing it, they agreed to the challenge. We put together the itinerary, produced a brochure and started selling the tour to our passengers and the wider London market. Our competitors were sceptical about our move, but at the same time concerned we had become a competitor on their sacred route.

The tour was planned in detail with us making all the necessary arrangements we could such as accommodation bookings and assisting the passengers in obtaining all the necessary visas and inoculations. The route was nothing like Europe and nothing like anything most of our passengers had ever experienced before. There would be the constant threat of food poisoning, diseases, accidents, crime and violence and always the unexpected. In some regions, the roads were atrocious and sometimes almost non-existent, medical services were limited and unsophisticated and communications sparse. Events could be so unpredictable with very real dangers around the next corner. Our staff were trained to be aware of the variety of the diverse religious customs and cultures that passengers needed to respect. We left nothing to chance as it was not just our reputation at stake; it was also the safety of our staff and passengers.

The first tour departed in October 1976 with Wayne as tour leader, a driver, a trainee and 24 passengers. Among the passengers was Wayne's fiancée whom he had met previously on a European tour (I guess he broke the rule of not fraternising with the passengers!). The tour travelled through Europe to Turkey then through Syria, Jordan, Iraq, Iran, Afghanistan, Pakistan, India, through to Nepal and finished in Calcutta.

The tour was not without difficulties, including one major incident. With the coach travelling at speed along one of the main highways in

Iran, just outside the town of Bonjnourd, the driver spotted in the distance a couple of donkeys on the road. It was raining heavily so he started to brake to slow the vehicle down. Inexplicably the back wheels of the coach locked. The coach swayed from left to right then rolled a full 360 degrees, landing back on its wheels. Tragically, one of the passengers was seriously injured and hospitalised in Meshed before her repatriation back to Australia. Wayne, our tour leader, was also hospitalised, however his injuries were minor and he was able to rejoin the tour a week later.

Over the years we introduced a choice of tour routes in both directions, ranging from 50 to 90 days. The latter included an air excursion from Athens to Cairo and down to Luxor in Egypt. We wanted to be the premier route operator on all fronts. Our programme became extremely popular with some departures having two coaches totalling 80 passengers.

Sadly, the number of unpleasant and unpredictable incidents occurring on the route increased. A civil war broke out in Afghanistan in April 1978, followed by the Soviet invasion. At the time two Contiki coaches and passengers were held under hotel arrest by the Russians. Fortunately, although an extremely worrying time, after few a days they were released with no harm done. As communication with our base was impossible, we were fortunate that the local Mercedes-Benz dealer could send a telex to Vermaat, letting them know all were safe and back on the road ready to move on to Pakistan and India.

Afghanistan was not the only place on the overland route that was becoming unpredictable. The Iranian revolution was brewing. Around the same time major demonstrations directed at the ruling Shah were held in Iran and then later that year, between August and December, strikes and demonstrations paralysed the country with the Shah going into exile, replaced two weeks later by Ayatollah Khomeini.

The Indian overland is one of the world's great travel adventures but with so much political and civil unrest throughout the region, we withdrew from the route. The safety of our passengers and staff in these areas had become too big a responsibility to continue carrying. The wear and tear on the coaches had also become unacceptable. The last tour departed for India on 27 September 1978.

Regrettably today many countries along that incredible route are still far too unpredictable and dangerous for the majority of travellers to chance. The few that have travelled that amazing overland journey are very privileged.

You will recall that my original business partner Peter Blake returned to his African homeland with his wife Marg in 1970, settling in Johannesburg. Peter soon opened an office in Twist Street, Joubert Park and began promoting Contiki through the South African travel trade. The number of young South Africans travelling to Europe was continuing to increase markedly. The shipping company Union Castle Line was running regular departures to the United Kingdom. In fact, a South African businessman Max Wilson who'd set up a travel club there started to charter the odd ship just for his club members. In the late fifties he had also been involved in setting up the Overseas Visitors Club (OVC) in London, where Contiki was born – thanks Max for the noticeboard opportunity!

Peter turned his attention to setting up an African overland tour starting in Nairobi and finishing in Cape Town. The route had been pioneered in 1967 by an English company called SIAFU Expeditions. Peter plotted his own route and test-drove it in late 1970. The more he researched the route, the more he realised how difficult, dangerous and unpredictable it would be. At the time, of course, the majority of African countries had an enormous amount of animosity towards South Africa and its apartheid régime, so anything that had a South African component was totally unacceptable. For example there was no way a South African registered vehicle could cross many of the other national borders in Africa. Peter persevered, and registered the vehicles in Botswana to overcome the obstacle.

The mode of transport chosen was long wheel-based Land Rover station wagons with heavy-duty suspensions. These were customised for the route and fitted with 12 seats, additional opening windows, radios, water carriers and full-length roof racks.

In the first year two north-bound and two south-bound seven-week tours were scheduled. The route was through Kenya, Uganda, Tanzania, Malawi, Mozambique, Zambia, and Rhodesia (Zimbabwe). Passengers would travel between London and Nairobi by air on East African airways. A series of 28-day tours around South Africa were also scheduled.

A two-colour brochure was produced with 'Overland Safari on a Mini Budget', emblazoned on the front cover, with a charging elephant in the background. We distributed the brochure to the travel agents and the London office.

The trips were not for the faint hearted. Virtually all the roads on the route were in total disrepair. The road between Lusaka in Zambia and Dar Es Salaam in Tanzania was so bad, strewn with broken down and abandoned vehicles, that it was famously known as the 'Hell Run'. Other roads were just tracks. This was on top of the enormous distances, lack of communication facilities, constant corruption at border outposts, and frequent difficulties obtaining entry and exit permits.

Typical of the difficulties was that Zambia in the early seventies would not permit South African passport holders or for that matter anyone with a Rhodesian stamp in their passport to enter their country. To assist in overcoming the problem the Rhodesian border officials rather than stamp the passports, alternatively stamped separate pieces of paper so there was no Rhodesian stamp in the passenger's passports. This led to some interesting conversations with immigration officials on the Zambian side of the Rhodesia/Zambia border. When a vehicle drove across the Zambezi River at either Victoria Falls or the Kariba Dam the conversation went something like this:

Zambia Immigration (after watching the Contiki vehicle drive across the bridge):

'Have you been to Rhodesia?'

Contiki Driver: 'No. See, we have no Rhodesian stamp in our passports.'

Zambia Immigration: 'But we just saw you drive across the bridge from Rhodesia.'

Contiki Driver: 'We can assure you that wasn't us, see, no stamps in the passports.'

Zambia Immigration: (perplexed) 'Wait over there!'

How long the tour waited depended on a number of scenarios. The authorities were well aware of the situation, so it normally necessitated some sort of reward being made to the officials to permit entry, which they inevitably did.

In January 1971, a group was travelling from Nairobi to Johannesburg. The tour tried to cross from Kenya into Uganda, but was told on the Ugandan side by officials, 'Sorry, you can't cross, as it is not convenient. We are having a coup today and the border is closed!' It was the day that Ugandan military dictator Idi Amin seized power from President Milton Obote.

The only choice was to put the vehicle and passengers on a barge and travel for two days down the river to Lake Victoria and come ashore at Mwanza in Tanzania.

On another occasion the vehicle was stopped at a remote Zambia/Tanzania border post because the engine number on the vehicle carnet did not correspond with the number on the engine. There was no way the vehicle was going to be allowed to enter the country. The nearest working telephone was 600 kilometres away in Lusaka, so the tour was forced to return there to sort the matter out.

The shocking state of the roads and crazy drivers meant accidents were inevitable, a constant worry for Peter, his drivers and passengers. On one occasion in Rwanda when his vehicle was edging past a truck, the road collapsed causing the vehicle to roll a couple of times, seriously injuring two passengers.

No matter how prepared, there were the inevitable vehicle breakdowns, with the breaking of springs, half shafts and shock absorbers on the Land Rovers, all due largely to the rough terrain and bad roads. Once, one of the vehicles had a serious gearbox breakdown in Goma, Eastern Zaire, which took a week to fix. There was a leper hospital nearby, so the stranded passengers all pitched in to work at the hospital for a week, doing whatever tasks they could. I don't doubt many of the passenger's friends and family have heard that story more than a few times.

In the early 1970s there were no restrictions as to where the tours could camp in the East African game reserves as there are now. They would find a suitable spot and pitch the tents in a circle, Wild West style, with the vehicle in the middle. One night the group was awoken by a couple of the female passengers screaming uncontrollably. With the others peeping from their tents, they saw a lioness standing on her hind legs with her paws resting on top of the girl's tent. The two terrified girls inside only had the flyscreen sheet between them and the lioness's belly! The driver ran to the vehicle and tried to open the door, but unbelievably it stuck shut. Next thing the lioness pounced towards him, then stopped and watched him from just a couple of metres away. He frantically forced open the door, and then proceeded to back up to each of the tents so the 11 passengers could get in. They all waited inside until dawn before getting out as the lionesses had pulled down a wildebeest only 50 metres away from the camp. While the lions had been feeding, the lioness had been amusing herself while waiting for her turn to feed on the kill before eventually leaving.

The number of African overland tour operators grew over the years, with the majority using converted trucks as transport. These included Aadvark Expeditions, Encounter Overland, Exodus Expeditions, Frontier Travel, Hughes Overland, Inter Trek, The Overlanders and Trans African.

After a couple of years, Peter, with no practical involvement with European operation parted ways with Contiki and changed the name of the overland company to Kimbla Travel. As a remaining connection with Contiki, the name Kimbla was created by taking the last two letters of Contiki (KI) the first letter of his wife's first name Margaret (M) and the first three letters of Pete's surname Blake (BLA). The African tours were terminated for not dissimilar reasons as the Indian overland – increasing unrest and too much risk for staff, passengers and vehicles. The last Kimbla African overland tour was operated in 1975. I purchased Pete's Contiki shares and although our business association was finished, our long and close friendship still remains.

16. UNCLE SAM BECKONS US

By 1981, with the European operation well established and profitable, we were acutely aware that we had all our eggs in the one basket – Europe. Perhaps we should look to diversify? We knew we were onto a winner with the product we had created, particularly as many passengers booked on another tour soon after they returned from the first. Why not replicate the concept to give our passengers yet another experience in a different part of the world?

North America and Canada had been tugging at me for some time. After all, Ali and I had taken that amazing road trip through North America in the name of research and had loved it. We believed it would also interest other young people and always had the view that one day Contiki would run tours through the country. So we reasoned it all through, listing the reasons why we should take on the mighty United States of America.

Many of our passengers from Australasia were either travelling on flights to or from the United Kingdom via America or Canada, so it was a logical step for them to stopover and to see something of those countries along the way.

Having already appointed travel wholesalers in both countries, we had experienced an explosion of young Americans and particularly Canadians booking on the European tours. They were not only very nationalistic, but raved about their respective countries, constantly encouraging their fellow passengers to visit. Looking at the size of the youth market in both countries we realised how big the potential could be for us to entice them to Europe. We imagined our eye-catching big yellow coaches with the winking sun on the side travelling the length and breadth of North America. What an amazing advertising billboard they would be as they travelled on the highways, byways and places like downtown New York, San Francisco or Toronto.

Expanding to North America would also give our staff the opportunity to expand their horizons. However, the underlying reason was to make Contiki a worldwide company. I had never forgotten my business plan from 1967 – I was going to Contiki-ise the world!

We had conquered Europe with operations in around 22 countries. We'd tackled obstacles such as different languages, onerous rules and regulations and diverse currencies. With belief in our product, determination and confidence in ourselves as a company, we had done it. America? It would be a doddle! At least they spoke English.

Little did we know how bumpy the road ahead was going to be.

*

Once the decision was made to expand to America, no time was wasted. First, we researched the competition. There were already three companies running camping tours around America, all of whom used minibuses: Americamp, Avontours and Trek America. They were not large in size, but appeared to be attracting passengers in small but growing numbers. A basic plan was established. Our American operation had to be significantly different, so for a start we would launch using coaches. Initially we would use tent and cabin accommodation in camp grounds, and once up and running, we'd introduce character accommodation in the form of special stopovers. Itineraries were drafted, influenced to a degree on what the existing operators were offering and adding mine and Ali's input from our experiences.

A young New Zealander, Euan Purdie – previously a primary school teacher – was about to be thrown his 'hunk of meat' as we gave him the task of researching and setting up the American operation. Euan had started out with us as a driver and moved into an operations role. He had proved his ability to solve problems and complete tasks effectively and efficiently, which was good enough for us. He, in turn, believed he was up to the task.

Euan took off for America on a tourist visa. On arrival, he applied for a green card (work visa) so he could stay in America to research the project. He booked, incognito, as a passenger on an Avontours trip. As the bus toured around the country, Euan noted all the information he could relating to the route travelled including details of the sights, excursions, accommodation and costs, writing everything down each evening; *Déjà vu*, again! I admit we were doing exactly what those early European competitors had done with us, and it sure helped fast track matters. He accumulated a stack of information, though he must have appeared to be a terribly studious stick-in-the-mud to the other passengers.

Euan soon found out that to carry fare-paying passengers on a bus through America you needed an International Chamber of Commerce (ICC) transport licence for every state the bus passed through. Such a licence wasn't required, however, if you carried eight or less passengers. Not all our soon-to-be competitors had licences, and managed to operate illegally by using unmarked minibuses with no identification. To the policing authorities they were seen as private touring groups. We were determined to find a way into the American market and offer a fully licensed operation and a far superior product.

Unlike them, there was no way Contiki could operate illegally with its conspicuous big yellow coaches. But an ICC licence shouldn't be too much of a problem, should it? After all we had our European coaching operation track record. Surely we just needed to fill in a few forms to show we satisfied the criteria? There were already three nationwide bus operators running: Trailways, Greyhound and Grayline, so if they could meet the requirements we certainly could – or so we thought.

To our utmost horror, it was confirmed we required a separate licence for every state we planned to visit or pass through. In our case, this would be 38 states. It could take up to two years we were told. The reality began to sink in – setting up in America was not going to be a doddle after all.

Two years? If we were going to fulfil our dreams of an American operation we needed to make a start, realising it could be a very long road. So, in 1981 we formed an American company to get the ball rolling. There was a legal requirement for us to have a minimum of one US resident director. As usual, we were already stretched and stuck for candidates. Luckily Jimmy Murphy, the owner of our American general sales agent, Brendan Tours, kindly agreed to step into the directorship role.

Off we set to hire the first of what was to become a legion of lawyers and the inevitable onslaught of legal fees. We found a Los Angeles-based lawyer who specialised in ICC licences. He reinforced the fact that licences for all 38 states would be required. Did that mean 38 lawyers? Heaven forbid! The estimated costs were unbelievable but we were determined to push on, knowing it might be a long, hard slog.

While we were pursuing the licences we approached the three existing National bus operators, Grayline, Greyhound and Trailways, to see if we could fast track an alternative option. Perhaps we could interest them in leasing us licensed coaches on a dry hire arrangement? After protracted discussions we concluded they were not interested in any sort of arrangement with a lowly camping tour operator with such grand plans.

Increasingly uncomfortable with the way we were being patronised, we comforted ourselves with the fact that their coaches were nowhere near the quality we aspired to anyway, even as a temporary arrangement. Could we work with these people? No we couldn't. We did, however, keep a distant relationship with them as they might be needed as a fall back plan.

One day we received a call from a very excited Euan.

'I've heard something on the grapevine, John,' he said.

'Yes? Tell me, Euan.' I asked.

'I think Americamp is having trouble with its creditors,' he said. 'They might have to cease trading.'

Americamp had minibus licences for a majority of the states it travelled through, although its permits restricted passengers to stay in camping accommodation only. With some rapid research and consultations with our legal eagles we realised there was an opportunity for us to help Americamp's owner and in turn help ourselves. We were advised its current licences could possibly, in time, be upgraded for coaches and regular accommodation.

Quietly we approached the owner of Americamp, suggesting we could bail him out of his predicament. His creditors were about to move in on him. In confidence, we told him of our grand plans in America, suggesting he could join us. We desperately wanted his licences. He agreed but drove a very hard deal. Lengthy negotiations later, we settled on a cash payment of US$20,000 together with him taking a 25 per cent shareholding in our American company. As a result he was able to settle his creditors and we had a new shareholder with operational expertise and his licences. We had advanced our original licence predicament by at least 18 months!

Our legal team immediately pounced on the licences and started the process of upgrading them. We looked at acquiring the four coaches required for the tours. Preferably we wanted to lease them but if absolutely necessary we would consider purchasing. We had learnt an enormous amount about the American bus industry through our discussions with the bus operators but hadn't quite realised how bad the vehicle quality was.

After several months of fruitless searching we hit a brick wall. The best coaches we could find were still vastly inferior compared with those in Europe. But we were not prepared to drop our quality standard. It seemed like an intractable dilemma.

Vermaat was called to the table for advice. As usual they were an incredible help and together we agreed the only solution was to have the coaches manufactured in Belgium by the same company that produced our European Mercedes-Benz coaches. We would ship them across the Atlantic to America. It would be extremely costly and fraught with risk, especially since at that point we didn't yet have the fully upgraded licences to even operate the coaches in America!

We entered into a three way financing deal with the coach building company, Vermaat and Contiki. It was a huge capital commitment but there was no alternative. On several occasions we reassessed the situation as to whether or not we pull the whole American project. On each occasion, our positive approach and longer term plans to expand internationally, won out. We convinced ourselves we could do it.

We ordered four state-of-the-art Mercedes-Benz coaches with Neoplan bodies and immediately started to search for a coach company or financial institution in America who might like to buy the coaches and lease them back to us. Time and time again, we were knocked back. Most times, those we approached would not even engage with us. After many false starts we found a bank based in Tacoma, Washington, called Rainier Bank. After a very complicated deal, Rainier eventually came on board.

By that stage we had set up an operations base in Anaheim, Los Angeles. A local tent manufacturer had been engaged to produce the tents, although the cook tents produced were unsuitable so we arranged to import some of our proven ones from Europe. In the meantime Euan, our man on the ground, was driving around the routes we planned to operate the first tours on. He chose suitable accommodation sites and booked them, confirmed the costings and wrote 'the bible' for future field staff.

While all this was in progress Alison Lloyd, our brilliant Marketing Director, and her team in London were working on the production of an American brochure. It was one of her toughest assignments so far. Neither she nor any of her team had been to America, let alone around the route we needed to promote. It was extremely difficult to know what to include in the brochure because so many details were still up in the air. We bit the bullet, however, and included photos of our European coaches on the brave assumption we would obtain the upgraded licences. Pricing the tours was also a challenge, since it was so far in advance and we didn't yet know how many departures or passengers we'd be carrying to spread the overheads.

We decided to operate eight different tours ranging from 18 to 49 days, quite bold for the inaugural year. But we wanted to make a big splash in our first year and also test the market appeal of a variety of tours. All departures were guaranteed to operate – again, a huge risk, but necessary for the travel agents to have confidence in booking their passengers, particularly as they could be nervous, it being our first year. We had to give a degree of certainty.

The initial tour programme consisted of itineraries around the West Coast taking in all the major sights and cities such as Los Angeles, San Francisco, Las Vegas, San Diego, Vancouver and the Canadian Rockies. The others were a combination of the Grand Tour heading East from Los Angeles through the south, then up to New York and back across the northern states.

*

Special stopovers were shelved until a later date. However, we did plan to include a few special nights' accommodation. We had found a teepee village at the Grand Canyon, pine wood chalets at a lakeside resort near Yosemite National Park in California, and accommodation at a genuine cowboy ranch in Texas.

Utmost secrecy was kept while we set up the American tours. We didn't want our competitors to get wind of what we were doing because when we launched we wanted to blow them out of the water. In late 1981, we launched our tours at a travel show in Philadelphia. Avontours and Trek America also had stands. They were truly flabbergasted and, as Contiki's plans became clear, began to make us feel most unwelcome. At the same time we introduced the new brochure to our worldwide travel agents in Australia, New Zealand and South Africa. Almost immediately the bookings began to trickle in.

Worryingly, the manufacture of the coaches was behind schedule and we were just months away from our first tour departure. But the brochure was on the market, so we had to deliver. You can imagine our alarm at the thought of the excited passengers arriving for Contiki's first-ever American tour only to find there was no coach for them to board. We knew how powerful word of mouth advertising was; it also worked in reverse. If we messed this up, the damage to Contiki's reputation could be irreparable. It was an intense nail-biting period as the risk of everything turning to custard was very real. Fortunately we knew that when (and if!) the coaches arrived, we'd actually be able to drive them, as our brilliant lawyers had earned their money by obtaining the upgraded licences.

The deadline for the first tour departure date continued to hurtle towards us at an alarming rate. It was all systems go. Six of our best European tour leaders and coach drivers were flown to America. Like Euan before them, they travelled on tourist visas and applied for green cards on arrival. Securing the green cards in the timeframe required gave us another unwelcome headache, but with sheer tenacity and another switched-on lawyer, they were granted and the drivers were free to obtain their American coach driving licences.

With just six weeks before the first tours were due to start we sent our American recruits out with Euan in a hired bus to learn the ropes and familiarise themselves with the route. The training trip skidded to a halt, back at our Anaheim base, with just ten days spare. Over the next week the passengers started arriving, all very excited. Everything was in place except for one small problem. We still had no coaches.

Although the shipment from Belgium had been delayed, the coaches had arrived, but at the port of New Jersey – 5000 kilometres away on the other coast! Not only that, but when we sent a couple of our drivers to collect them we discovered the coaches' sophisticated state-of-the-art sound systems had been stolen en route. But there was no time to investigate the theft. The moment each coach was cleared by Customs it was driven directly across America, non-stop, day and night.

In March 1982, the first American tour departed from Los Angeles with tour leader Gus Maher at the helm. As the coach disappeared down the road, Euan has told me he sat down on the kerb, and with an overwhelming emotional feeling of the moment, cried. Contiki was operational in America – we had done it!

The first three-week tour had overnight stops in Las Vegas, Grand Canyon National Park, Durango, Santa Fe, El Paso, Bandera, San Antonio, Houston, New Orleans, Memphis, Nashville, Winston Salem, Williamsburg, Washington and, finally, New York.

The first trips were fraught with problems, primarily relating to issues with the coach. Owing to their unusual height, several detours were required as some bridges were too low to pass under. The air conditioning systems broke down and there were a number of problems with the advanced Mercedes-Benz engines. In Europe, this would not have been a problem but in America, there were no appointed Mercedes service agents to help out, so repairs were difficult. And, of course, with no sound system it was a pretty quiet trip – music-wise. Other teething pains included the massively long distances. The drivers and tour leaders were not accustomed to such long days and lengthy gaps between sights, coming from their tour of duty in the comparatively small and action-packed Europe.

By the end of 1982, Contiki was a fully licensed *bona fide* American tour operator. We had established an operating base and had hired a good number of local American staff. An excellent working relationship was underway with accommodation providers, food suppliers, and activity and entertainment operators. Better prices were in store for the year ahead, thanks to some persistent negotiating, and we had flown out specialised Mercedes-Benz mechanics from Europe to deal with the coaches' mechanical problems.

Most of all, we had learned a huge amount about the American way of business. It was surprisingly highly regulated with a painfully slow bureaucracy. We'd become accustomed to doing business in Europe, where rules were bent a little more often and, if they weren't, you could at least offer to pay to expedite the matter. In America, the officialdom was rigid and its word was final. So much for the great land of entrepreneurial opportunity, but to be fair, America had given us an opportunity, which we grabbed with both hands.

But our new operations in America provided several other benefits. We could now boast we were an international tour operator. We had four huge billboards travelling through the towns and cities of America and Canada. Our uniquely painted European coaches were a crowdstopper everywhere they went. Thousands of young Americans, their parents and travel agents were being introduced to Contiki this way. But above all we had proved to everyone, no matter how tough the challenges, we had met them head on and succeeded.

In 1983, we expanded the American business considerably by adding a further six coaches. We had learnt from our trials with the last four coaches, however, and this time we chose an Eagle Chassis, a Detroit 6V92 engine with a Jonckheere body. The capital required was enormous and well beyond our capabilities at the time so we set out again to find funding for them in America. Once again this turned out to be extremely difficult, but suffice to say, with perseverance we found a solution, with a bank buying the coaches and leasing them back us.

Having proved we were up and running, we approached a number of airlines including TWA, Qantas and Air Canada to assist us with the huge cost of transporting our American brochures around the world. They did this on the condition we put a full-page advertisement in each version of the American brochure. Naturally we agreed. Being endorsed by these highly respected airlines also gave our new American product just that little bit of added credibility.

We soon started a serious hunt for some character accommodation. One of the most popular tour destinations was New Orleans, always a two-night stop. Whether it was a trip on a Mississippi paddle steamer, an historical stroll around the French Quarter and all that jazz, or a taste of Creole cooking, New Orleans was always a hit. We had noticed several magnificent Southern mansions around the area. What a treat it would be for our passengers if they could sleep in one! Several months of searching passed until we found a grand looking mansion in the Garden District. The building was almost within walking distance of downtown New Orleans and streetcars passed by outside the front door. It was owned by an historical society who agreed to lease it to us. We spent US$150,000 on upgrades to accommodate two coach loads, and called it the Mardi Gras Mansion.

In the same year, we lifted the product up a huge notch and dispensed with tents altogether. Passengers would be accommodated in what was called 'hard-top' accommodation such as cabins, motels, hotels, and even a casino hotel in Las Vegas. Costs would be only marginally higher than camping, but the continuing problem of inclement weather would be removed, not to mention the enormous amount of time saved. We disposed of the tents and camping equipment at knockdown prices, sustaining a significant loss. This only added to the huge losses we had accumulated in setting up the American operation over those first three years, which ran in excess of US$2 million.

At the end of the fourth year we made our first profit. Passenger numbers were growing and we were now running tours to Eastern Canada, plus a few extra excursions like visiting the Bahamas from Miami. We opened our own sales office in Anaheim to deal with the increasing number of bookings coming through from the American travel agents. Our giant, roaming billboards were clearly paying off.

From a standing start, Contiki was now a well respected American tour operator. We were getting even closer to Contiki-ising the world!

17. BRINGING CONTIKI HOME

By 1979, Ali and I had two school-aged children. After my 18 years in London we decided to move back to New Zealand, and settle in Auckland. We wanted to bring up our children in the lifestyle we had both been privileged enough to experience. The presence of our extended families, the favourable climate, excellent education system plus a family home for us to settle down in permanently confirmed our decision to return.

Over the years I lived in London, I met hundreds of travellers from Australia and New Zealand. I was always surprised by how few had seen their own country before heading overseas. As the years passed, I observed that after enjoying Europe, many expressed a strong desire to see their home countries on return, perhaps travelling with some of the new found friends they had met on tour.

I'm a very proud New Zealander and love my beautiful country with a passion. Being in the Southern Hemisphere, New Zealand was an ideal country to continue Contiki's geographical diversification as it had the opposite weather patterns to Europe. Many of our European staff were laid off at the end of the Northern summer, until the tours began the following season. Operations in New Zealand would enable us to transfer them and provide year round work.

At the time, tourism in New Zealand was a sunrise industry with huge potential. Now was an opportunity to enter on the ground floor before it really took off. I began to thoroughly research the market. There were already a number of established companies operating camping tours through the country, specifically for the youth market. These included Freedom Holidays, Value Tours, Southern Cross, Guthrie's and Moatrek, the latter having been started by one of my original European minibus drivers.

With me being Mr Johnny-on-the-spot I embarked on another challenge: to bring Contiki to New Zealand. I could hardly wait to show it off to others! So I made a start to turn it into a reality

To operate tours carrying fare paying passengers in New Zealand the appropriate road transport licences were again required. However, I soon discovered they were extremely difficult to obtain and very restrictive relating to travel areas, the size of vehicle and even the type of overnight accommodation passengers could stay in, not dissimilar to America. How archaic it all seemed compared with Europe!

The licences were issued by a body called The Authority – a one-man band whose power was absolute. The Authority decided who won and who lost. All the existing operators vigorously opposed my licence application, determined to protect their patch at all costs. After taking legal advice it became clear this was going to be a tough, drawn-out affair with no guarantee of success. It turned out New Zealand had a highly protectionist business culture and did not welcome a big new player like Contiki coming in to throw its weight around, as they perceived it.

If you can't beat them – join them. I approached the owners of Moatrek which had minibus licences to operate throughout the country, although restricted to camping accommodation. We reached agreement for the New Zealand company I'd formed to buy a 50 per cent interest in Moatrek. The other competitors had lost the first round.

The plan was to carry on with the existing operation while we upgraded the current licences to full-sized coaches and eventually change the name of Moatrek to Contiki New Zealand. Two straightforward objectives right? Wrong!

*

We appointed legal counsel to represent our application to The Authority to upgrade the licences and were confident our request would be favourably considered. After all, we had the backing of Contiki in Europe which was considerably larger and more successful than any other tour operator in New Zealand.

But the competition ganged up to fight us, appointing the top specialist lawyer in transport licensing to bat for them. It was an open court and within an hour we realised we were on a hiding to nothing. We had made a mistake in not appointing a similar transport specialist. Our lawyer opened our case but had little knowledge of the subject and was no match for the other side. The opposition literally took to our man. I'd never been in a court before, let alone experienced an attack as venomous as the one he unleashed. He tore our case to bits in such an aggressive manner it left our man standing there almost whimpering. I've never forgotten that opposition lawyer's name and face. The experience helped create the start of an aversion (with a simmering respect) that I would eventually form about the legal profession, which to some degree I still hold. And from that day onwards whenever we needed professional advice, be it legal, financial or specialised expertise, we always went for the very best, as there is no substitute for quality – even though the cost, on some occasions, seemed excessive.

Our application to upgrade the licences failed but we didn't give up. We appealed and this time had a break through, with The Authority granting us a licence to run coaches in the North Island but only minibuses in the South Island! How clever of the opposition to achieve this result but how stupid of The Authority. We battled again and eventually obtained upgraded licences New Zealand-wide. The fiasco put us back a year in introducing coaches.

As our legal battles simmered away, some smart Alec (a local tour operator in Wellington) was off registering the name Kontiki, (yes with a K) for himself. When we moved to do the same, we were of course refused the use of the Contiki name. We tracked him down and although he wasn't using it, he forced us to buy the name from him. He drove a hard bargain and we ended up shelling out NZ$5000! We had learnt yet another costly but very valuable business lesson: protect your brand name. We immediately set about registering the Contiki name around the world where we thought it should be protected. It was an expensive exercise but proved to be a great investment later on.

With the now valuable coach licences in hand, we had to find suitable coaches to run the upgraded operation. Like America, the overall standard of these and the operators were sub-standard compared to Europe. We tried a couple of different companies, operating with their equipment but we had nothing but trouble with their inferior vehicles. We weren't prepared to compromise any longer so decided to have new coaches built to our own high criteria and specifications, just as we had done in America. We chose Volvos and painted their exterior bodies in the Contiki yellow, again with the winking sun logo on the side.

Some hard lessons in Europe had taught us we were tour operators not coach operators. It therefore made sense to partner with Newmans, the top coach operator in New Zealand, to take over the coaches so we could lease them back. There was, however, one condition. Newmans had started a camping tour operation in competition to Contiki called 'Tearaway' by hiring one of our ex-European staff. We requested they close down Tearaway, which thankfully they did.

In 1982 we bought the remaining 50 per cent stake in Moatrek. Contiki now had a fledgling coach tour operation in New Zealand!

The first Big Yellow coach departed from Auckland in December 1983.

Owing to the country's shape we designed what we called a 'Mother Itinerary'. This was a single route that started in New Zealand's largest city (Auckland), looped up the west coast to the northern tip where the Tasman Sea meets the Pacific Ocean, went back down the East coast to Auckland and travelled south through Rotorua to Wellington, crossed the Cook Strait from the North Island to the South Island, travelled down the West Coast to Fox Glacier, went over the Southern Alps to the adventure capital of Queenstown, south to Te Anau and Milford Sound, north through Dunedin and Mount Cook and finished in the garden city (Christchurch). The route would return from Christchurch to Auckland in the reverse direction so passengers had the option to start their tour in either city. We based six different tours off this Mother Itinerary, ranging from seven to 21 days.

New Zealand has so much to offer in such a small space – it truly is a compact wonderland. We encouraged travellers to experience it all, such as New Zealand's unique Maori culture through Hangi feasts (where food is buried and cooked in the ground), and staying at a Marae (a Maori meeting house) and enjoying the unique concerts, with Queenstown offering several world famous adventure options like jet boat rides, paragliding, white water rafting and the adrenalin rush of bungee jumping.

Moatrek was a camping tour operator when we purchased it. We decided to upgrade the new Contiki brand to operate without tents. In the three major cities we used hotels and around the rest of the route we used cabins, chalets, lodges and introduced special stopovers. In addition hard-top accommodation also made it possible to run tours throughout the winter months as well.

Auckland was the starting or finishing point for the majority of passengers where they stayed a few nights before or after their tour. The New Station Hotel on Beach Road dated back to the 1930s and was situated directly opposite Auckland's main railway station. It was a brick building with six levels, 60 rooms with communal bathrooms on each floor, three bars, and a dining room with an enormous kitchen attached. It could sleep up to 130 guests and we believed it was perfect for our requirements. With a hefty mortgage and a lot of faith, we bought the hotel and surrounding land for NZ$1million. 'What a bargain!' So we thought.

A frightening reality check was soon to follow. We knew the hotel was in receivership – that's how we'd nabbed the low price. But we hadn't really done our homework on the underlying reasons *why* it was in trouble. What a lesson. If something's cheap look hard for the reasons ... it's never a coincidence. The New Station Hotel was an entertainment in itself starting from day one. And this was only the first instalment of a number of sagas that would begin to unfold.

We set about completely refurbishing the hotel. Fifteen new rooms with private facilities were added, the public areas were upgraded, the kitchen refitted and a new restaurant built. We could now accommodate 174 guests, at a squeeze, and would hopefully benefit from the improved economy of scale.

On the touring front we were determined to have a far superior programme than our competitors. We wanted to be a young person's obvious first choice when touring New Zealand. By introducing a quality coach fleet and cutting out tent accommodation, we'd already lifted the bar – now we wanted to introduce special stopovers to seal the deal.

Orakei Korako was an exclusive thermal hideaway near the North Island's famous Rotorua geothermal area. There, passengers were able to relax in newly constructed, authentic log cabins overlooking a tranquil lake. Orakei Korako even had its own hot pools and a small geyser. It turned out to be an absolute hit with the passengers.

Another popular stopover was the overnight stay on the Maori Tarawera Marae in Rotorua, where the passengers slept in a magnificently carved sleeping house, called a Wharenui. Yet another great stopover was the mountain base camp at Makarora in the Mount Aspiring National Park in the South Island where the passengers spent a pleasant night in A frame chalets dotted amidst the natural bush. No one ever forgot the eerie silence at night, and the blowflies as big as bumble bees!

On the outskirts of the southern city of Dunedin (as Scottish as any city in Scotland) was the magnificent Larnach Castle. Originally built in 1871 it had been faithfully restored. Beside the castle was the old coach house, next in line for restoration. The owners didn't quite have the funds available, so together we agreed to develop the coach house into an accommodation facility. With our guarantee to fill it, plus a loan to facilitate its restoration and construction, it was built, giving Contiki passengers the wonderful experience of staying in the grounds of Larnach Castle. Like the Von Allum family's purpose-built chalet in Lauterbrunnen, Switzerland, this was another perfect example of two interested parties cooperating to achieve a mutually beneficial result.

Queenstown is the tourist mecca of New Zealand. Our tours lingered there the longest as there was so much to see and do. Initially we stayed in the municipal motor camp and later in a rundown hotel. While the hotel was on the shores of the magnificent Lake Wakatipu with to-die-for views of the Remarkable Mountains, it was not up to our standards.

Budget accommodation, however, was becoming increasingly scarce in Queenstown, which was getting more popular with tourists by the day. In addition, there were very few facilities that could accommodate a full coach load of 45, let alone two coach loads on the nights where our tours overlapped. 'Why not build our own special stopover?' we figured. It would only get more and more expensive to build as time passed, so we thought, 'Let's jump at the opportunity!'

In 1984, on a hillside overlooking Lake Wakatipu we found five acres of magnificent land, up for sale. It was in a dress circle position in Fernhill on the outskirts of Queenstown, just an eight minute drive from the town centre. It had been an old strawberry farm and, as a bonus, still featured the original homestead. The only other item on the site was an enormous pine tree. Five acres was much more than we required but the seller was only interested in disposing of the whole block. We bit the bullet and bought it for NZ$250,000.

On the evening we took possession of the land, Contiki colleague Hewitt Harrison and I stood on the middle of the site, looking down on the unimpeded views of Lake Wakatipu. It was simply breathtaking!

'We're going to build the most magnificent lodge here, Hewitt!' I told him.

Funding, planning permissions, architects, builders, and furnishing what finally emerged as the wonderful Queenstown Lodge proved to be an enormous challenge. What's more we only needed half of the land to build it.

Seeing it all come together, from the original blueprint I had spent hours looking over, to a structure that could accommodate 120 people was an amazing feeling. It was this feeling, and watching other people enjoy the results, that constantly encouraged me and the Contiki team to take on even bigger challenges.

The success of building the Queenstown Lodge was thanks largely to Hewitt, who took overall responsibility for the project. Prior to joining the company he had been a stock and station agent, meaning he would visit farmers to see if they needed supplies such as fertiliser, fence posts, wire or perhaps some item of farm machinery. He was a very organised, meticulous individual, always dotting the i's and crossing the t's. He had absolutely no experience in building tourist lodges, yet I had trust in him, and he rose to the challenge magnificently, like so many Contiki staff. The Lodge was opened for its first guests in December 1985.

In those days I was so busy that I 'managed by exception'. I entrusted people with tasks, big tasks, and we would draw up the plan together. Off they would go and unless I heard back I would assume everything was progressing to plan. If something unexpected happened, they reported back and we would sort out the problem together. I simply had too many things happening at once to manage things any other way. That said, at times I also liked to be involved in some of the detail; the Lodge being a good example. I remember helping to select things such as the furnishings, right down to details relating to the choice of fabric and colour of the curtains.

With the Queenstown Lodge operational we leapt at the opportunity to introduce ski tours to the Queenstown region, catering exclusively to the 18–35 year old age group. No other company had done this previously; we would again be the first. Why not enjoy your ski holiday experience with other young people from all around the world?

Ski tours in New Zealand would not only assist with the Lodge occupancy in the winter and give summer staff work, it also meant we could tap into another market – the young skier, particularly from Australia. However, if we were going to be taken seriously as a ski tour operator we also needed to extend our product range to the other major ski resort area in the South Island – the Mount Hutt ski field. We found Pudding Hill, an accommodation complex on the outskirts of Methven, at the base of the ski field. We purchased it, upgraded the facilities to sleep 140 guests and opened it for business in the winter of 1986. By the following winter with the two properties in operation we had nabbed a 15 per cent share of the total packaged ski market.

In the meantime, The New Station Hotel had become the backdrop for weekly dramas. The hotel was covered by two police stations and we turned out to be an excellent customer! To my horror, my proud new acquisition seemed to have sirens blaring towards it every other day. And if it wasn't the police, it was the fire brigade.

We had a major drama soon after we had taken over the hotel. The hotel employed a chef and two cooks. The chef was married to one of the hotel's barmaids, and they lived together with one of the cooks in an outer suburb of Auckland. One day the chef came home a little earlier than usual to find his wife in bed with the cook. Naturally an unpleasant altercation ensued and his wife moved out.

One night the chef and the adulterous cook were home alone and a heated argument started between them. It became physical and the chef hit the cook in the face with a loose brick from the fireplace. The cook went into the bathroom to clean up the blood pouring from his face and the chef followed him, grabbed his head and bashed it against the side of the cast iron bath. This resulted in the cook's untimely demise. Subsequently the chef used a knife to cut off the deceased's hands, head, feet and, rumour has it, his penis.

The chef proceeded to dump the body's torso in Puhoi, north of Auckland. The hands and feet were thrown off the Birkenhead wharf on Auckland's inner harbour. He placed the head in a plastic bag, wrapped it in newspaper and placed it the boot of the hotel's car. A few days later the hotel's remaining cook took the car to fetch food supplies. On opening the boot, he found the package, picked it up and put it on the pavement to load the supplies. The package rolled away and the gruesome discovery was made. The torso, hands and feet were eventually located but no one seems to know what might have happened to the penis. A rumour went around town suggesting it may not be such a good idea to eat at the New Station Hotel …

There was always a large cross-section of humanity passing through the hotel. We soon discovered it was an active brothel. There was a second entrance to the hotel on the top floor, which had a bar and a restaurant off Anzac Avenue. The girls' clients would check in at the hotel's ground floor reception for a room, and the girls entered through the top to service them.

There was a public bar on ground level that turned out to be one of Auckland's major gathering places for low-level criminals. Here they conducted their business, more often than not arranging the distribution of stolen goodies. Fights between these patrons were some of the best spectacles in town – some went several rounds!

When you cater for the general public you never know much about a customer prior to dealing with them – hotel guests were typical of this dilemma. The odd guest would check in with a couple of large but empty suitcases, go to their room, pack the cases with everything they could possibly squeeze in – including bed linen, towels and window drapes – then take the lift to the top floor and leave. On one occasion we had an intoxicated guest who checked into his room, lit a cigarette, and immediately fell asleep on his bed in a drunken stupor. The bed blankets began to smoulder and the room caught on fire tragically causing the unpaid-up guest to die of smoke inhalation.

We had a number of visiting sports teams staying at the hotel. We were centrally located and – more importantly – one of the few hotels prepared to accommodate them. Most were no problem, but there was always the odd group with a few too many beers onboard that caused us much aggravation. The room parties, noise and aftermath of mess were a continuing problem. It was not unusual for the people who threw up in their room to innocently check out. Occasionally guests would kick-in the lift doors, putting the lift out of action. Once this happened from the inside, which left the guilty perpetrator trapped there for almost a day.

One day I received a call from the police stating the hotel was about to be held up by an armed criminal. The police had been tipped off and were following the robber as he drove around the city towards his intended target. A police contingent had arrived ahead of him at the hotel to prepare for his 'arrival'. It was a courtesy phone call to let the hotel owner know about the situation. They assured me all was in hand.

An armed officer crouched behind the reception counter ready for our unwelcome guest to show up. Other officers spread around chameleon-like, ready to take whatever action was necessary. Our brave young receptionist was asked to stay behind the counter and act normal. Sure enough the robber fronted up with a gun, at which point the police swarmed and arrested him.

New Station Hotel dramas aside, in just three short years we had established a Contiki presence at the other end of the world, the South Pacific country of New Zealand. After 18 years away from my homeland I had returned and achieved another dream. I was a very proud New Zealander indeed.

18. WE'VE COME TO THE LAND DOWNUNDER

Way back in 1968 one of my early European minibus drivers returned home to Melbourne. Coincidently he had been the driver of the European tour with that first passenger who had given me a problem (now Ali Anderson). He was keen to help promote Contiki in Australia by visiting the local travel agents and holding slide evenings for young people considering a trip to Europe. To give a professional impression we registered an Australian company, Contiki Travel Pty Limited, and opened a small one-room office in the city at 397 Little Collins Street. It was quite a momentous occasion as Contiki had opened its first overseas office! He set about promoting Contiki and started to take the occasional tour booking, which he then sent through to the London office.

He was quite an entrepreneurial sort of guy and proposed we run weekend ski tours to Falls Creek, a resort around four hours north-east of Melbourne. The profits from this venture would help defray the costs of running the Little Collins Street office. It seemed like a good idea. I funded the purchase of a 15-seat Ford Transit minibus and he had the Contiki name and logo painted proudly on the sides. Our man put together the ski packages and started to promote them. Every weekend over the winter he reported setting off with a near full bus. However, he continually asked for more funds, which seemed odd. With the tours constantly full, surely we should be making profits, not losses.

On my next trip to Melbourne I investigated why the losses kept stacking up. It soon became clear. On the Tuesday before the tour was to depart, he often found the bus was only half full for its Friday evening departure. So he would advertise in the local newspaper and successfully fill the vehicle. But the money spent on the extra advertising was more than the total projected profit for the trip. He was, in fact, buying the extra passengers. At the end of the winter season, we stopped the ski tours, sold the bus and closed the office.

Fifteen years later, in 1983 we were back, opening a sales office in Clarence Street, in the business district of Sydney. Before we could sell tours we had to obtain a Travel Agency Regulation Board (TARB) licence. One of the requirements was to place advertisements in a local newspaper for five consecutive weeks advising the public of our intentions, in case anyone had objections. This responsibility rested with our lawyers, a prominent Australian firm. First, they delayed weeks before placing the required advertisements. And second, they omitted to place the final one, forcing us to start again from scratch.

For three frustrating months, our sales booking staff were unable to deal with the public. The cost of the delay was considerable, so we sued the law firm, won, and recouped our losses. There was an irony in the case as the lawyer we hired to act for us had been a previous disgruntled employee of the defendants. He relished the opportunity to 'get one back' on his former employer, as we did.

With the office up and running we had a base in Australia and decided to extend our international tour operation to include Australia. This wouldn't be too difficult as our local staff, like all Australians, had this natural positive attitude to life. I'd seen them in action with us in Europe and America resolving major obstacles, time and time again. We were confident they were up to the challenge. As a bonus, the Aussies are very nationalistic and love their country (and their sport) with a passion. They, like me, love to show the world their country, which is almost as good as New Zealand!

We knew we wouldn't be lacking in the range of compelling sights and activities for the itinerary. Australia is the most amazing country. It has an incredibly diverse landscape, from the parched deserts in the red centre to the lush rain forests in the north-east and the World Heritage wetlands in the north-west. It's packed full of beautiful surf beaches, dreamy off shore islands, sleepy outback towns and, of course, the incredible Great Barrier Reef. Its cities are diverse too, from pulsating Sydney with its breath-taking harbour to the Northern Territory's tropical, multicultural capital of Darwin to the beautiful city of Melbourne situated on the banks of the Yarra River.

It's also a huge continent. It's one thing to appreciate this on a map, and quite another to begin drawing up practical and entertaining travel itineraries. We soon discovered just how enormous the distances were between some towns and cities.

Two tours along the east coast and two around the red centre of Alice Springs and Uluru and up to Darwin were agreed. To help bridge the distances Ansett Airlines offered special airfares to our passengers for travel within Australia.

We found a suitable coach operator with quality coaches and the all-important transport licences who we could lease the coaches from. They agreed to paint them in Contiki yellow with our name and winking sun on the sides with the tag line, 'As much fun as you can handle'.

As with New Zealand, we decided not to accommodate the passengers in tents. We located a unique mix of cabins, cheap hotels, motels and resorts. The first of our special stopovers were introduced and included a stay in an outback homestead, in a typical Aussie pub and in beachside cabins on beautiful Fraser Island. We scouted for unique experiences for the passengers to enjoy, such as an Aboriginal Corroboree, a re-enactment of Ned Kelly's last stand and learning how to throw a boomerang. We included special meal experiences such as cooking and tasting damper (a flour and water mixture cooked on an open fire), sampling kangaroo meat, and alligator burgers (known as Ali burgers). Barbecues were also a frequent occurrence.

Our ever-resourceful marketing department in London produced another brilliant sales brochure and the bookings started to roll in. The first Australian tour departed on 12 January 1985.

Over the years the Australian operation grew to offer an extensive range of concept tours plus adventure tours in four-wheel drive vehicles exploring the magnificent Cape York Peninsula, flotilla sailing around the spectacular Whitsunday Islands and eventually a stay on the company's own island resort. More about this later.

At the time of our entry into the market there was another well-established Australian camping tour company, Centralian, running tours for the youth market. We had heard it had a few financial problems and thought it would be a great opportunity to buy into a competitor. After protracted negotiations we bought 50 per cent of Centralian and injected funds to assist it through its current predicament. It was decided to continue to promote Centralian as an independent competitor with a slightly different product range.

But Centralian was in a more serious financial situation than we had been led to believe. To give the company a solid chance to survive, we had to put in even more funding. The owners of the company, two brothers who appeared wealthy on paper, had given us personal guarantees in exchange for the funds.

We tried to restructure and improve the company's trading situation but the Managing Director, who had started the company, proved to be a little intransigent. He still ran the company as though it was his own and did not take too kindly to the improvements we suggested be made. No one was going to tell him what to do, after all he was the veteran tour operator and always knew best!

The writing was on the wall. After a couple of years of total frustration Centralian went bust. Then came the kick in the head. The brothers who had guaranteed our loan refused to honour their agreement. We planned to take them to court only to find out we were not the first to have a similar problem. We lost our total investment. I've often heard it said 'Never invest cash into a business you have no control over'. If you are going to do that, make sure it is speculative money at risk, money you can afford to lose. On many occasions I've often looked back and thought, 'If only I'd followed that advice'.

This was a real lesson and a wake-up call. We had put in good money, trusted a couple of individuals we didn't really know and realised what we all ready knew – you can't change a leopard's spots. Entrepreneurs are hard to control, they don't like being told what to do, they like to call the shots. I should have known better – I was a classic example!

But unlike Centralian's Managing Director, I had slowly learnt to listen and take advice from those far wiser than me and act accordingly, although sometimes reluctantly. I do, however, admit on occasions I did not, at a heavy cost to myself and the company. I'd also learnt to delegate and give total autonomy to those I trusted and had confidence in. I'd had no choice due to Contiki's rapid growth and increasing global stretch.

With me living in New Zealand I was far away from the front line action. I left the day to day responsibility of running the entire group to our very capable Managing Director Garry Draffin and his fellow directors. A reporting system was put in place, where Garry and I would speak to each other twice a week by phone. Sometimes with a pressing matter, either would call without hesitation.

In addition we had an excellent accounts reporting system with monthly accounts providing updated forecasts and cash flows. Andrew Fleming our Finance Director had a massive responsibility and managed to keep our heads above water, although a couple of times we dipped below the line due to the company's rapid expansion. We implemented strict timelines to adhere to the accounts being completed. To have these completed all the relevant information had to be input, so it brought a real discipline to the business to ensure the figures were constantly up to date. It was so important to have up-to-date financial information so we could continually plot our progress and keep an eye out for any cash pitfalls that may lie ahead.

Delegating and feeling control slipping away can be a huge challenge for business owners, especially if the company is one you've nurtured from scratch and it's in your blood. But I came around to understanding that if you choose the right people to help manage your business, you have to let part of it go, and to trust them to do their jobs. This is a lesson many business owners never learn. I personally found it very difficult.

With Australia up and running we had completed the circle. In just 22 years, from that original European tour, Contiki had operations around the world in Europe, North America, New Zealand and Australia. The company was now a truly international tour operator. As always, standing still was not an option for us, we had to keep moving, and keep developing the business to keep up with the changing times ahead.

19. HONG KONG CENTRAL

On 29 July 1981, a 600,000-strong crowd filled the streets around St Paul's Cathedral in London, trying to catch a glimpse of Prince Charles and Lady Diana Spencer on their wedding day. The date was also an important one for our London-based director responsible for Personnel and Special Projects, Richard Lewis, but he, his wife and their young children would miss the wedding. The family had flown out from Heathrow that morning heading for their new home: Hong Kong.

Why? After nearly 20 years based in London, the directors of Contiki had decided to move the company's residency. With our international operations now being established and planned, we wanted to minimise our exposure to the high UK company tax rates and secure a geographic centre for our future worldwide operations. Hong Kong was central to both our northern and southern hemisphere planned operations and had a very favourable tax environment.

Such a move was a brave decision. On advice we were told it would be extremely difficult to move the residency with such strict criteria and restrictions imposed by the UK tax authorities. It would also be an expensive manoeuvre to pull off with no certainty of success. It was a risk, but we calculated that with our plans to turn the company into a truly international one the benefits down the line were well worth it. Of course we could do it!

There was another reason to move the company's residency. We had experienced a number of situations where we had been sued by opportunistic passengers. Nothing too concerning but it had been enough to push us to take reasonable steps as a safeguard. We'd watched as another well-known and well-established tour operator was sued over an accident which had forced them to cease trading. We realised how vulnerable Contiki could be in a similar situation.

It was highly unlikely that such a situation would occur because we took our responsibilities for our passengers extremely seriously, and were well insured. But the risk of a similar occurrence and the prospect of losing everything outweighed our confidence. At anytime we could be sued for millions. With the move to Hong Kong we would create a complex octopus-type corporate structure that would minimise our vulnerability and exposure. If we were successfully sued and not covered by insurance, only one arm of the octopus would be vulnerable and, in a worst case scenario, cut off without affecting the other arms of the business.

Our professional financial advisors were a local UK accounting firm. As we spread our wings internationally we also appointed local accounting firms in America, New Zealand and Australia. However, as our accounting requirements became more and more complex we decided to hire one of the best international accounting firms, Arthur Andersen (later of Enron fame). This firm began to streamline our corporate and accounting structure and assist us with shifting our residency from the United Kingdom to Hong Kong. We also engaged the top legal advisors in both London and Hong Kong experienced in making such a move.

A plan and timetable was set down. With the residency move well in hand we began to create the 'octopus' structure. We started to create a whole raft of new companies including one in The Dutch Antilles and another in the Cayman Islands in the Caribbean. We sure endorsed the latter as we figured it might be a good place to have the odd Board meeting!

The first of our invoices from Arthur Andersen arrived. It was astronomical! And we soon found we could do little without our newly appointed specialist legal teams poring over every single move we planned to make. Even larger fees headed our way; would they ever end? But we had learnt if you want the best, you pay for it.

One of the partners at Arthur Andersen in Hong Kong had a brother, Mark Fong, who had his own accounting practice. Since we needed a local accounting firm as well, we appointed his firm to help deal with local matters and form a local Contiki company, with him as the required resident director (temporary) and Company Secretary.

After months of preparation and fancy fees the green light flashed. We were given another detailed timetable of transaction deadlines for all parties involved to scrupulously meet. Every step of the move had been choreographed. The final transaction required one of the UK's company directors to physically sign the final documents in Hong Kong by 5 pm on 30 July 1981. However, there was another condition. That person would need to become a director of the new Hong Kong Company and reside there for a couple of months. We were very grateful to Richard and his family for missing Charles and Diana's wedding and rising to the occasion.

Family Lewis's Cathay Pacific flight that morning suffered technical problems delaying the departure by several hours. The flight departed, stopped over in Bombay (Mumbai) India, unexpectedly incurring another extensive delay. The clock was ticking and Richard was becoming concerned. As the flight was about to touch down at Hong Kong's Kai Tak Airport, the pilot aborted the landing, took off at full throttle, and returned to land another hour later. Richard was beside himself with worry, as all our hard work depended on him completing the final chess move. By this time just under two hours remained between his arrival and the 5 pm document-signing deadline. The family rushed to grab the first taxi available, sped to Arthur Andersen's office in the city and, with just 20 minutes to spare, Richard signed the critical documents. The company and Richard's family became residents of Hong Kong.

At the time of our move, a company resident in Hong Kong paid a 15 per cent tax rate on any profits derived from trading in the Colony. We did not actually trade there so we had no profits, just costs. At the outset it was made very clear to us how imperative it was to ensure this new-found status as residents of Hong Kong was protected unequivocally. There were a number of strict requirements we had to fulfil at all times. The most important was to clearly demonstrate that *'the mind and management of the company was in Hong Kong'*. To ensure this happened, we scheduled regular three monthly Board meetings in Hong Kong.

A month after the successful move, the directors arrived at the Hilton Hotel in Hong Kong the evening before the inaugural Board meeting. It had been a busy and stressful few months and we were all elated about the successful move of the company's residency. It had been a major achievement and the future was looking bright. That night we went out on the town to celebrate. And celebrate we did! We went from one drinking hole to a girly bar to another drinking hole to another girly bar and so on until we finally collapsed into our hotel beds as the sun was rising.

Our meeting was scheduled for 10 am that day – just a few hours after most of us had hit the hay! Our new Company Secretary, Mark Fong, had not been out celebrating with us the evening before and arrived on time to discover a completely empty hotel board room, which he'd booked for the occasion. Calls to our rooms had no effect, so Mark dutifully proceeded to track us down one by one, knocking on our respective bedroom doors. Without exception we opened the door, bleary-eyed, breathing alcohol fumes and no doubt mumbling incoherently. Barring Richard, none of us had met Mark before and, since he was Chinese, a couple of us mistook him for housekeeping staff and told him (in no uncertain terms!) to come back later. To this day I can't remember the meeting, but I've seen the minutes and my name is on the list of those who were present!

International Board meetings occurred regularly after the relocation. On most occasions we flew in and out either first or business class. As recognised tour operators and travel agents we were entitled to our agent's discount of 75 per cent on the airfare cost ... so why not? We stayed in Hong Kong's top hotels because we received an agent's discount of around 50 per cent. As Chairman, I was often accommodated in an extravagant suite where the meetings were usually conducted.

It was our good fortune that Mark Fong and his wife were well heeled and well connected. We were often treated to a number of special experiences whether it be lunch on his family's private junk on the fascinating harbour, dinner at Hong Kong's exclusive Yacht Club, or horse races ensconced in his family's private box at the plush Hong Kong Jockey Club.

On the last night of our Board meetings we made a tradition of the 'Chairman's Dinner' where I would take the Board somewhere unique, and usually bloody expensive! Sometimes it would be an authentic Chinese restaurant with a round table and an enormous array of exotic dishes. Other times we'd choose a European-style fine dining establishment. One evening in one of the latter, a few of us ordered oysters as an entree. When the bill arrived it transpired that the delicacies we had so innocently consumed had cost US$7 each! The black-suited Maître d' politely justified the exorbitant price by saying, 'But Sir, you will appreciate they were the finest Blue Point oysters, flown in from New York this morning'.

The tradition at the end of our Chairman's Dinner was to select a port, often followed by a fine cognac or Armagnac. The trolley would be rolled up to the table with an enormous range to select from. One night we selected a port we all agreed was the finest we had ever tasted. We knocked off the whole bottle, no trouble. It turned out each glass cost US$35! When we later remonstrated, we were informed very courteously 'But Sir, you will appreciate it was a Taylors '45!' But of course!

No meal was complete without a fine Havana cigar selected from the humidifier. These special dinners carried a certain irony. Here we were treating ourselves to the finest cuisine at the finest restaurants when our business was basic camping tours and camping food! Two completely different worlds. However, we reckoned we should treat ourselves occasionally – so we did!

To take control of our fledging international operation we divided it into four geographical regions, appointing a Managing Director with total autonomy for each. Europe was headed by Richard Peate, a qualified accountant who could understand and grapple with the complex web of financial transactions in this region. And the bonus was his excellent management skills. America had Dave Hosking who had the ability to tackle any problem or task by thinking outside the square. He already had an exceptional track record with the company. Australia was headed up by Peter De Maria, a streetwise Australian with a strong background in the travel industry. His proven strength was in sales and marketing; a real asset in the country where we sourced the majority of our customers. New Zealand was the responsibilty of Kit Nixon whose all round ability to deal with the diverse interests there suited perfectly.

Over the years the Hong Kong Company Contiki International, accumulated a number of subsidiaries, primarily those of each of the three regions. However, a number of other companies were also formed for specific purposes, so in 1983 we decided to form a master holding company to own the whole shebang. JAGWAR Holdings Limited was formed and reflected the name of the original directors, each of whom had a prime responsibility.

John Anderson – Chairman

Andrew Fleming – Finance Director

Garry Draffin – Managing Director

Wayne Page – Operations Director

Alison Lloyd – Marketing Director

Richard Lewis – Personnel & Special Projects Director

With the constant increase in the number of brochures being produced, we decided Alison Lloyd should concentrate on the marketing side of the business and appoint a dedicated sales director. In 1981 we appointed Geoff Phillips who had owned and run CCT, the company we had bought that year, to take responsibility of our sales worldwide.

Dave Hosking, who had originally joined the company as a tour leader in 1976 had over the years successfully undertaken a number of diverse tasks for the company and clearly had the X-factor of a leader. Some years later he too was appointed a director, responsible for Research and Development worldwide.

To say the dealings of our finance departments around the world were complicated is a huge understatement. We sold our tours in 10 different currencies and operated them through 38 countries – meaning 38 different currencies! With currency values shifting the way they do with the odd devaluation thrown in for good measure, you can imagine how difficult it was. Sometimes the movements were so material, we had to surcharge our selling prices which had already been set up to a year in advance. Anticipating the value of a currency that far ahead was immeasurably hard. We had a treasury section, which bought, sold and hedged currencies. There was always millions of dollars washing around the world, both incoming and outgoing.

In 1982, I instigated an arrangement that was to change things forever. As an entrepreneur I liked to be in control. But I had become torn on this issue as I wanted my directors to feel the company was theirs too. They'd all worked so hard to achieve the position we were in. I'd moved back to New Zealand three years previously and now they were the ones constantly at the coalface. I decided to offer the original five directors the opportunity to buy 21 per cent of the company between them. After agreeing on a fair price, they all accepted the offer, some borrowing to make the payment.

In just a month, in a funny sort of way, I had created five other John Andersons. Now it was not just my money at risk but theirs too. After the deal was complete the first thing I noticed was their change in attitude from that of employee to employer. The other change was the Board became very risk adverse. Some of the ideas that arose were knocked back as the other directors were less prepared to risk their own money, now they had a stake in the company. The biggest difficulty I had to face was that I had lost the total autonomy I'd enjoyed. I still had overall control but I had to factor in the reality that my directors were now shareholders. It was no longer my company but our company. I felt I couldn't override them on decisions as they would feel as though nothing had changed. It was, perhaps, the start of a succession plan for me. All business owners at some stage should prepare such a plan in advance, yet so few do.

One day while in Hong Kong for one of our early board meetings, I went to Nathans Road. I stood alone on the pavement and looked across the street. The Shamrock Hotel was still there and so too were my memories. This was the hotel I had stayed at in 1962, shocked by the girl in my bed. Some 20 years had passed since this adventurous yet naïve young man had stayed there, not knowing what lay ahead. It was an emotional moment. What a journey, and it wasn't nearly finished yet!

At the end of 1983 I seriously considered the possibility of listing the company on the Australian and New Zealand stock exchanges. Tourism there was gaining increasing interest as an investment option and there were few tourism companies listed and certainly none with the international spread and potential growth of Contiki. The annual turnover of the group at the time was US$22 million. The European operation that year produced an audited after tax profit of US$4 million. It was this region that was funding our international expansion. I could clearly see with Europe's continued growth and our new operating areas still to come on stream, the future looked very rosy – very rosy indeed. I put the idea on the back burner deciding to take another look once the other areas were in full operation.

In early 1987, we were surprised to be approached by a highflying investment company called Omnicorp, which was publically listed on the New Zealand Stock Exchange. At the time Omnicorp was well funded with a number of high profile shareholders. It had decided to specialise by investing in tourism companies and become the only such company on the New Zealand Stock Exchange. It had already made a number of international tourism investments.

The Chairman, at the time, was a young, up-and-coming business executive; Lloyd Morrison. I took an immediate liking to him and he took me into his confidence regarding Omnicorp's long-term plans. There appeared to be an enormous number of synergies that could arise from Contiki being part of their developing group. They had already carried out their research on us but since our business interests were spread so widely around the world, they had a lot of information gaps. When they heard the extent of our operations and plans they offered to buy the whole group outright.

Initially I didn't want to sell. I had worked so incredibly hard for 25 years to develop Contiki into the worldwide operation it had become. Together with my key staff we had overcome huge hurdles, continually reinvested the profits back into the company and fully believed that in another year or two our efforts would be handsomely rewarded. There was no way we, as a board and shareholders, were prepared to watch someone else reap the potential benefits if we sold too early.

After protracted negotiations a deal was struck for Omnicorp to buy 50 per cent of the company, which would still allow us to benefit on the upside potential. The cash injection would give us an opportunity to develop the company further and allow us to build the resort hotels that were on the drawing board at the time. An arrangement was written into the agreement where the JAGWAR director shareholders kept control of the Board. New shares were issued and Omnicorp invested in excess of US$15 million dollars. The Company gained two new directors representing Omnicorp – Lloyd Morrison and Ray Thompson – two great assets as they brought extra expertise and a new dimension we needed to take the company to another level.

I did not sell any of my shares. In fact I had to buy some of the newly issued shares to bring my percentage equal to 40 per cent, with the other Contiki directors holding 10 per cent of the increased capital. I had some cash but not sufficient to cover the amount required. So I took out a large mortgage on the debt-free family home Ali and I owned. It was a substantial residence on two acres of land, with a tennis court and swimming pool in a prime location of Auckland. I borrowed several million dollars, never having borrowed in my life. But I believed it was critical to keep my shareholding percentage. Ali, always the cautious one, was not convinced it was a good idea, but reluctantly agreed. For the first time Ali and I had a substantial multi-million dollar debt.

Omnicorp bought its 50 per cent on the understanding that within a reasonable period of time I would sell my remaining shareholding. It was a gentleman's agreement – with nothing in writing. It did, however, suit me as over the next few years I could see the company's profitability increasing considerably and together with my fellow shareholders, if they decided to sell, we would all reap the rewards.

20. FLY AND FLOP RESORTS

In the mid eighties my family and I enjoyed a Club Med holiday at a beach resort in Pattaya, Thailand. The vast majority of the other guests were also young families. Club Med offered package deals to exotic destinations where everything such as accommodation, food, wine, entertainment and activities were all included in the price. I remember thinking that it was a brilliant concept.

The thought crossed my mind that Contiki could create similar resorts, exclusively for 18–35 year olds. I knew the secret to our continued success was simple: 'young people love to travel and experience things together'. Why wouldn't they enjoy a holiday somewhere exotic with people their own age? The 'Contiki Fly and Flop Holidays' were born.

We had several hundred thousand ex-Contiki passengers with the numbers growing continually. If they had enjoyed their previous Contiki experience, we reasoned they may also consider taking their annual holiday with us, or perhaps arrange a reunion of their tour group at one of our resorts.

There had never been a resort built anywhere in the world catering exclusively for 18–35 year olds. It would also expose our brand to a whole new market of young people who either didn't have the time, money or inclination to travel overseas, but would love to meet and holiday with other young people in an exclusive resort. We anticipated huge benefits for our tour programme through cross-fertilisation, as past Contiki passengers mingled with others and influenced them to travel as they had.

All the benefits seemed to stack up, so we convinced ourselves it was a good idea. We faced the daunting prospect of turning the idea into a reality, but the thought of building resorts was almost too big for us to contemplate as it was an area in which we had no expertise. We knew we would be venturing into the unknown and it would be capital intensive, but we had taken on similar challenges before, so felt reasonably confident. The Board's decision was not unanimous. However, we decided to do it anyway.

The Contiki brand was strongest in Australia and New Zealand and where our largest ex-passenger base lived making it clear that was where we should open the first of our resorts. If they proved successful, we could extend them to Europe and the rest of the world as we had with the tours.

In 1986 we began to research what was available. No sooner had we started when an opportunity came out of the blue to buy an existing resort in the Whitsunday Islands, just off the northern Queensland coast of Australia. The area boasts 74 islands with seven resorts, the largest of which is Hamilton Island. The Whitsunday 100 Resort was available, situated on Long Island's Happy Bay. Westpac Bank's venture capital arm, BLE Capital, had considerable loan funds invested in the property which was not trading well. The bank was desperately looking for a new investor who could develop the resort to its full potential.

After inspecting the resort it soon became clear why it was not performing. It was rundown, in disrepair, had poor management, low staff morale and no direction. It was a disaster. But there were a number of redeeming factors. It was located on the most beautiful, secluded, palm fringed, white sandy beach on a National Park island, and unlike the other more remote islands, it was just 20 minutes by water taxi from Shute Harbour at Airlie Beach on the mainland.

It was agreed the only hope for the resort was to completely knock it down and start all over again. BLE Capital was very keen for us to become involved. We fitted their criteria perfectly, so together we negotiated to purchase the property.

Contiki soon owned an island resort holding 80 per cent of the shares in the owning company with BLE holding on to 20 per cent. The loan the bank had advanced previously on the property was transferred and retained by us. We hired the very best architects with previous experience in building island resorts to design a purpose-built one for our target market. We also engaged similarly experienced engineers and builders. Contiki had just entered the brave new world of property development.

Building a resort on the mainland is quite straightforward. Building a resort on an island is not. If you have ever stayed on an island resort you take the facilities for granted. When you turn on the tap in your bathroom, where do you think that fresh water comes from? When you turn on the electric light, where does the power come from? When you go to the loo, where does the sewage and wastewater go? What about the waste from the kitchens and the guests' rubbish? These were just some of the problems to be addressed.

Access onto the island was another major headache. Happy Bay had a very shallow seabed, which made it impossible for any reasonably sized boat to pull up to the small wharf to discharge or embark passengers – let alone supplies. Passengers were brought to the island by water taxi which, on arrival, tied up to a buoy in the middle of the bay while the passengers were transferred onto a flat bottomed barge and brought ashore onto the beach. To solve this problem we needed a walkway built at one end of the resort that would extend several hundred metres out into the bay. We had another unwelcome complication. Pulling down the existing resort meant we had to take it off the island before we could start to build the new one. No small task.

The plans were completed and the project costed. We could have a 150-room resort with 300 plus beds for a cost of just $24 million

Australian dollars! In addition to the existing BLE loan, Contiki would have to find the balance of funds required for the development and once the resort was built, the initial operating costs.

It was an Australian development, so the Australian office was given the responsibility to raise the necessary funds. Offers of funding were obtained from several Australian banks. As a wild card, I approached New Zealand's largest bank, Bank of New Zealand, to gauge their interest. Unexpectedly, they fell over themselves at the opportunity and offered a deal with a lower interest rate and more favourable conditions that were far superior to any the Australian banks could offer. They almost pleaded with us to take their money. While the Aussie team didn't like it, no matter how hard they tried, they couldn't better it. The Bank of New Zealand offer was too good to refuse. We pushed the 'start' button.

The old resort was closed, demolished and removed from the island. Every piece of heavy machinery and equipment needed to be barged in, as did all the building supplies. An accommodation facility was set up to house and feed the 300 workers. We fixed the water supply shortage by building an enormous dam in the National Park. We faced huge difficulties dealing with environmentalists' objections and in obtaining permission from the bureaucrats to do this. The issue was publicised and much-discussed in the local newspapers and radio.

We upgraded the original generators to supply the increased electricity load. These were replaced later with power from a cable installed from the mainland to nearby Hamilton Island. We contributed to the cost to route it through to Long Island. 'We could cut off your power at the flick of a switch!' we used to joke with Keith Williams, the entrepreneur who created the Hamilton Island resort.

We modernised the existing sewerage treatment ponds and built a broad walkway several hundred metres in length along the side of a hill and out into the deeper water, with a floating pontoon at the end to better cope with the extreme tides in the area. This would enable our passengers to have direct access to the resort.

Meanwhile, a busy team of architects and builders worked on creating the resort. The 150 rooms were constructed in a series of two-storey blocks, plus a huge restaurant and kitchen to cater for around 300 guests (in two sittings), a couple of bars, a games room, an entertainment area, a lounge, a shop, two swimming pools, a gym and two tennis courts. In later years, we built staff accommodation blocks and a fine dining restaurant. The building of the resort and its set up for operation was overseen by one of Contiki's staff, Simon Wan, who had been employed specifically for the job.

We were grossly over-capitalised if we didn't get the occupancy we had budgeted for. During construction, the 1987 sharemarket crash hit. We were concerned, but kept building and just 14 frenetic months later, it was completed. We named it 'Contiki Whitsunday Resort' – perhaps not the most imaginative of names, but naturally we wanted to associate it with our brand name.

We felt confident we could operate the resort ourselves from the experience we'd gained from our other properties such as the problematic New Station Hotel in Auckland, the Queenstown Lodge, the European château, villa and the others we operated around Europe. We hired the hotel manager who had previously managed our hotel in Auckland, Terry Short. Terry came onboard during the construction phase and was responsible for accommodating and feeding the workers who stayed on the island. He also hired and trained 110 resort staff for their new responsibilities which was an immense task – especially since he had no previous experience running a resort, let alone an island one – but he did it. We had thrown Terry his hunk of meat and he had risen to the occasion. (He was subsequently headhunted by a major five-star hotel chain and went on to have an extremely successful career in the industry.)

Back at Contiki HQ, Alison Lloyd and her team were creating a brochure filled with colourful photographs of young people having fun in the sun. We teamed up with Ansett, the domestic airline who had regular flights into the nearby airport on Hamilton Island and Proserpine on the mainland. We were included in the Ansett Holidays brochure and promoted as a preferred product by their sales force. Our Whitsunday Resort brochures were distributed to our worldwide sales network and, within a few weeks, the vast majority of agents in our key selling areas had the brochure on their racks. We also promoted heavily to our past and present passengers. The bookings started to trickle and then began to flood in.

We opened the resort on 15 July 1988 with a huge party to celebrate the occasion. Everyone was there, including the key people responsible for the resort's construction, managers of the other Whitsunday Island resorts, local dignitaries, Contiki and Ansett staff, travel industry representatives and journalists from every conceivable publication. A TV crew was choppered in, filming as the Minister of Queensland Tourism cut the ribbon, for a programme called *Live at 5*. The Contiki Whitsunday Resort was open for business!

I remember feeling, yet again, a sense of incredible pride. We had built the first resort in the world designed exclusively for the 18–35 year age group and had achieved it through sheer determination and perseverance. It had, however, come at a heavy cost as its development proved to be more expensive than originally budgeted. We had to make our resort a resounding commercial success.

We discovered that operating an island resort was more expensive than originally advised and had forecast for. We were plagued by access issues, primarily through inclement weather, as everything, and everybody, had to be shipped in and out. Frustratingly, we were limited to the extent at which we could recoup our costs through the room rate, as there was a limit to what the market was prepared to pay. The rate had to offer value for money and be competitive. We opted to copy our other island resort competitors by making the tariff 'full board', just like Club Med, which included three meals a day. This was to ensure we captured the guests' spend on food.

The odd cyclones that hit the area were never taken lightly. With all the guests pinned down and the resort virtually boarded up in preparation, heavy damage was still inflicted when they hit, which proved expensive, not just in extra repairs, but loss of business. Staff turnover was relatively high, making the costs of training higher than usual. The fixed operating costs were high, making us dependent on consistently high occupancy levels. However, this was patchy; some nights we would have 250 in-house and on others, just 25.

We spent hours nutting out ways to encourage our guests to spend, spend, spend during their stay. Once they landed on Long Island we wanted to offer them every opportunity to put their hand in their pocket; cash or credit, both were gratefully accepted!

We set up what we secretly called the 'Rape and Pillage' department whose objective was to empty the guests' pockets with attractive options. For starters, we opened the main bar and lounge 22 hours a day, offering substantial food snacks. To attract constant patronage we had afternoon and evening entertainment. A games room flaunted every conceivable pay-per-play game and the shop was stacked with attractive merchandise. We offered paid excursions to anywhere and everywhere such as the magnificent Whitehaven Beach and other island resorts. We introduced a popular sunset cruise on 'Gretel' (named after the wife of Australian media mogul Frank Packer), a 12-metre ex-America's Cup yacht which had unsuccessfully challenged for the 'old mug' in '62. It was easy for guests to spend money with their plastic magnetic strip-coded room key card (a first in Australia) that could be used to charge items directly to their room. We tempered the onslaught of paid activities with the free use of the water sports equipment, tennis courts, gym and aerobic classes. The walks through the National Park were always a highlight.

The entertainment on the resort was the responsibility of the 'crazy crew' who constantly arranged activities, put on shows in the evening and kept the guests amused. We even had some top line acts visit and perform. I recall, amongst others, Tina Arena as she was just starting out on her singing career. On these occasions with visitors from the mainland there could be up to 1000 people attending. The Contiki tour groups stayed giving us some guaranteed patronage. I always remember one of the island's staff rules. 'Whenever you pass a guest anywhere, at anytime on the resort, always smile and acknowledge them.' So simple but so effective.

Occupancy in the first year grew steadily and, although the resort was not yet breaking even, the financial trend was looking positive. In August 1989, we had a major shock: Ansett Airline's 1300 pilots went on strike, demanding a 30 per cent pay rise! This prolonged strike was devastating for the resort because, at the stroke of a pen, access to the Whitsunday resorts from the lucrative southern states in Australia – New South Wales, Victoria and South Australia – was cut off. There was still a skeleton schedule but the number of airline seats available was minimal. The resort struggled, then began haemorrhaging financially. We activated an emergency sales campaign to attract guests from the nearby Queensland mainland by introducing all manner of initiatives but, although the strike was finally resolved, the momentum we had built up had stopped. We had to start again and rebuild the patronage we had worked so hard to create over the previous year.

At the same time we were building the Whitsunday resort we were also building another resort in New Zealand, on the other half of the land we owned adjacent to the Queenstown Lodge. At the time, the New Zealand Government was keen to develop the country's burgeoning tourism industry and wanted to ensure the supporting infrastructure kept up with projected growth. More new hotels had to be built so they generously offered developers a very juicy carrot. They offered a grant of 10 per cent on the total construction cost of any new hotels in resort areas. We put up our hand, presented our plans and soon had our grant approved and received a cheque for just over NZ$2 million dollars.

We appointed the architectural firm that had carried out alterations to The New Station Hotel in Auckland, asking them to design a hotel to exploit the land's stunning position overlooking Lake Wakatipu. They produced plans for a hotel with 150 rooms, complete with two restaurants, a gym, swimming pool, even a commercial laundry. To take full advantage of the magnificent view, I requested the restaurant have floor to ceiling windows, based on a similar design I'd seen at the Regent Hotel overlooking Hong Kong's Harbour.

Once again, Hewitt Harrison, who had taken responsibility for building the Queenstown Lodge, was given the task of overseeing this project – yes, he had been thrown another hunk of meat. Construction began, but after two-thirds of the hotel had been built, it became clear the hotel was of a standard far too superior to suit our target youth market. Realising this, we decided to take advantage of the situation. As Queenstown was desperate for more high-quality hotels, we changed direction and decided to turn it into a four to five-star hotel, thinking it would make a great investment. But we had stepped outside our area of expertise – the youth market. We were caught in a major dilemma, entirely of our own making.

We had no option but to appoint a professional hotel management company to take over the marketing and running of the hotel. Initially the Sheraton Group, which was keen to have a presence in the area, was interested. However, their fire protection criteria required too many changes to be made at the point of construction we'd reached. Holiday Inn jumped at our offer. This was the first Holiday Inn in New Zealand and would be their flagship property, the start of their plans to roll the brand rapidly throughout the country. This was very attractive to us as the cost of sales and marketing could be spread over a number of properties and each would feed the other with guests.

We opened the hotel with great fanfare on 20 August 1988, just one month after the Contiki Whitsunday Resort. An exclusive dinner was held with all those involved in the property's construction, together with dignitaries such as the Minister of Tourism and a couple of celebrity guests. We received extensive media coverage. Again, I was a very proud owner that evening looking at what we had created. It was a much needed asset to the Queenstown tourism industry.

The relationship with Holiday Inn proved to be tenuous. Their promise to open other hotels in the country never eventuated. Unlike the Whitsunday Resort, where sales and marketing costs could be spread over the entire Contiki brand, this situation meant the entire cost was carried by the single Queenstown property. The sales and marketing costs were hefty but the sales they achieved were slow and low. The management fees seemed excessive in relation to the results they achieved. It was not a happy marriage.

With the sharemarket crash the year before, in October 1987, we had already decided the Queenstown and Whitsunday Island resorts would be our only two. We'd been unlucky to have built them when we were unaware of the impending crash and the continued fallout that was to follow. We survived but the mistakes we had made with the two resorts were crystal clear. It highlighted the premise 'stick to what you know'. Contiki were tour operators, not hotel owners. We had shifted from our original focus.

21. ANOTHER BRILLIANT IDEA?

In the early eighties, Contiki passenger numbers were multiplying at an extraordinary rate. The activities around the London scene, which the Contiki Travel Club was managing, were booming.

We decided to separate out all the London activities that were not tours such as accommodation, social events and excursions, and carry them under a new separate entity. A new club would take over all the responsibilities of the previous Contiki Travel Club and extend its activities.

We named the new club 'Farthings'. The idea sprang from the penny-farthing bicycle, which we initially used as the logo. The name, Farthings, was also synonymous with our long-term plans as it spelt out 'Far Things' and we planned for the club to go far! Huge plans were afoot to develop it into an entity that could offer members unique opportunities all around the world. Like Contiki, the club was to be exclusive to 18–35 year olds. A small membership fee was to be charged. A separate company was set up with its own personnel, board of directors and offices in London. Contiki consciously began to distance itself from Farthings, as we had a hidden agenda; to develop a whole new range of products under the Farthings name.

Virtually all of Contiki's passengers were now arriving by air, landing at London's Heathrow Airport. Putting ourselves in their shoes we thought carefully about what their first need would be. Previously we'd

MV Artemis dockside in Greece.

The cook, the wife, the chef and the lover.
The infamous Station Hotel, Auckland.

A typical training trip in Dutch
national costume. Such gorgeous girls!

Our winking sun balloon tethered
at the Chateau de Cruix.

Board members enjoying testing 'the product' in Queenstown. John leading the charge!

The Board of Directors and Regional Directors (back row): A temporary member of staff, Peter De Maria, Richard Peate, Richard Lewis, Dave Hosking, John. (Front row): Alison Loyd, Gary Draffin, Kit Nixon, Andrew Fleming, Wayne Page.

A Chinese Chairman's dinner - left to right Dick Vermaat, Geoff Phillips, Richard Lewis, Mark Fong, Andrew Flemming, Dave Hosking. John and Ali Anderson with backs to camera.

International Board Meeting
Hamilton Island, February 1986

'Go West Young Man'- Trying desperate to head in the same direction!

Lloyd Morrison (Omnicorp Director) and John sealing 'the deal'.

Kimbla African Safari, 1970.

The 'Hell Run' between Lusaka (Zambia) and Dar Es Salaam (Tanzania). The so called roads were a driver's nightmare.

An elevated view as a local waves to an Indian Overland tour.

The visiting Contiki & Lodge staff outside the newly opened Queenstown Lodge.

First New Zealand owned coach, Auckland, 1983.

The Mardi Gras Mansion, with a Mercedes-Benz coach, New Orleans, USA.

First Australian coach, Sydney, 1985.

Part of the European coach fleet parked off season at Vermaat's base - Hellevoetsluis, Holland.

The Contiki Whitsunday Resort, Queensland, Australia.

Toasting the opening of the Whitsunday Resort with first Manager Terry Short (far right).

A watery welcome to the new seasons' staff at Whitsunday Resort.

What a setting! Our second resort, The Holiday Inn – Queenstown, NZ.

'Three Bees' and 'Freetime' logos on an Agents Manual.

Cute and iconic Dropkick mascot.

Farthings Worldpass and Discount Book.

John-Alison-Gary-Wayne-Andrew-Richard
JAGWAR logo – the original key board member

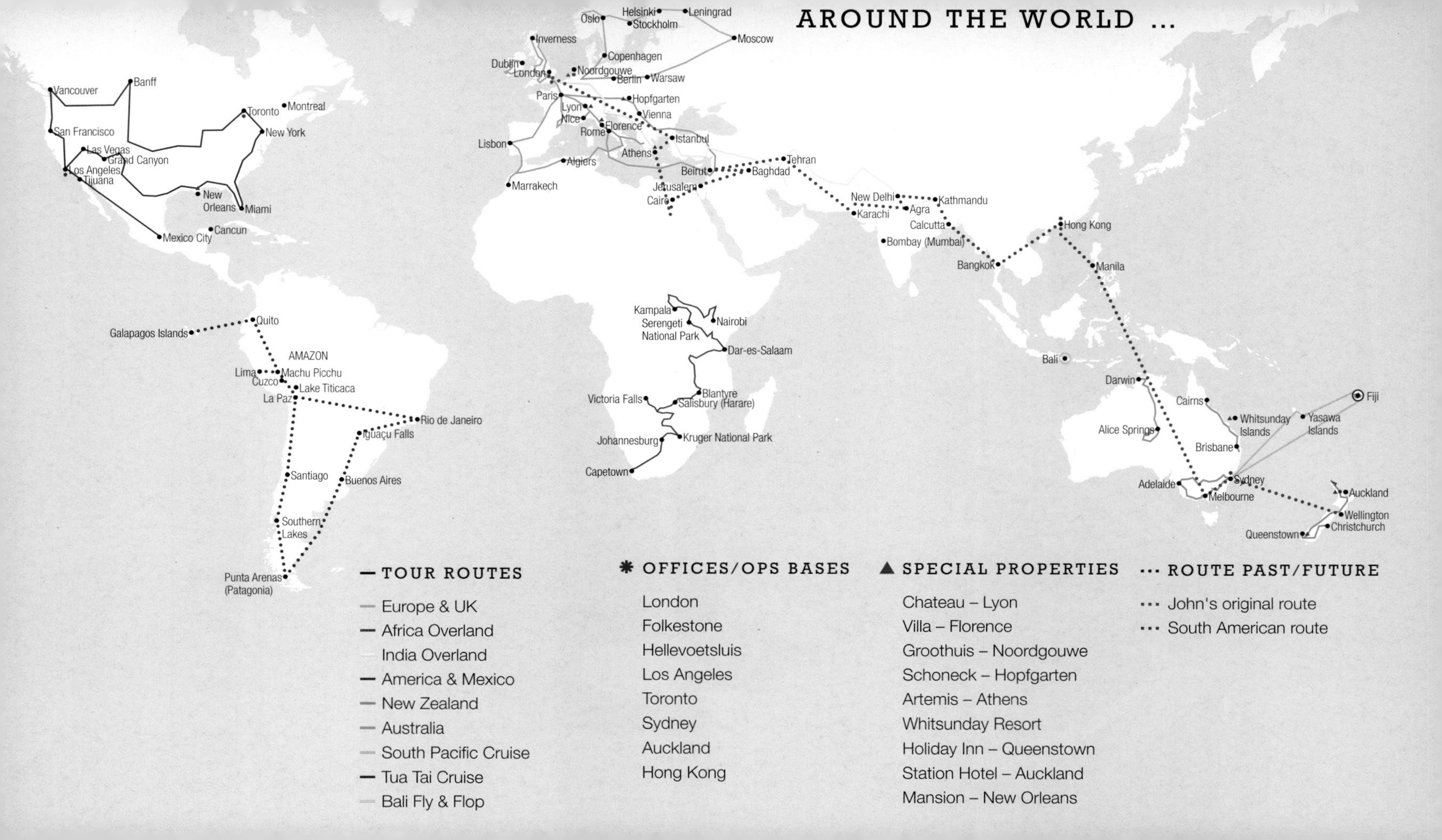
AROUND THE WORLD ...
Vancouver
Banff
San Francisco
Las Vegas
Grand Canyon
Los Angeles
Tijuana
Toronto
Montreal
New York
New Orleans
Miami
Mexico City
Cancun
Galapagos Islands
Quito
AMAZON
Lima
Machu Picchu
Cuzco
Lake Titicaca
La Paz
Rio de Janeiro
Iguaçu Falls
Santiago
Buenos Aires
Southern Lakes
Punta Arenas (Patagonia)
Helsinki
Leningrad
Oslo
Stockholm
Moscow
Inverness
Copenhagen
Dublin
London
Noordgouwe
Berlin
Warsaw
Paris
Hopfgarten
Lyon
Vienna
Nice
Florence
Rome
Istanbul
Lisbon
Athens
Algiers
Tehran
Beirut
Baghdad
Marrakech
Jerusalem
Cairo
Kampala
Nairobi
Serengeti National Park
Dar-es-Salaam
Victoria Falls
Blantyre
Salisbury (Harare)
Johannesburg
Kruger National Park
Capetown
New Delhi
Kathmandu
Agra
Karachi
Calcutta
Bombay (Mumbai)
Bangkok
Hong Kong
Manila
Bali
Darwin
Cairns
Whitsunday Islands
Yasawa Islands
Fiji
Alice Springs
Brisbane
Adelaide
Sydney
Melbourne
Auckland
Wellington
Christchurch
Queenstown
TOUR ROUTES
Europe & UK
Africa Overland
India Overland
America & Mexico
New Zealand
Australia
South Pacific Cruise
Tua Tai Cruise
Bali Fly & Flop
OFFICES/OPS BASES
London
Folkestone
Hellevoetsluis
Los Angeles
Toronto
Sydney
Auckland
Hong Kong
SPECIAL PROPERTIES
Chateau – Lyon
Villa – Florence
Groothuis – Noordgouwe
Schoneck – Hopfgarten
Artemis – Athens
Whitsunday Resort
Holiday Inn – Queenstown
Station Hotel – Auckland
Mansion – New Orleans
ROUTE PAST/FUTURE
John's original route
South American route

A tighter fit for the same staff 35 years later at the Sydr
Reunion 2005! And still they don't want to be identified

Promo shot with staff as models 1970.
No one wishes to be identified!

Eight of the original drivers and the original
troublesome passenger, Sydney Reunion 2005.

CONTIKI

The original Contiki lozenge logo 1967.

contiki
HOLIDAYS for 18-35's

The new millennium Contiki logo.

assumed it was accommodation, but first our jetlagged new arrivals actually needed to get into London. They needed a ride. In response to this we introduced a unique service. If arrivals were booked on a Contiki tour or were a member of the Farthings Club they'd be met at the airport by a representative and offered free transport into London. A hard offer to refuse when you've got a heavy suitcase and you're in a new and foreign city …

Free Farthings membership was given to everyone who booked their Contiki tour from overseas. This added value to our tour price and was something new the other operators weren't offering. The immediate advantage of membership was the meet-and-greet service, free transfer, and access to our special accommodation rates for those first few nights in London. On arrival at Heathrow passengers were given a ticket for the A2 bus, which took them to the Farthings' Plaza hotel in Bayswater. Almost unbelievably we managed to convince London Transport to add an extra stop near our hotel to their bus route to accommodate the passengers. This was yet another way of adding to our service.

Another reason for Contiki distancing itself from Farthings was to catch new prospective passengers that had not considered a Contiki tour. Travel agents overseas could offer membership to all their young clients (not booked with Contiki) but travelling to the United Kingdom for a small membership fee. The new Club member would be staying alongside our converted passengers, giving us another opportunity to influence their decision to see Europe with us. It was an effective cross-promotion. We gave a strong incentive to the agents to sign people up as we'd record the membership sale against the agent's name and, if that member booked a Contiki tour after their London arrival, the agent would receive a five per cent commission. It was a win-win situation.

We extended the number of excursions out of London to include major European events such as the Running of the Bulls in Pamplona, the Grand Prix in Monaco, the Oktoberfest in Munich, even tulips in Holland weekends. The Club had its own reception at the Farthings

Hotel, along with disco, TV room, reading and writing room, and travel desk. We produced a travel guide and discount directory for members that included exclusive deals and discounts at a huge range of establishments. We produced a regular newsletter too and unbelievably called it 'The Thing'!

Once Farthings was established in London we extended it worldwide. As Contiki started tour operations in America, New Zealand and Australia, the Farthings Club followed. We replicated what we were doing in London adapting it to suit each area. Within two years we added hotels and activities in Auckland, Sydney and Los Angeles. We started to recommend hotels suitable for the 18–35 year age group in places such as San Francisco, Miami Beach, Honolulu and Singapore, the latter two being popular stopovers for those flying to London. We introduced a new club card, the Farthings World Pass. One of our long-term plans was to have a network of hotels all around the world the Club could recommend and even book for members.

We then set about offering a whole new range of travel products designed exclusively for the 18–35 age group under the Farthings name. These were essentially short-haul package tours which could be sold directly to Club members or through travel agents. No one had ever designed short-haul holiday packages (a one-destination holiday as opposed to Contiki's multi-destination tours) specifically for a limited age group before.

Our target market was huge. First, we could target several hundred thousand satisfied Contiki passengers, predominately Australians and New Zealanders and Canadians, when they returned home. Second, our market had expanded to a wider range of young people: those who had no intention of going overseas or couldn't afford to. These people still wanted to travel, but were more tempted by destinations closer to home. After all, everyone had annual holidays. The travel agents were very supportive as they had seen the success of Contiki over the years, and were excited about a new range of options they could sell to the youth market.

Farthings products in America included excursions from Los Angeles to Mexico, and a 'Sleep and Beep' package, which included the cost of a rental car and recommended places to stay in and around America's west coast. We trialled some pilot products under the Farthings brand in Australia. Why not a cruise around the South Pacific? The first 18–35s cruise ever undertaken.

We approached Sitmar who owned the *Fairstar*, a ship that ran a series of cruises out of Sydney. Farthings negotiated a special price to take 1000 of the 1280 berths on one of their departures. As insurance, or should I say, a fall back position, any unsold berths could be released back to Sitmar for sale.

'There is no way you will fill the 1000 berths,' Sitmar's executives assured us. The Farthings team responded with, 'Just you watch us' or something to that effect! Suva, Yasawa Islands, Noumea, Isle of Pines and Lautoka … here we come!

Leveraging our support from Qantas and Air New Zealand, we put a brochure on the market. It was promoted to Farthings members, ex-Contiki passengers and through travel agents.

We did minimal advertising but ran a competition in *Cosmopolitan* magazine offering the prize of a cruise for two. The response was overwhelming resulting in thousands of entries. In fact, *Cosmopolitan* said it was the biggest response they'd ever had to a competition. There was an unexpected bonus, as Farthings scored a mailing list of 18–35 year olds to tempt them with future offerings. The only other promotion we paid for was advertising at some drive-in movie theatres, which were very popular at the time.

The first cruise departed from Sydney on 21 March 1984 with just under 1000 Farthings passengers onboard, with another one the following October. One of our long standing Contiki field staff, John Graham was the cruise director with eight Farthings staff supplementing the regular *Fairstar* crew who ensured it was the huge success it turned out to be – a 24-hour party day in day out. We then gave cruising a break for a couple of years. However, in 1987 we returned running four cruises on the 750-berth *Alexandr Pushkin* (named after the Russian poet *Alexander Pushkin*, yes, but without the 'e') out of Sydney, but on these occasions they operated under the Contiki brand name.

In 1985 Farthings leased the Fijian schooner *Tua Tai* for a series of cruises around the Fijian Islands and introduced the first package tours to the Indonesian island of Bali.

Then, we hit on another idea! Our relationship with Qantas and Air New Zealand was continuing to grow in strength as we were successfully targeting the youth market, a market the airlines were keen to attract. For people to buy an airline ticket they needed a reason to travel. Contiki gave them that reason.

Farthings, with the support of Contiki, approached Qantas with their idea. They suggested that each week one of their London-bound flights out of Australia should be designated an 18–35 year old flight. The back cabin of a 747 jumbo could be reserved exclusively for that age group. A flight that departed Melbourne and went via Sydney was chosen as an example. It was suggested the flight entertainment be modified to suit the age group. To really make the flight unique they suggested a fashion show down the aisles between the Sydney and Perth leg. The models would disembark in Perth and be followed by live entertainment, such as a comedian and a passenger talent show throughout the next sector. Finally, on the last leg of the flight just prior to arrival in London, a Farthings representative onboard would present an information session with questions and answers about London and the different options available. The flights were to be called 'Farthings Flight Fantastic'.

Qantas was extremely enthusiastic but there were a number of hurdles we needed to jump before the idea could become a reality, the biggest of which was the airline unions. On meeting them, they were not at all happy with the concept, although surprisingly good progress was made, but there appeared to be a number of issues that were insurmountable. At the time we were also talking with Air New Zealand.

After many promising discussions, the hurdles grew higher. The main concerns centred on the safety of handling a large group of young people, alcohol and the possibly of them having a bit too much fun. With a great sense of opportunity lost, we abandoned the Farthings Flight Fantastic idea.

At the end of 1985, at considerable cost, Farthings had been established in London, Auckland, Sydney and Los Angeles. It had a team on the ground in each location, developing products and producing brochures. Membership was taking off. It would, however, be some time before Farthings' new products and services including a discount book for each area would produce a profit and become cash positive. At the same time we were developing and expanding the Contiki tour operation in the same areas. The constant call on our precious cash resources for Farthings' rapid growth was putting Contiki under pressure. As with our other developments it was all being funded from our successful European operations. Farthings was also struggling to find the right personnel to take it to the next level.

The situation had become untenable. Contiki was our core business and we didn't want anything to threaten it. We regrettably pulled the plug on Farthings soon after.

It was a courageous, gut-wrenching decision, as so many dedicated people had put an incredible amount of effort into creating the Club which, we believed at the time, had the potential to eclipse Contiki. Over the next 18 months we wound it down to the point where it ceased to exist. To this day I still believe it was a brilliant idea and there is still an opportunity for a venture such as this.

On reflection it was clear why Farthings failed. It grew too fast with insufficient resources to keep it going. We were impatient to get it up and running and had not appreciated how much cash and personnel would be required before it generated a realistic return related to the investment and effort made. We had learnt another lesson the hard way.

22. YOU WIN SOME, YOU LOSE SOME

We constantly analysed what our passengers spent their money on while touring. We discovered personal shopping, gifts, souvenirs, alcohol, food snacks, entertainment, excursions and tourist activities were lightening their pockets by up to 50 per cent of their original tour fare, sometimes considerably more. It became clear 'the little extras' amounted to a vast sum of money.

It added up to millions of dollars, millions that other businesses were taking from our passengers' pockets. Sure, we were getting a cut through some commissions but nothing substantial. So why not look at providing some of the tourist activities and services ourselves? Quite frankly we knew we could lift the quality of many and, in turn, receive the full revenue – a win for the passengers with a better product and a win for us with the extra resulting income. In addition it would diversify our operations and we'd become a major player not just in the tour business, but in the provision of tourism goods and services. In the business world it's known as horizontal integration.

With me based in New Zealand, we decided to trial the idea there first since tourism was predicted to grow rapidly. The aim was to get in on the ground floor before the boom, with our advantage of a guaranteed number of customers through our tours. We had already done some solid market research through our observation of what passengers regularly spent money on – a big bonus for us, since it meant a lot of the guesswork was removed. We also analysed the spending habits of other tour operators' passengers and that of independent tourists. Queenstown and Rotorua, the two main tourist destinations in the country, were selected as the best places to focus our efforts.

We set up a separate holding company called Worldmark and an intricate chain of nominee companies to disguise their true ownership. There was absolutely no association with Contiki. Why? We wanted our competitors to use our tourism services as well.

Queenstown offers a plethora of tourism activities such as white-water rafting, jet boating, bungee jumping, helicopter flights, horse riding, trekking and boat excursions on Lake Wakatipu. In 1984 we purchased an interest in one of the main Queenstown white-water rafting companies, Challenge Rafting, a successful operator on the Kawarau River. We implemented a brief business plan, put in some funding, delivered the Contiki passengers and left the business in the hands of the original owner to take advantage of the new and improved situation. In 1986 we purchased an interest in Queenstown's Helijet Adventures, which operated jet boats on the river and helicopter flights. Again we put in a plan, funding and introduced our passengers. In each case we left the operation in the hands of the original owners with whom we had confidence in their proven ability and specialised expertise to take our now jointly owned companies to another level.

Passengers enjoying such activities, usually a first-time experience, wanted to have the occasion recorded with a photograph. A company called Smile Click provided this service so we bought a 50 per cent interest. It had exclusive photographic rights with a majority of the activity and tour operators. In winter it had similar rights on the ski fields. As tourism grew, so did Smile Click, to the point where it opened its own retail shop with photographic equipment available for sale as well.

In Europe, every Contiki tour group as a matter of tradition had a tour T-shirt produced for each passenger as a trip souvenir. Usually the design would encompass something with special significance to their particular tour, often relating to some sort of in-tour joke or incident. The production of these was almost exclusively in the hands of a young entrepreneur who had set up his operation called 'Gooses T-Shirts' in Venice, Italy.

The T-shirts were to become a similar tradition on the New Zealand tours. In Queenstown, Impact Screen Prints was supplying tour groups with T-shirts. It also produced shirts for local sporting groups, other organisations and a few of the local retailers. It appeared to be an absolute goldmine, so we bought the company.

While these acquisitions were going on in Queenstown, we turned our attention to Rotorua. This city with a large Maori population was at the centre of a unique wonderland of hot thermal pools, bubbling mud pools and geysers. While in the area, tourists could visit a rainbow trout hatchery, a wild life park, the Agradome to see sheep shorn, take flights over stunning lakes and volcanoes or experience the Maori culture.

Our first acquisition was the purchase of Waimangu Thermal Reserve. This amazing place originated from the ashes of the Mount Tarawera volcanic eruption in 1886. It has the largest hot spring in the world, Frying Pan Lake, the pink and white terraces (a geological phenomenon), a buried Maori village, the obligatory hot thermal and bubbling mud pools and a geyser. Waimangu was a unique experience all the other tour groups, public and our passengers could enjoy.

I never thought we would end up owning an airline but by 1986 we did! We purchased Floatplane Air, based on Lake Rotorua. Amongst other assets, Floatplane owned three Cessna floatplanes and, of course, the licences to operate them. We now owned buses, boats and planes!

Challenge Rafting was going well in Queenstown so we started looking at other rafting operations around the Rotorua area. The largest, River Rats, catered primarily to the Auckland domestic market and, to a lesser extent, the tourist market. It was well managed and we saw the potential of our involvement by increasing their number of tourist customers through our sales network. So we bought a stake in the company and, as a result, became the largest white water rafting operators in the country.

The only place where visitors to New Zealand could obtain information about tourist attractions was through the New Zealand Government Tourist Information Bureau. We reckoned we could do a far better job with an alternative visitor centre. We figured it could be improved by hiring switched-on staff and offering complementary services like film development, souvenir shopping and the ability to book tourist services and activities.

As such, two 'Activity Centres' were set up, one in the heart of Queenstown and the other in Rotorua. After two years however, the large labour costs associated with running them, plus the huge cost of setting them up, was not commensurate with the revenue they were generating. The losses being incurred were only going to increase so regrettably we bit the bullet and closed them down. It was a lesson in being too optimistic and not looking at the practical reality of how we could make them profitable.

I'd like to say we always learnt from all our mistakes – but we didn't! There was always a temptation to take a risk, to step out of the comfort zone and explore new ideas that might be fresh and new and, more importantly, profitable. Contiki had successfully expanded from a two minibus operation into so much more across the globe, yet we always had to find the balance with making a considered decision on things while still hanging onto that sense of innovation. Any entrepreneurial business will always struggle with this kind of balance.

We also invested in a few other tourism operations such as 'Willowbank Wild Life Park' on the outskirts of Christchurch, which had, amongst its other fauna, a kiwi bird breeding colony.

Then came an idea we thought could revolutionise camping as we knew it ...

*

For around 25 years we had been using camp grounds all over Europe. The quality varied enormously. Some were outstanding, others were total dumps. Over the years we had been responsible for dramatically improving many by demanding a certain standard for our patronage. New Zealand and Australian camp grounds had a similar variety of quality.

When Ali and I had travelled around America we discovered the Kampgrounds of America (KOA) chain, an impressive franchise stretched throughout America. KOA camp grounds were beautifully kept and professionally run with a consistently high standard of facilities. They also had unique features such as specially designed log cabins as an alternative to tents, high quality communal amenity blocks, communal kitchens and a recreation centre where people could relax together.

In 1986 we decided to create a high quality chain of unique camp grounds throughout New Zealand. If successful, we could export the concept to Europe. The potential was mind boggling. In addition, we believed any camp grounds we purchased would make a great real estate investment that would appreciate in value over time. We began to identify locations in towns and cities throughout the country.

First, we approached established camp grounds. Some were owned and operated by local councils, so we offered to buy or takeover the lease of these. Where there wasn't a suitable camp ground available we would find the land and build a new one.

The first established camp ground we bought was The Rotorua Thermal Motor Camp which, at the time, was the largest camp ground in New Zealand, accommodating up to 1500 guests per night. We immediately commenced an upgrade of the facilities, with the building of twelve KOA designed log cabins which could sleep two to four people. We built new amenity blocks and communal kitchens, the most modern in the country. A facility to cater for campervans was built. As if that was not enough, we also built a self-contained lodge to accommodate Contiki groups. This was to be our flagship showpiece.

Like some of our other construction projects, it was fraught with unanticipated difficulties. But in this case, two-thirds of the way through the makeover, our builder went bust! But we persevered and created a wonderful asset.

We progressed through the country negotiating to invest in a number of key sights such as Queenstown, Christchurch, the outskirts of Wellington, and the Bay of Islands. In early 1987 we purchased five acres of land on the outskirts of Auckland at East Tamiki to build the city's first and finest camp ground.

There was only one campsite in Queenstown, owned by the local council, but they were not interested in any of our proposals. Since Queenstown was critical to our overall plan, we had to find an alternative site. We found one just outside of town at Frankton. What's more, it was already zoned to allow use as an accommodation business. But approaches to the owner, a small publicly listed company on the New Zealand stock exchange called Lakeland Properties, were fruitless. We desperately wanted the site so had to find an alternative way of obtaining it. Why not buy the company?

As we thought the idea through, another reason to buy Lakeland Properties dawned on us. If we could obtain control of it, we would not only get the site but we could also turn it into the first listed tourism company in the country, as opposed to the property company it was. Lakeland Properties had other land holdings we could sell. We would put all the tourism ventures we already had interests in, plus future ones, into the company. We could use the company's script to buy into other ventures and eventually raise further capital on the market. It was such an exciting scenario.

We consulted with a notable stockbroker to hatch a plan. Lakeland Properties' share price had been languishing whilst the rest of the market was on fire. The company had a well-spread share register and, as a result, was ripe for the picking. It was agreed we would 'stand in the market', offering to buy as many shares as possible up to a value of NZ$1.1 million at a price some 30 per cent above the current market price. As a matter of courtesy I rang the Chairman about our intended action the evening prior to our stand. The response I received was blunt and to the point: 'We do not welcome your offer,' he told me.

Through a nominee company we launched our offer the next day, keeping our identity anonymous. The market was abuzz and a handful of shares came into our hands. Within a couple of hours another stockbroker came into the market, offering a higher price on behalf of his client. At the end of the day, not wanting to pay more, or enter into an auction, we withdrew our offer. But what an exciting day it had been! The shares purchased were sold. Back to square one.

The development of the camp grounds concept was gathering pace. The Rotorua camp was doing a roaring trade and we knew that the concept was a winner. There were a number of other locations around New Zealand we were negotiating with to become part of the chain. While all this was all going on, we sent one of our researchers to Europe to scout for possibilities to introduce our proposed camp ground franchise there.

*

A NZ publicly listed company, Fullers Corporation, ran cruises on Auckland Harbour and in the Bay of Islands, with a fleet of around 25 boats. In May 1987 we were approached by Fullers Corporation to take a significant stake in them. With the encouragement of our new shareholder, Omnicorp, we carried out limited due diligence and, primarily based on the recently audited accounts of the company by Price Waterhouse Coopers, we agreed to take a 26.7 per cent shareholding. The cost was around NZ$5 million dollars.

At the time of our acquisition, Fulllers was predicting an after tax annual profit of NZ$1.5 million dollars. Three months later it announced a profit warning, stating the company would make a loss. The share price collapsed. We rushed to cancel the original purchase without success. We believed we had been totally misled by the directors of Fullers and, more importantly, by the firm's auditors. Some six months later the company announced a loss of NZ$4 million plus NZ$3 million in write offs. Soon after this, Fullers went into receivership.

This was an exhilarating period for the Contiki group. We were firing on all fronts and felt invincible, with not just the growing tour operations but developing interests in other tourism ventures. Nothing ventured, nothing gained.

23. WHAT HAPPENS ON THE BUS, STAYS ON THE BUS

Kleptomaniacs, nymphomaniacs, agoraphobics, arachnophobics, alcoholics, psychotics and womanisers. No, not the local psych ward, just some of the many personality types our field staff had to deal with over the years. To think I started off in 1962 interviewing each and every passenger to see if they were suitable!

Originally, the majority of our passengers, (colloquially known as punters), travelling in Europe were Australians and New Zealanders with the odd South African and Canadian soon starting to appear on the passenger lists. Slowly a number of other diverse nationalities joined them, until eventually it was not unusual for a coach to have as many as a dozen different nationalities or more onboard. All spoke English, often with a distinctive accent. There were always many more females than males but, over the years, the imbalance improved.

Passengers' backgrounds were as diverse as you could imagine. We had the sons or daughters of governor-generals, presidents, prime ministers, royalty (although never English royalty to my knowledge), and famous or well-known individuals in their own right. There was the odd beauty queen, including the occasional ex-Miss World or ex-Miss Universe and even a Miss Te Kuiti from New Zealand. From America we toured with a stream of pageant winners such as Miss Strawberry

Fair, Miss Cherry Blossom Festival, or Mr and Miss Hoedown Kentucky. The tour was their prize for winning.

There was always a smattering of honeymooners and married couples onboard. Since they have no need to 'play the field' like the singles, these couples often teamed up as a group. Inevitably, some started the tour as a couple but didn't end as such, as one or the other found someone else they found irresistibly more attractive.

While I was writing this book a passenger wrote to me with a story of her own.

'I took my husband on a Contiki European tour and after a few weeks I saw another unexpected side of him. With all his philandering I realised what an arsehole of a man I'd married. Soon after the tour we were divorced. I remarried and am now so happy. Thank you Contiki!'

The exact opposite to the usual reason of thanks continually received relating to match-making.

There were many varied reasons why passengers were travelling. There were the genuine travellers, who wanted to see the world and meet people of other nationalities and cultures. Some wanted to escape a situation at home, the further away the better. Some, to get out of their comfort zone and take on a totally new challenge, adventure or new life experience. Others taking a holiday break or gap year before starting a new job or study course. Some were either drifting or looking for 'greener pastures' in another part of the world. Finally, there were those wanting to meet new people and make new friends, perhaps even the possibility of meeting a future partner was the main reason to travel.

The personalities onboard were even more diverse. Tour leaders and drivers rarely see their passengers until they turned up for a pre-departure meeting or at the coach door on the morning of departure. They never knew what hidden characteristics lay dormant in any individual but they soon found out.

Some passengers are very difficult as they are not used to the new situation they find themselves in. Some dislike the necessity of going with majority rule and therefore resist conforming or being told what to do. This often happens with passengers who are only children, who have always been the centre of attention and are used to having their own way. It's often a beneficial wake up call for them. Some try to assert their authority, some are self-centred, and some are downright objectionable. It's hard enough running a tour with so many personalities let alone with some in the mix who constantly attempt to disrupt the tour and make it hard for everyone. These folk are a tiny minority, but usually the other passengers sort them out. The majority of the passengers have one common aim – to make their tour the success they want it to be.

Some passengers have physical disabilities or health problems such as allergies, asthma, diabetes and the like. As the years went by there were increasing numbers of vegetarians, vegans and those wanting gluten-free meals. People from different ethnic backgrounds or religious beliefs also joined the tours in ever-growing numbers, many with differing values and opinions. I received this comment from a passenger who travelled in Europe in 1978.

'As a 27 year old polio survivor, travelling solo was my first test that I could make it and cope alone. I wasn't out to conquer the world as I knew I had physical limitations. I really appreciated the staff on my Grand European tour as they constantly watched out for me and stopped me doing anything foolish.'

For most passengers it was their first time away from home, their first time overseas and the first time they had experienced total freedom and anonymity. This also meant it was, for many, the first time they had to really think about and take responsibility for their actions, make major decisions and budget their finances. Also, the first time they had to make a real effort to integrate and get on well with a group of complete strangers.

In the early years, passengers had four or five weeks onboard a boat coming to the United Kingdom to become accustomed to leaving the security of home and adapting to their new environment. With the end of the boat era, the passengers took to the air. A teary mum, dad, family, friends and relations would gather, with last-minute advice, hugs and kisses and wave them goodbye. Just 36 hours later they would be in London, all alone. Contiki was often their only contact.

On tour there were three broad groups of passengers. The Culture Vultures liked to sit at the front of the coach where they could see everything they passed and prise information from the driver or tour leader. The Party Animals preferred to sit down the back where they could be a bit more rowdy, play cards, or sleep last night's party off. If there was an interesting sight along the way, often they would ask to be woken so they could briefly take in the scene, perhaps taking photos before drifting off again. Most passengers wanted an all-round experience and sat somewhere in the middle.

Every tour has similar traditions which have been religiously carried on year in, year out. On the first day each passenger is required to stand with the microphone at the front of the coach to introduce themselves. A daunting task for some. There is always the trip song, more often than not the wake-up call, played first thing every morning, or a song written by the passengers reflecting their own special trip. Both songs are written to fit with a popular, well known tune. Then there was the trip diary, which was devotedly written up every day by either the appointed author or everyone taking a turn. This is raffled of at the end of the tour and is a highly prized possession. And who will ever forget being a 'coach packer' in Europe or a 'room mouse' (housekeeping staff) on the Whitsunday Resort.

Whether it be cross-dressing or a challenging theme, the regular dress-up party evenings are notorious for bringing out passengers' daring, flair and individuality, often with a totally different side of a passenger emerging. These are hilarious occasions, remembered for many years. Each touring area had its own special places for these traditional events.

Each also had its own special activities, memorable ones which passengers often recall as highlights of their tour. Typical in Europe would be the ouzo cruise on George's boat or the scary scooters – both in Corfu. The evenings at 'Space Electronic' or 'The Red Garter' in Florence. The evenings at the Mathauser (now extinct) or Hofbrauhaus beer halls in Munich, dressing up in the Dutch National costume or for the salt mine excursion out of Salzburg and so on.

With such a diverse mix it was inevitable passengers on tour got up to a lot of mischief. Many did not know how to handle their newfound freedom and soon came a little unstuck especially with too much alcohol. So many stories from the road were fuelled by people drinking a little too liberally, which gave them the false bravado to do crazy things. As one passenger recently said to me: *'I was voted the most likely to need a holiday after my holiday!'*

Occasionally passengers took matters into their own hands. It was related to me that a renegade passenger on a tour in 1983, passing through Turkey, obtained directions to Gallipoli. Clearly quite a charismatic chap, he convinced the other passengers (obviously from the ANZAC nations!) that although Gallipoli wasn't on the route they should go anyway. When the passenger told the tour leader of the plans, he responded with 'We can't as it's not on the itinerary'.

'Well, you tell the passengers then,' the stubborn passenger responded. 'I have already told them we're definitely going.'

Backed into a corner, the tour leader worked out a way to cut some time and head to Gallipoli at 4 am the following morning. From all accounts it was an emotional day and a wonderful experience. Most of the Australians on the trip didn't know the words to their national Anthem so they sang *Waltzing Matilda* instead. The passenger involved in this 'grand group coup', recalls *'Not being able to talk about it with other tours brought us together and the feeling onboard was special. We never did get potted for it!'*

Another group on a ski tour in 1982 went tobogganing one night. They took the ski lift to the top and indulged in some gluwein (mulled wine). Probably as a direct result, everyone had trouble getting down the mountain with one passenger needing to be carried due to frostbite! A South African girl on a toboggan crashed twice and ended up with two broken wrists. Her brother had to feed her for the rest of the trip.

Friendships made on tour are legendary. Living together for a period of time people get to know each other extremely well. The longer the tour, the closer the friendships become. Sometimes passengers start out with a false veneer, but this is soon stripped away. The realisation that everyone is in it together to have a good time soon makes people relax, join in, and go with the flow.

Typical of the sometimes hilarious close bonds that were formed was the friendship formed between two passengers, one of whom drunk the other's glass of water in the night, only to discover the next morning he'd also drunk the passenger's contact lenses!

A passenger wrote to me recently about his first Contiki European Concept Tour. *'A young lady onboard believed she had booked on a hotel tour. She arrived with a suitcase full of cocktail dresses and stilettos. She was a solicitor no doubt hoping to find and marry a successful barrister. After a few days of tottering across grass fields in high heels, much to the amusement of the other more down-to-earth passengers, they loaned her some more appropriate attire, which she accepted with relief.'*

Here are a few memories sent in by passengers that you may enjoy.

'Our driver lost his passport in the red light area of Athens. We were delayed four days while he sorted it out.' MJ

'Keeping ahead of two "nymphomaniacs" on the tour – who tried everything possible to lure this 23 year old "virgin" into bed!! They NEVER succeeded!' CC

'I recall drinking beer and Jägermeister chasers in Camping Fusina, Venice while standing naked at the bar. The mossies, however, were a bit of a menace.' SH

'Our tour was the last to leave most sites, so became known as the "turn the lights out when you leave" tour by staff.' SW

'We were all in fits of laughter at Clara Cluck's comment on first sighting the replica of Michelangelo's David: "Oooh look at Dave baby with all his accoutrements showing!" which became one of our many sayings. The lasting friendships we made and how vivid the memories are still, even though it was over forty years ago. Our group had no arguments, fights or rivalries and we have some great reunions. The drivers were special young men and looked after us so well, like big brothers. Local lads always asked their permission to take us out to other places.' PS

'More fucking castles and churches than a hung over Aussie chick could handle!! Laughs, drama, backstabbing, bitchiness and shagging – what a great holiday!' KW

'Maybe the 18–35s of today's Contiki tours don't have to flap their plates to dry or sleep in those infamous tents like we did, but I do know that they share the same sense of wonder and friendship that I know I did. Viva la Contiki!' SN

'I became the chunder photographer as the competition became quite fierce and we needed more evidence.' L McK

'In the early minibus days I was a driver on the Russian tours. Contiki had "run out" of my passport photos so they pasted one that looked like me, on my Russian visa for pick-up in Stockholm. Getting into Russia at Vyborg was ok as the young (20) officer was more interested in my predominantly female passengers than me. However, leaving Russia at Brest going into Poland was a far different story. I was interrogated by screaming officers, it was frightening, but I didn't understand a word. I made it through.' NM

'I had the Contiki logo and the places we visited tattooed on my bum. Contiki got hold of a photo and I signed a release form so they could use my bum in future advertising.' GF

'We took two of the new Mercedes V8 coaches for a 'chariot race' around Circus Maximus.' PC

'All these years later I could go back and have that holiday again! How did I ever get my luggage to fit that tiny Contiki suitcase?' J O'H

In the early minibus days I personally met the returning tours. To watch such happy groups returning as close friends, people who had started out as total strangers, was always very special to me. Together they had shared an experience the memories of which would last a lifetime. Their fond farewells, hugging, kissing and crying were always an emotional moment for me. In later years, unbeknown to anyone, I would often stand in a corner watching the return of coaches. I always felt a huge amount of pride that Contiki, in some small way, had made a difference to their lives.

24. BRAND AND BROCHURES

I believe a company's brand is its biggest asset. Many people disagree and say that 'people are the most important asset of any organisation'. Yes, I agree they are extremely important, but not as important as the brand. 'People move on, but the brand is there forever.' People only have temporary ownership of a brand before they pass it on to the next generation. They have a duty and a responsibility to protect the brand, enhance the brand and ensure no damage ever comes to the brand.

A brand is not just a name and a logo. Yes, a company originally starts out with just a name but, out of the millions that exist, very few last the test of time. An established brand has depth, history, and a character all of its own that is ingrained within the products and services of a company.

I recently spoke to the CEO of McDonalds Australia. Both Contiki and McDonalds are internationally established brands that have been around for a similar length of time. Both are well respected and continue to grow in their own highly competitive markets. Together we asked ourselves why our two brands had lasted the test of time? We agreed it came down to five basic reasons: quality, consistency, innovation, value for money and trust. Perhaps the most important of all is trust.

I am passionate about brands and have very firm ideas what makes a good brand name. Ideally it should be one or two words maximum, easy to spell, pronounce and remember, such as AXA, Westpac or Viva. It can be an advantage if it is also a little unusual. It shouldn't be too close to another name, where it could become confused. A brand's colours are also an important element and should be consistent across all marketing materials. Just think of the strength of Shell's colours (yellow and red) or BP's (green and yellow).

The constant protection of our brand name was paramount. We initially registered the Contiki name in the United Kingdom and subsequently in all our key areas around the world. It was an extremely expensive and time-consuming exercise as the name, in some countries, had to be registered under all the different categories it was associated with, such as travel, accommodation and transport, to name just a few. Someone else could still use the brand name in any category omitted – for example in food – Contiki biscuits. Yes, biscuits!

Some names are self-explanatory such as Air New Zealand or BP Oil. If they're not descriptive on their own, it is imperative to somehow say or illustrate what the brand relates to. Contiki on its own could be anything so we added the word 'travel' to be more explicit. Contiki Travel became the name used on all our stationery, brochures, publicity material, signage – everything.

To clearly define what Contiki Travel was, we added a strap line. In the early years we used 'Europe on a Mini Budget' under the name. Later we deleted the word 'travel' and just used the name 'Contiki' with a series of changing strap lines such as 'European Camping Holidays', 'We Show You Europe', 'For the 18 to 35s' and 'As much fun as you can handle'. Eventually we settled with 'Contiki Holidays for 18 to 35s' which is exactly what the company was all about. The name Contiki has become an iconic brand in many countries around the world, in some even a household name, and needs no explanation as to what it represents.

A company logo is often an added advantage and can add value. Sometimes this is imbedded in the brand name, like 'Coca-Cola' (in the way it is written). Some logos have become so strong: they are even recognised without any words. The McDonald's 'M', the Mercedes-Benz three pointed star or Nike tick are perfect examples. In its 46-year history, the Contiki brand has had four logos. Originally, it was a C with a T shaped like an arrow, followed by the Contiki 'lozenge'. It was later refreshed with Contiki in written script and eventually revamped into the current one of today, a blue name with a touch of yellow in the background.

There is a parallel between a brand name and a person's individual name. Either can be destroyed by carelessness or taking the wrong course. I believe your name (brand), next to your health, is the most valuable asset you have. It carries you all the way through your life. Your name is about integrity, about honesty, about credibility, about reputation. I say to young people 'You must protect your name, enhance your name, and never let any damage come to your name'.

An example of how seriously some of our staff took our brand name was the time one of our coaches was involved in an accident. The coach bodywork took a pounding, but fortunately, nobody was hurt badly but some of the passengers and passers-by began to take photos of the sight. Our tour leader stepped forward to cover the Contiki name on the side of the coach by throwing a tent over it to protect our brand. While I didn't condone such acts, the sentiment behind what he did was important. We wanted staff to instinctively understand the importance of our good reputation and to strive to protect it at all times.

The brochure was our most valuable selling tool. In the first 30 years we didn't have the luxury of the internet, which didn't gain popularity until the mid 1990s, although I believe the internet is not a total substitute for travel brochures. People still like the option to hold and read through them away from a computer, not unlike newspapers, magazines and books.

The annual production of our brochures was a massive task. It was an ongoing, year-round operation. The brochures had to be produced and distributed at least six months before the season started in each of our tour operating areas. Brochure production brought huge pressures and enormous discipline to our decision-making processes. We had to decide on the tour programmes at least nine months ahead of the following year to allow for production, distribution and sales time. We also had to cost the tours and decide on the selling prices. This was compounded with difficulty by the myriad of different currencies we traded in.

Originally I started with a four-sided card in one print colour – blue. Each year the brochures lifted to a new level starting with an extra colour – red, then black and white photos were added. Over the years these became massive multi-page full colour brochures with a variety of different versions for specific countries. Each brochure was carefully tailored to suit each major selling country and was priced in the currency of that country, featuring the local selling office address and supporting airline.

Those given the task of producing the brochures were a dedicated team who worked so hard, more often than not late into the night to meet print deadlines. When each brochure came off the presses everyone was so keen to see the result. But I've never forgotten the way people, not involved with their challenging and complicated production, would flick through them looking for mistakes or criticise the layout or choice of photos. Instead of praise and positive comments, so often they gave negative ones. No doubt I will suffer the same with this book!

We reaped enormous advantages by being associated with the key airlines I've already mentioned. Every brand must have credibility for people to have confidence in it. This must be earned and can take a long time to achieve, but it can be accelerated by piggy-backing on another company's proven reputation. So we also hooked onto the banks by stating for example, 'The Bank of New South Wales (now Westpac) travel department highly recommends Contiki'. This added to the brand's credibility.

The airlines assisted us with air freighting our brochures globally, which was a huge bonus. Some provided our passengers with preferential airfares and paid us a marketing fee based on the number of our passengers who booked on their flights. These fees ran into several hundred thousand dollars each year. We, in turn, would exclusively promote and recommend the airline in our brochures.

Our brochures were very carefully and cleverly crafted. We knew our customers' main reason to travel was 'to meet other young people and experience things together', preferably in a new or exotic environment. So the brochures reflected just that. They were always packed full of images of young people having fun together with those enticing backgrounds. We avoided using models in the brochure photographs by using shots of our own passengers, so prospective passengers, particularly the females, were not intimidated. Most passengers would prefer not to be accommodated in tents but this had to be an essential ingredient to keep the price of the tours down to an affordable level. So, our use of tent photos and camp grounds was kept to a minimum.

We knew our potential customers would be comparing our brochures with the competition, so we designed them to highlight all the unique features of our tours. We made sure we had the largest range of tour options and the largest number of departure dates to choose from, endeavouring to guarantee these dates to give confidence to the customer and the travel agent.

Early on I made the decision not to take on the lower priced end of the market, where everyone brings the quality down to achieve a lower price and then proceed to discount each other out of business. I realised it was far better to go for the quality, upper end with the tours appearing on the surface to be more expensive. I also had a theory that many prospective passengers who had saved and planned for their trip for years, did not want to buy a tour just because it was the cheapest, they wanted the best deal. This was their trip of a lifetime and by paying a little more they hopefully would receive extra benefits. As a result our tours were never the cheapest but always offered the best value.

In 1974 we decided to lighten up our brochures with a little humour and introduce something different. We created a character named 'Dropkick' – a cartoon figure who became the much-loved mascot of the company for around ten years. As a fringe benefit Dropkick gave us loads of merchandising opportunities such as T-shirts, key rings and silver charms for bracelets.

An established brand doesn't just *happen* to still be in existence 50 or 100 years after its inception. There's very little chance or luck involved. It takes years of research, trial and error to gain long-term respect. The Contiki brand has been established for 46 years – I believe it will still be around for another 46!

25. A WORLDWIDE SALES WEB

If you create a quality product that people want – they will buy it. Sounds simple enough, but how do you let them know your product exists? Passengers don't just materialise out of thin air, you have to tell them what you are offering.

To attract passengers we had five basic rules:

First, we clearly identified who was our target market. You can't be all to everyone so we chose a specific age group: 18–35 year olds. We then identified where they lived. Initially it was the old Commonwealth countries of Australia, New Zealand, Canada and South Africa. Later of course, it was worldwide.

Second, we delivered a product that the target market wanted. We constantly observed and listened to what our passengers were saying. From this we developed tour options, tailored and tweaked to suit each market. Australasians coming to Europe wanted longer tours, yet those coming from Canada and America shorter ones. Often the market doesn't know what it wants, so we continually trialled a whole range of new products on them. They soon let us know which ones they liked, as they bought them. Giving a new tour sufficient time to gather steam was important, but we also had the courage to withdraw it if it didn't gain sufficient momentum.

The third rule was to brand the product. I've already mentioned the huge importance of branding, so I'll say no more here but to repeat again 'It's the company's biggest asset'.

The fourth rule was to tell the potential customer that our product existed. Avoiding the scattering shotgun approach we used a pinpoint rifle one. We chose the travel industry – airlines and travel agents. As a combined force supporting each other we believed we could achieve the best results and, of course, we did.

The fifth was to hold onto our customers. It was hard enough to get them in the first place, so once we had them onboard we tried to keep them, by recognising them and encouraging them to book again. For example if they booked a second tour we rewarded them with a 5 per cent discount. I met a passenger recently who had taken 15 Contiki tours, (admittedly a couple were excursions, like the Oktoberfest) and I know there are many others like him! Interestingly a huge number of those passengers' children have now travelled Contiki. And subsequently the children of those children – the third generation – are now starting to travel with Contiki, often on their parents' recommendation as they recounted the memories of the time they also travelled with the company.

In 1966, my first driver Jet returned to New Zealand and offered to help promote Contiki. I'd already had a couple of enquiries from travel agents, including Mitchell International Tours which had six offices throughout New Zealand. I'd corresponded with them by aerogramme (no faxes, emails or text messages in those days!) and eventually they made a tour booking. I asked Jet to call on them, which resulted in their appointment as our first New Zealand travel agent with a commission of 10 per cent payable on every booking they made. I still have the original letter of appointment in which it states the following:

'We normally prefer to meet clients before confirming a booking, however, we are willing to accept your booking clerk's approval of a suitable client but do ask that they make sure the client is within the age limit of 19–29 years and is of good character.'

Can you imagine doing that today, ensuring the client was of good character as a condition of travel, and discriminating on age as well? My how things have changed! Further bookings from Mitchells turned out to be minimal, so I appointed another agency, Holm & Co., based in Wellington, with the same result. I had to find an agent who would promote Contiki aggressively to the whole New Zealand travel industry.

White Heron Holidays, based in Auckland represented a number of other high quality overseas travel companies, had an excellent reputation and a proven track record. I particularly liked their key personnel so in 1969 I appointed them as a master General Sales Agent (GSA) to wholesale the tours to all the other travel agents in New Zealand. The GSAs were to become a very important aspect of our business. It meant Contiki only had to deal with one agency, instead of hundreds, and we could channel our promotional efforts through them. With White Heron the bookings lifted dramatically but, unfortunately, they exited the representation business a few years later.

Atlantic & Pacific Travel (A&P) was my next GSA appointment, the largest and most successful travel company in New Zealand at the time. They had a great management team, including their CEO Duncan Hamilton who became a personal mentor to me. Bookings really took off. The association was a long and fruitful one.

In Australia I appointed the top travel wholesaler, World Travel Headquarters (WTHQ), as our GSA. The company was long established and highly respected in the travel industry. Their CEO John Webb also became one of my mentors. John knew the travel industry inside out and taught me so much about establishing and selling a new product in a new market. Fortunately for us, Qantas was seriously looking at initiatives to tap into the youth market for its Kangaroo route to London at the time.

In the seventies and early eighties the majority of overseas travel booked by Australians was made through the travel departments of the five major banks. So, with the combined endorsement of WTHQ, Qantas and the big banks, Australian sales increased dramatically. Contiki was therefore well established with the travel industry in Australia and New Zealand before the competitors woke up. We were well ahead of the game already.

Our bubble was somewhat burst when we went on to appoint a GSA in Canada, Fairways Travel, that went bust and cost us more than CAN$40,000. On the upside, it was a real lesson in credit control! From that point on we monitored our GSA agents vigorously. We subsequently appointed Kenway Travel based in Toronto and Air Canada agreed to endorse our brand. In America we selected Brendan Tours based in Los Angeles with British Airways and TWA coming onboard. In South Africa we appointed Budget Travel and gained the support of South African Airways.

It was a winning formula. Over time, we became a 'preferred product' in the vast majority of travel agents in the areas we were represented.

The GSA model served us well but eventually, we grew out of it. In the early 1980s, with our tour operations in America, Australia, New Zealand, and Canada we decided to progressively take over the sales role in each area ourselves. It was a difficult period. Our GSA representatives had been very loyal and put so much hard work into establishing Contiki in their areas. There was no way to soften the blow – they were now going to suffer as a result of their success. Most were very unhappy at the loss of their representation but realised it made sense for Contiki to be in charge of its own destiny.

The first of our own sales offices to open overseas was in Sydney (Clarence Street) followed by Auckland (Anzac Avenue), Toronto (Young Street), Vancouver (6th Avenue) and Los Angeles (Katella Avenue). It sounds so straightforward, but I can assure you in each case it wasn't just a matter of leasing an office and opening the doors as each was a major challenge. We had to satisfy the regulatory authorities we were financially sound and met the very strict criteria to trade – sometimes a long and arduous process! We retained the GSA in South Africa and to spread the sales net even wider appointed a GSA to represent us in Mexico, Singapore, Malaysia, Philippines, Israel, Hong Kong, Holland, Germany, Switzerland, Austria, Italy and Scandinavia.

There were huge benefits in having such a broad range of representation as we were not reliant totally on any one country's market for sales. And, as a bonus, we were also receiving a more diverse range of passenger nationalities, instead of just Australians and New Zealanders, which made the tours even more interesting for everyone!

In the seventies, every year in October and November, I would set off for my annual six-week sales trip around the world – affectionately known as the 'milk run' (for the number of regular stops made) – armed with the new European brochure for the following year. In the early days, I would set off alone, leaving super capable Ali and our children at home. In later years I was accompanied by Contiki's CEO.

Typically I would travel to Perth, Adelaide, Melbourne, Hobart, Sydney, Newcastle, Brisbane, Auckland, Hamilton, Wellington, Christchurch, Dunedin, Los Angeles, San Francisco, Vancouver, Edmonton, Calgary, Toronto, Quebec City, Montreal and sometimes to smaller towns where thought appropriate. These trips were an outstanding opportunity to meet with the agents on the 'coal face'. I always liked to keep in touch with those on the front line. It's amazing what you pick up, both good and bad.

The entire circus was a masterpiece of organisation, coordinated through our GSA offices and later our own. At each stop a luncheon was arranged to thank the top ten or 20 travel agents for the year and, in the evening, there'd be a function to which all the travel industry, particularly the front line travel agency's selling staff, were invited.

These were huge affairs, often with well over 1000 people attending. Sometimes we'd take over an entire nightclub or disco. Once, we took over a cinema for the premiere of the film *Educating Rita* with the star of the film, Julie Walters, attending. Other times we'd hire a boat for a cruise around the harbour. We always made sure our functions were the very best, quality affairs that were different and unique, just like our tours.

On each occasion I would present the new programmeme, highlighting all the exciting additions such as new 'special stopovers', routes and destinations. In the early years I had a slide show, and from 1969, we produced a full colour movie. I did the 'milk run' every year for around ten years, always aiming to be in Brisbane for the Melbourne Cup horse race. Why Brisbane? Because I had a close affiliation with the travel industry there, who always went to the same pub for the event, year in, year out. The pub's still there and whenever I visit Brisbane I always drop in for a beer. I'm a sucker for memories.

We paid the travel agents a basic commission for the Contiki sales they made, with an extra incentive payment if they achieved higher sales. We had a huge advantage over our competitors because of our worldwide range of products. It was in the agents' interest to sell Contiki exclusively because it would increase their chances for a bonus payment. A majority of our advertising budget was spent in association with travel agents as in this way we helped each other. We would support their marketing efforts often by matching dollar for dollar. We needed them, they needed us.

We took advantage of our strong market position when we set up operations in New Zealand, where we faced a number of existing competitors. We told the agents in Australia where most of the New Zealand tour bookings were sourced, 'If you don't sell our New Zealand product in preference to our competitors you will not be able to sell our European product'. On reflection this was quite a bold and arrogant stance, something that would not be tolerated today. But these competitors had reacted very aggressively to our entry into the market in the early eighties and, as you will recall, had dragged us through a very unpleasant period with 'The Authority' when trying to gain our transport licences. As such, when the time came we had no qualms pursuing our own business just as aggressively.

Every year we took up to 100 front line travel agents from around the world on 'familiarisation' tours. Most would join a regular tour to experience what Contiki was all about from the perspective of a passenger. It was an excellent way to educate them about our product and equip them with powerful first hand knowledge when selling to potential customers. It's all about word of mouth advertising, even if the mouth belongs to the travel agent!

We introduced another form of secret shopper. We had young people visit travel agencies and pretend to be considering a trip to one of our operating regions. They would ask the agent to recommend the tour that suited them best. If Contiki was recommended they'd ask why, and also elicit the agent's opinions of our tours. If the agent recommended a competitor, they would ask similar questions. This practice gave us insight into the agent and, above all, why they might recommend a competitor.

In our main selling areas we had Contiki sales representatives visiting the agents to educate them on our latest offerings. We had videos made featuring our tours, which they could loan to potential customers.

Acquainting ourselves with the editors and journalists of the travel industry publications around the world, we communicated through them to the travel agents. Often it was one of our brochures on the front page of a travel trade publication. Our strong belief in proactive PR and working with the media saw us issuing frequent press releases to stimulate magazine and newspaper articles. We experimented with all formats of advertising changing with the times and technology, from cinema slides to television.

Our promotional ideas were often 'outside the square'. In the early seventies we advertised in the *Australian Women's Weekly* magazine, a publication which was certainly not read by our target market, but by their mothers. Young people in those days were strongly influenced by their parents, so we figured we should appeal to them as well. In so doing, they may encourage their children who were contemplating a trip to Europe, to book with Contiki.

Our advertisements and editorial content emphasised our endorsement by Qantas, and the banks, to give us credibility. We focused on our industry experience and the fact that we only used safe, reliable Mercedes-Benz coaches. In essence, we appealed to a parent's innate desire to protect their children by stressing our credibility and safety-first approach. We also knew that parents often chipped in to pay for the tours so, in a way, they were also our customers.

We never attempted to increase sales by discounting. I had always believed discounting would have a detrimental effect on our brand's image. In fact if it had not been for the volume of passengers we were carrying, the prices would have been considerably higher. We wanted to give value for money and receive a reasonable return for our efforts. In the end you get what you pay for.

In the early years, in a desperate effort to attract business, I had seen some of my competitors discount their tour prices, as to them it was all about price. No doubt this contributed to their demise. Although I said we never discounted, we did have three exceptions. If a passenger booked and paid in full in the year preceding their tour they were entitled to an earlybird discount. If a group of four or more booked together on the same tour they received a discount and if a passenger booked on a second tour they were recognised accordingly. This made good commercial sense.

Our worldwide, year-round moving advertising billboards (the coaches!) were not neglected in our promotional efforts. Our Contiki name was splashed both on the sides, front and back, with the Contiki office address and telephone number. The coaches were always pristine and sparkling clean and were never sent out with any body damage showing. Our field service vehicles were given the same treatment.

We produced stickers of the Contiki logo and the cartoon figure, Dropkick, to be stuck on the passenger's suitcases. Often I would be at an airport luggage carousel watching for my bag when suitcases would circle by with our stickers on display, always a proud moment for me. Dropkick was even painted on the roof of our American coaches so anyone looking out a skyscraper window would see him.

Whenever a tour group photo was taken we would ensure the Contiki name was somewhere in the photo. It may have been a sign in the front or a coach parked in the background. When passengers proudly showed the photo of their group, there was our Contiki logo on display – for free!

With all the sales ideas and initiatives we introduced there was one more important and more valuable than all the others put together – 'word of mouth' advertising. I know I've said this before, but I can't over emphasise its importance. We learnt fast, that if someone has had a good experience, they'll tell others – there is no other more powerful form of advertising and what's more it's free!

The number of passengers and therefore sales kept increasing. Our first objective each year was to hold onto the previous year's increase, then endeavour to improve on it. But at the end of the day, no matter how well or how cleverly you promote your product, or how much you spend, there is one fundamental objective you must fulfil to achieve increased sales. You have to ensure you have a quality product or service that people want to buy. Simple as that.

26. WE GAVE THINGS A GO

Looking back, I can see I've always been a risk-taker and this attitude infused Contiki's culture completely. Remember how, in 1961, I had plunged everything I owned into a company on the stockmarket in the belief it would pay my way to Europe? It did, and off I went. Was this a formative experience? Did it teach me that the bigger the risk, the bigger the gain? Yes, I think it did. Our maxim at Contiki became to always give things a go. If you don't try something you'll never know the result. But over the next 28 years I was also to learn that the bigger the risk, the bigger the fall. I have always said 'Beware of failure, but never ever fear it'.

During the period 1981 to 1983, Contiki's resources were incredibly stretched. Having moved residence to Hong Kong and begun investigating or establishing operations and sales offices in New Zealand, America and Australia, personnel and cash were at a premium. The European Concept Tour initiative had sparked a growth spurt of over 50 per cent more passengers each season, and our Farthings Club was spreading its tentacles across other parts of the world.

Unlike 20 years before – a time when I believed myself to be *terribly* busy selling plants, eggs, chicken poo and sorting mail – I was now multitasking on three different continents, making decisions that risked the rise or fall of millions of dollars.

With operations in so many different time zones, finding time to relax was tough. It was a 24-hour operation: as New Zealand and Australian businesses closed for the day, the European offices were just opening their doors. But the tour operations never stopped, never closed. Many of my calls were made or received in the middle of the night. In addition, by 1982 I had four young children: Sarah (one), James (three), Peter (nine) and Susie (ten).

But the thrill and excitement of taking a risk and turning an idea into a reality was addictive. Our research of new ideas and business opportunities showed no sign of abating.

The European concept tours had proved to be ideally suited to a large segment of the youth market. But with the cost rising for passengers, we decided to reintroduce the original camping tours for a couple of years for the more budget-conscious tourist. It turned out the price differential was not great enough, however, with most passengers opting to pay the difference for the superior concept tour.

We knew there was a bigger market out there not tempted by any current Contiki options. Many couldn't bear the thought of travelling on an organised tour at all. They did, however, still require transport around Europe. So we put our minds to catching this new market in our ever-expanding net.

In the late seventies, the Eurail pass was gaining in popularity. It appeared to be ideally suited to the free-wheeling independent travellers we were looking at. It allowed them to buy a pass of varying value and step on and off trains operating virtually anywhere on the vast European rail network. It had the added advantage of not only being very cheap but also gave tourists the chance to mingle with the locals in a more natural environment.

We talked to a number of people who had travelled using Eurail. Their overall comments were very positive, particularly relating to the flexibility and freedom of choice. They liked the fact that there were no restrictions as to the duration of their stay in any given place, or the activities and places they experienced once there. The downsides were hard to prise out of them, as they were surprisingly defensive about their choice of transport.

However, the more we dug, the more negatives arose. A large number admitted each day they constantly worried about where to stay on arrival, how much things would cost and where they would eat. They rarely had enough information to prioritise the tourist sights in any given place, let alone how to find or get to them. Bouts of loneliness were common for Eurail passengers, due to not being able to share their experience with other young English-speaking travellers.

In 1983 we decided to replicate the Eurail concept as a cheap alternative option to our organised tours. We designed a bus route around central Europe taking in the towns and cities where our regular tours stopped overnight. For transport we would use some of the older but still reliable Mercedes-Benz coaches, as they were cheaper to run. No accommodation, tent villages, special stopovers, meals, sightseeing or other activities were included. It would, quite simply, act as a transport network with some commentary along the route. Advice would be provided on accommodation, restaurants and sightseeing and so on.

Initially, the coaches would leave London every five days and drive around the route, stopping over each night at the towns and cities and moving on to the next the following day. Passengers would have the freedom to stay in each place as long as they liked and move on when the next bus that suited them came through. If patronage increased we planned to have a bus coming through every two days. Eurail's ticketing system would be adopted – tickets could be purchased for a set sum and set periods of time from two to six months. If it worked in Europe we would consider replicating it in other locations.

The new product was branded 'Freetime', again with an age group limited to 18–35 year olds. We designed and registered a logo and a basic brochure was produced and promoted throughout our sales network. It was received very positively.

Although we had almost everything in place, we struck a major obstacle. We had gained permission to transport passengers through the majority of countries, but a couple, including France, refused point blank to allow us to drive through their territory on what is called an open-door operation. Our regular tours were classified as closed-door operations because the same passengers started and finished their tour at the same point and place. Open door operations were perceived as too similar to some countries' domestic transport services, and therefore competitive. It soon became clear the French authorities weren't planning to budge, no matter how much effort, lobbying and pleading we tried. We'd hit a brick wall!

Devastated, with no other option, we canned the whole Freetime concept. It cost us dearly both financially and in reputation, since we had to inform passengers and our valued travel agents that the new programmeme had been cancelled. Ironically, many years later a company in New Zealand, Kiwi Experience, successfully adopted a similar idea.

As we were developing Freetime we were also creating another product – a cross between Freetime and the all-inclusive concept tours. This was a regular coach tour, with set departures and set routes, again using the cheaper coaches, camping accommodation, but no sightseeing, no meals (except a continental breakfast), or other inclusions. It was branded 'Three Bees – Bus, Bed and Breakfast'. Again, we developed the brand and brochure but, at the last moment, with the collapse of Freetime, we lost our nerve and pulled the plug. It was again costly, but with so many other endeavours on the table we decided to concentrate on what we were currently developing in Europe and around the world including the Farthings Club.

With the successful introduction of our ski tours in Austria in the late sixties, we started to offer other options in Europe in the seventies, beginning with a pilot ski trip to the tiny mountain kingdom of Andorra (nestled between France and Spain) and an Italian resort in the Dolomites. In the early eighties, we also started ski tours in New Zealand and began eyeing the ski districts of Australia and America. We considered becoming a worldwide ski tour operator specifically catering to the youth market but the idea never got legs, probably for the simple reason that too few of the directors had an interest in skiing!

In 1972, however, another ski idea did take off – literally. We had become concerned about the long bus drive passengers had to endure from London to our Austrian resorts. In the brochure, we disguised the long journey by focusing on all the beautiful scenery the passengers would see, and the twinkling lights of the beautiful little villages they'd pass through during the night. In reality, it was a ghastly 24-hour road trip, especially in the early days when passengers were cramped up in minibuses.

The majority of the English mainstream ski tour operators who offered ski tours to Austria had begun, by then, to fly their passengers to Munich and then coach them to the Austrian resorts. We figured this had to be the way to go. So, we contracted to buy the majority of charter seats on a Court Line BAC 111 jetliner for a weekly return flight from London to Munich over the ski season. With a full aircraft the cost per seat was almost as cheap as road transport. Although it would make our tour a little more expensive, the fly and ski package would be a far superior product, even giving our passengers an extra day at the resort with the time saved. It would pull us way ahead of our camping tour competitors who also offered ski trips and were using minibus transport. We thought the number of bookings would escalate and believed we were onto a winner.

We didn't give even a passing thought to the possibility of disruptive weather or the reliability of our aircraft operator. It turned out that bad weather constantly played havoc with our schedule and the operator we had selected was unbelievably unreliable. From late departures, mechanical breakdowns and overbooked flights – this operator ticked all the wrong boxes! In addition, we fell well short of our projected passenger numbers, so with a half filled flight the seat cost doubled. It was an unmitigated disaster, we'd lost our shirt and we were forced to return to buses. The only consolation was that the journey did improve with the introduction of coaches, with reclining seats, and later TV and an inbuilt toilet.

It's worth mentioning here that we didn't make the switch to flights on a whim. We wanted to stay ahead of the pack – something that had paid off many times over in the past, such as introducing coaches. Yes, the 'fly and ski' package failed, but had we not tried, we risked being left behind. Taking risks only seems foolish in retrospect when it doesn't work. When risks do pay off, they are viewed as a stroke of genius! Either way, risk-taking is a necessary part of business.

Another time we had contracted accommodation in a newly built hotel complex in St Johann, Austria, for the peak Christmas/New Year season. We had been so pleased to be taking the passengers to this brand new complex confirming and ensuring the beds by paying in full in advance. On arrival with a full complement of passengers, we found the hotelier had gone bust and the hotel was closed for business. It was freezing cold and we had a bus full of bed-less refugees! We had to scramble around the village finding beds for passengers anywhere we could, with many ending up in private homes.

With the success of our tent villages, we put together some budget family holidays for the English domestic market under a different brand name. We intended to set up villages in the popular Mediterranean coastal camp grounds, bus them in, and accommodate them for a week or two at a time in pre-erected frame tents. But, again it was not our core target market. We decided not to stray from the 18–35 age group and canned the idea at the last minute.

In 1972, ten years before we set up our American business, one of our experienced European field staff members, having met his American wife on one of his European tours, decided to take off and live in California. It was suggested he research the possibility of Contiki operating there. As he was particularly fond of Mexico it was agreed he would pioneer a series of three-week and five-week tours from Los Angeles, down through California to Mexico and back.

He purchased a Dodge minibus, camping gear and produced a small brochure, which we distributed to our sales network. All started well with the number of passengers increasing on each trip, predominately Californians. But it was not long before border authorities noticed we were regularly transporting groups without the appropriate transport licence. The budding venture came to an abrupt halt and the operation had to be closed down. This was, of course, one of the reasons why I was always so particular in later years about securing the correct transport licences – so at least there was a lesson in it!

With our major investment in the water-based operation of Fullers Corporation in Auckland and our presence in the Whitsunday Islands in Australia, we looked at the possibility of investing in the water taxi business that served our island resort. In addition, we looked at investing in Quicksilver, one of the boat companies in Northern Queensland that took tourists out to the Great Barrier Reef. Now all we needed to complete the water-based investments was an interest in a Sydney-based operation.

Again out of the blue, an Australian-based company building a paddle steamer for cruises on Sydney Harbour approached us. The company, Blue Line Cruises, was about to list on the Australian Stock Exchange and offered us a 30 per cent stake. It all looked very attractive, so we decided to take the punt. We also encouraged many of our personal friends and associates to invest in the float.

The paddle steamer was built in Singapore and towed to Sydney. It commenced cruises and, for a while, all went well. But within a short period of time operating costs went up, as passenger numbers went down – an ominous combination. The share price started to slide, as did our interest. We sold out at a loss realising it had been a terrible mistake to invest in the first place. We didn't pursue the other water-based investments we'd been eyeing as we'd now had our fingers well and truly burnt! (Interestingly enough, our paddle steamer, *Showboat*, still paddles around Sydney Harbour.)

In New Zealand we had an idea to fill a niche in another market. Because of our expertise with young people, we set up a separate company called 'Students World'. This would specialise in offering schools customised, educational group tours to our operating areas of Europe, Australia and America. We had the expertise on the ground so it was just a matter of marketing. We had an ex-school teacher head up the operation but, while he did manage to get one group away to Europe, dealing with school committees became very tiresome. They wanted us to incorporate all their special requirements at little or no extra cost, plus run the tours so cheaply, it would turn out to be virtually at cost. The concept was worth a try but we soon realised the effort required meant it would not be commercially viable. Another one bit the dust!

To ensure we covered all segments of the youth market, in the early 1980s we started to develop a product in association with Farthings Club aimed at the growing backpacker market. We could see the potential of this new sector (how right we were!) and started scoping a worldwide network of back packer hostels. We planned to name the new product 'SuperTramp', which we thought was an appropriate moniker. Unfortunately, we had too many other projects on the boil at the time and were not able to follow through with this.

The mistakes, failures, stuff-ups and ideas that didn't see the light of day all had a number of common elements. The main mistake was investing time, money and energy in ventures that were not within our core area of expertise. We wasted valuable personnel and cash resources on new endeavours when they could have been better directed improving our core businesses. The other was investing in businesses we could not completely control. We also took on too many initiatives at once, instead of just one or two at a time. Of course, this can be countered by the fact that if opportunities are not taken at the time, they can be lost.

It's all about taking calculated risks and where possible having a fall back position – something we did not always adhere to. We often fell over, but each time we had the courage to get back up and try again – sometimes we even learned from the experience and didn't make the same mistake again! We were always aware of failure, but never feared it. For me in particular it also took some time to learn not to allow your heart to rule your head. In business, an idea, no matter how brilliant it may seem at the time, must in the end be commercial or add value to a product or service to be successful.

27. A LITIGIOUS SOCIETY

There was simply no way I could anticipate some of the situations the company would encounter, especially with regard to lawyers and litigation. A typical tale involves a young American lawyer and his newly wed wife, who joined a European hotel tour for their honeymoon.

On the first night, the tour stayed in a hotel in the Pigalle quarter of Paris. When the innocent wife peered out the window she was horrified to see prostitutes plying their trade on the street below. Mortified, upset and almost inconsolable she became convinced their hotel bed had been 'used' by one of these women of the night. The couple checked out immediately and moved to an upmarket hotel.

So affected by the incident, they flew back to America the next day. The lawyer husband then proceeded to throw the book at us for destroying their honeymoon. He sued for the full refund of their tour fares, return airfares and damages for hurt, humiliation and loss of enjoyment – way over the top with his demands. He aggressively threatened to broadcast to the world what a cheap and lousy tour operator we were, clearly trying to prove to his darling wife what a fine man she had married.

There was no way we were going to give in to his ridiculous demands and the publicity blackmail, and decided to defend the case just as aggressively. He welcomed the challenge with open arms. First we tried the concilliatory approach, bending over backwards to reach some sort of ex gratia settlement. It didn't work. He wanted full compensation and, above all, a notch on his belt. We instructed both an American and English lawyer and set out on the long path to resolve the matter. The bills started to mount as it became clear our adversary was going to take us to the wire, and he started to get some publicity about the case.

At that point we took stock of the commercial reality. As with any court case, the legal fees are just a portion of the cost. It's also a massive amount of wasted company and staff time. We regrettably settled out of court and refunded the tour costs, airfares and a token sweetener, without admitting any liability. He had his notch!

We learnt early on the importance of treating customer complaints, no matter how small, very seriously. One bad apple can contaminate a whole bunch. The first rule was to identify an issue before it became major. Often problem passengers show signs of dissatisfaction early on. We advised our field staff to watch for this and try to diffuse any situation as quickly as possible. Often the sting can be drawn by simply asking the person to talk about the problem and hopefully it can be resolved there and then. Our staff were advised to never be confrontational, where possible agree with the passenger within reason and offer a solution. But there were times when placating certain individuals was impossible and the matter couldn't be resolved amicably.

There are certain nationalities that are extremely impatient and threaten to sue if they do not get their own way immediately. Often, the most difficult individuals are newly graduated lawyers who, full of their new-found arrogance, knew it all and wanted to make us one of their first test cases. The vast majority of passengers, however, would at least listen to reason and resolve a matter before making legal threats.

Contrary to my tone so far, I do have enormous respect for the legal fraternity. We all need a lawyer's advice or assistance at some time in our lives and overall, I have been reasonably well serviced. However, I still have a jaundiced view of the profession due to my countless encounters with them over the last 45 years. I've had more than sufficient experience, because, after all, my companies and I have shelled out millions of dollars in legal fees. Yes millions!

The excessive fees which I believe are sometimes heaped onto an unsuspecting client's tab, have always been a concern to me. I've been told by a budding lawyer, the first lesson taught at law school is: 'Before you even start to discuss the situation with your client, take down their name and address, so you know where to send the bill.'

More often than not it's impossible to check a lawyer's bill. It might list all the work done, but who knows how many hours were actually involved? I'm aware that some lawyers (and accountants) charge a fee based on what the client will bear. Wealthy? Charge 'em. Poor? Be a little gentle. And why aren't legal documents written in plain understandable English instead of in flowery ye olde English? Beats me. The profession is a law unto themselves.

Now here's an unusual story. We had a case where a male passenger took a liking to one of our male tour leaders. The tour leader was not interested in reciprocating. One evening he was minding his own business, sitting on the loo in one the camp's ablution block cubicles. The passenger came in and made advances. An altercation took place and, in desperation, our leader nearly bit off the other guy's thumb! I suppose it could have been worse with something else bitten off! The matter was eventually resolved with an appropriate cash settlement being made to the aggrieved passenger.

Below is an idea of the sorts of cases tour operators have to deal with. The following anecdotes are by no means the only cases we came up against.

Here's a case of misunderstanding. In 1982 we had a Canadian charter group, of 217 boy scouts, plus a few parents, on a European camping tour. Five coaches picked up the group in Belgium and the tour commenced. Later in the day, to their total dismay, they were taken to the camp ground for their overnight accommodation. They claimed to have had no idea they would be camping, and had assumed their accommodation was to be in hotels.

The reaction was explosive as they were adamant they had not paid for a camping tour and we were instructed to correct the situation forthwith. It became very ugly, with us being threatened with terrible consequences if we did not accommodate them in hotels. For the price they had paid there was no way this could be contemplated. Within two days several had left the tour and a couple had even flown back to Canada. The tour that survived was a disaster as the remaining parents complained incessantly, making it difficult for the boys to enjoy their experience. It turned out the travel agent had assumed that being boy scouts, they knew it was a camping tour. Yes, inevitably, both the travel agent and Contiki were sued.

Here's a case of sexual discrimination. Our coaches required fully licensed Public Service Vehicle (PSV) drivers to take the huge responsibility of driving 50 or so young passengers safely around Europe. They were also an integral part of the team, running the tour in conjunction with the tour leader. It was, therefore, necessary to hand pick drivers with the right attitude and personality to assist with the successful operation of each tour. In the 1970s the passenger mix averaged around 85 per cent female and 15 per cent male. As such, we only hired male drivers as it was essential that both crew members were male since situations often arose that required the attention of a man, particularly in countries such as Turkey and further East. In these countries, it was common for women to not receive the same respect and authority as men. Passengers preferred a male crew at times like this, as they felt a little more secure, particularly when major incidents occurred. Dealing with the authorities in certain countries was also easier with male tour leaders.

Of course, the inevitable occurred in the seventies in London, when a woman with a coach driver's licence applied for a driving position. We refused her the opportunity, reasoning with her on the grounds detailed above. She was not at all happy with our decision. We had discriminated on her gender – big, big mistake! Two days later we received a call from a women's rights organisation, asking us to confirm our decision and state our reasons.

'Would you re-consider this decision?' they asked.

'No, we would not!' we replied flatly, giving our reasoned explanation.

'Well if that's your final decision, you will be hearing from us again shortly.'

A week later we were informed that the case was going to court. It had been taken up by the organisation as a test gender discrimination case. We immediately hired a woman barrister to bat on our behalf and came up with ten defences we confidently thought would resolve the matter.

A few nights later, I was sitting in front of the TV watching the BBC news, when incredulously one of the items was our test case. The next day it was on the radio and I was interviewed for comments. Interest in the case was gathering momentum all around us. We just wanted it to go away! Eventually the case came to an end with us losing on nine of our defences but winning on the very last. As we employed our drivers in Holland at our base in Hellevoetsluis, the English law at that time did not stretch to Holland. Phew!

The woman who had originally applied for the job and started the whole circus had the courage and character to front up in person later to apologise for what she had put us through. At the time of her complaint she understandably felt rejected but had been railroaded into taking up the case against us. She had no idea it would become such a high profile case and added she now understood the reasons for our original decision. However, we had learnt a lesson. In later years when the female/male ratio became more balanced, we hired female drivers and tour leaders. It turned out that many of our female field staff were often our best. Why? They were often more conscientious, very good with detail and, importantly, could keep their mind above their belt!

How about one based on age discrimination? When we advertised for a sales representative for the Queenstown Lodge in New Zealand, we had a huge response. We ended up hiring a young lady in her mid twenties to represent the property. She was the perfect image. The lodge was built primarily as an accommodation facility for 18–35 year olds and everything was geared for this age group. We had young, vibrant staff and projected an image to the market that said: 'If you are 18–35, and visiting Queenstown, there is only one place to stay'. After the interviews, we let the unsuccessful candidates know and thought that was the end of the story. It was not to be. One of the rejected rang the company, asking why he had not been successful. It was explained to him that although he was well qualified, we had found someone else more suitable. Then came the question: 'Was my age a factor?' He was informed it was one of the factors. The immediate response was 'So I was discriminated against, due to my age? You will be hearing more about this'. We didn't have to tell people why they had not been chosen – we did it to be fair and honest. Big mistake!

A week later we received a letter from the New Zealand Human Rights Commission telling us we were facing prosecution. To avoid going to court, we ate humble pie, wrote a groveling letter to the Commission and gave an undertaking to never discriminate on age again. Given this assurance we avoided court but were required to pay the unsuccessful candidate a substantial sum to lessen his hurt feelings. The candidate, incidentally, was 62 years old!

How about one based on supposed false advertising? Originally Contiki Tours was promoted as 'exclusively' for 18–35 year olds. On one occasion we had a 22 year old passenger who demanded her money back. Her justification? There had been another female passenger on the same tour aged 37. The younger woman had not had a particularly good tour. The tour leader may have rejected her advances or maybe she'd fallen out with the older passenger … who knows? Anyway, she claimed we had falsely advertised the tour and we were forced to repay a portion of her tour fare. Ironically, if we had refused to book the older passenger, *she* could have sued us for discrimination! You can't win! After that encounter, all Contiki publicity material was hastily switched to say 'recommended' for 18–35s.

Here's a case based on racial discrimination. We advertised for an accounts clerk for our London office and one applicant, a West Indian with totally unsuitable English speaking skills and presentation, applied for the job. He made it clear that he had an accounting qualification suited to the position. A few days later we rang to inform him he had not been successful and that we'd given the job to another applicant. This latter part, admittedly, was not true, because at that stage we had not yet filled the position. An hour or so later we received a call from a man asking if the position was still available. We responded that indeed it was and we would be only too happy to interview him.

'My friend has just been told he didn't get the job and that you had filled the position,' came the chilling reply. 'He has the right qualifications so we believe this is a blatant case of discrimination due to his colour. You will be hearing more about this.' Luckily, we didn't, but it was another wake up call and goes to show how very tenuous it can be hiring the staff you actually want.

Over the years the company has been involved in a number of major accidents, some extremely tragic. Contiki treated the safety of its passengers as its top priority – just like the major airlines – but accidents still occur, some of which are self-inflicted, as the following incident illustrates. Yet, we were held accountable.

In 1989 an American guest was staying at the Whitsunday Island resort. He spent a considerable amount of his time at the bar and often became quite inebriated. Late one night he decided to take a swim in the resort's main swimming pool. He dived into the shallow end hitting his head on the bottom of the pool, tragically breaking his neck. He was flown home and now faced life as a quadriplegic. He sued us for around US$5 million, claiming we should not have allowed him to become intoxicated to the point where he decided to dive into the pool. We handed the case over to our insurance company, who fortunately settled the matter on our behalf. If ever there was a perfect example for having comprehensive insurance this was it.

I have always believed in taking full insurance to cover for the unexpected. We had insurance brokers in all of our operating regions. Each time we would fully brief them on our activities and ask them to prioritise the cover we needed for any eventuality. Our worldwide premiums came at a significant cost but in reality it was simply a case of having a 'fall back position'.

How about one of litigation the other way around? You will recall we invested around NZ$5 million in Fullers Corporation, the company that operated cruises on Auckland Harbour and the Bay of Islands? We felt extremely aggrieved, to say the least, at the demise of the company, particularly so soon after our investment had been made. We had relied on the PricewaterhouseCoopers audited accounts, which we subsequently believed did not reflect the true position of the company. We took the very best legal advice, which encouraged us to go after all the parties concerned and sue them for the amount we had lost. So we appointed legal council and brought charges against all the partners of PricewaterhouseCoopers, all the directors of Fullers in the Auckland operation, and the directors of the Bay of Islands one.

Our legal advisors were extremely confident of our position. We left no stone unturned and appointed one of New Zealand's top Queen's Counsel to act for us. He was incredibly expensive, but we considered it a good investment as surely we would get the costs back? Initially we endeavoured to settle out of court to avoid the potential of a long, drawn-out court case. Immediately one group of defendants (The Bay of Islands directors), settled without accepting any liability, but unfortunately, the others did not. No doubt they had received advice from their legal advisors that they too would win, as we had.

We went to court almost a year to the day after we had made our original share purchase in 1987. It was a long and extremely acrimonious case. We only won against three of the Fullers Auckland defendants, one of whom had conveniently left the country for good, so we couldn't claim on him. The other two planned to appeal, so the case would continue ad infinitum. In the interests of commercial reality and common sense we withdrew the case. In the end, with Fullers going into receivership, we lost our entire investment of NZ$5 million plus added legal fees of NZ$3 million.

The financial cost was only one penalty, the other was the enormous stress I was placed under, and with so much at stake it was almost unbearable. Day in, day out, I sat in that acrimonious courtroom, listening to the lawyers tearing everyone apart. The lesson learnt was simple. Litigation is an extremely costly and personally crippling way to settle a matter. So often, the only winners are the lawyers.

28. A LIFE-CHANGING EXPERIENCE

In 2005, a crew from TV New Zealand filmed a reunion for Contiki staff and passengers from the early years, held over an April weekend at the Convention Centre in Sydney. More than 500 people attended, many flying in from places such as South Africa, Europe, Canada and America and, of course, New Zealand. The event was so significant that the footage was aired on a nightly current affairs show on TV 1, the main TV channel in New Zealand.

Before the event, I had set about tracking down the original 11 passengers from that legendary minibus trip around Europe in 1962. With help, unbelievably, I managed to track down all 11 passengers! Regrettably one was deceased but the other 10 were living in Australia and New Zealand. All are now aged in their late sixties, the majority of whom are married and can account for over a score of children between them. Five of the original passengers attended the reunion, it being the first time we had met for 44 years! And, of the original 10 minibus drivers from that early period, eight were present. None of them had appreciated how large and successful Contiki had become. They were the pioneers and on listening to Dave Hosking's presentation (the current Managing Director of Contiki) about the company in the present day – they were quite simply blown away.

Of special significance was the attendance of the original gang of six: John and Ali Anderson, John and Mary Tingey, Peter Blake and Marg Thornton (Peter's first wife). Our friendship is still as it was all those years ago. Can you just imagine the emotion and elation we all shared; the passengers, staff and the gang of six meeting again after all those years? There was a lot of hugging and many emotional tears flowed. The memories seemed as vivid as if it all happened yesterday. We all had something in common – we had experienced Europe in our early twenties. Contiki had for the vast majority of us changed our lives.

But although this was a big affair, it wasn't out of the ordinary. The number of Contiki reunions held every year around the world is countless. There are reunions still being held by groups who travelled in the early 1960s, right up to those who travelled last year. I attended one a couple of years ago in Taupo with a tour group I drove in 1964 – 45 years ago. We watched the colour slides of the trip, crying with laughter as we relived our experiences together. More recently I was invited to attend a reunion in 2011, of a group who travelled on SP/1 (Spain Portugal & Morocco) in 1976. Of the original 26 passengers, 22 have confirmed they will be attending plus the crew of three and the trainee! The memories of those tours are still indelibly imprinted on the passengers' minds to this day.

The number of marriages the company has been the catalyst for runs into the thousands, with me, and my old friends Peter and Jet being typical examples! But it's not just the passengers who have found their future partners, but also the staff. Of course the field staff were forbidden to fraternise with the passengers – a lost cause! It was inevitable, particularly with the male staff, many of whom had temporary relationships while on tour with our female passengers (known as 'flowers') where the relationship would bloom into a permanent arrangement. I am unable to quantify how many marriages Contiki has been responsible for – perhaps 10,000? However, with regular stories of a single tour being responsible for five or six, perhaps the number could be closer to 20,000!

The lifetime friendships made by passengers and staff on tour are legendary. Absolute strangers from all over the world, from varying backgrounds, are thrown together in a totally foreign environment. The friendships that subsequently emerge, I believe, are one of the greatest contributions Contiki has made to those passengers' lives. If it was not for the product that brought them together, they would never have met.

I am aware of many passengers who met on tour, not only became friends, but went into business together. Often passengers already in business comment that their Contiki tour opened up opportunities for them. They may be negotiating a contract with a total stranger or attempting to sell them something, only to find they had both travelled Contiki in the past. With an experience they could both relate to, the relationship enters a new and different plane. There are similar stories of passengers or staff applying for jobs. It's almost like belonging to a secret club.

I still travel a lot today on speaking engagements and constantly meet people – both staff and passengers – who say their Contiki experience is 'still one of the highlights of my life'. Many go so far as to say that 'It is still the highlight, because it changed my life'.

I believe this is because they travelled or worked with Contiki at such an early and impressionable age and associate so many 'first-time' experiences with the tour they will never forget. It was perhaps the first time they felt exhilarated by total freedom, saw things they'd never seen before, or met new and amazing people. No one forgets their formative years, and Contiki contributed to that period in many young people's lives in such a positive way.

Over the years I've met many ex-Contiki tour leaders and drivers who in later years have gone on to be incredibly successful in their chosen career. Some have achieved way beyond their original dreams and sure, some have fallen by the wayside. But success is not just what you achieve in your chosen vocation, it's also what you achieve in your own personal life. I believe their time working for the company made an enormous difference and helped mould them into the people they are today.

I've asked many of them what they learned from Contiki in those early days of their adult lives, the majority then in their early twenties. They have said that through the experience, they learned patience, tolerance, negotiating skills both with people and suppliers, planning ahead, self belief – the list is endless. I have narrowed down the most important things that they have told me they learnt.

- We learnt leadership.
- We learnt to make decisions.
- We learnt to take responsibility.
- We learnt to have confidence in our own ability to do the job we'd been trained to do.

But above all there was one thing more important than the other four combined.

- We learnt how to communicate and get along with people.

And that's what I reckon life is all about!

*

I'd now like to swing the spotlight over to some of the passengers, and ex-Contiki staff, to let you as the reader hear from them in their own words, not in mine, how Contiki was a life-changing experience.

'I worked for Contiki for 23 years and married a beautiful woman who also worked for the company. I've been to Contiki weddings, funerals, reunions and count amongst my lifelong friends many, many ex-Contiki-ites. To say Contiki has played a significant part in my life is an understatement. I'm eternally grateful. The many thousands of smiling faces that I have seen and still see today – the brand and legend of Contiki is alive and well!' MS

'As a tour manager I learnt a great deal about people. There are so many different types and we all have something to offer. How lucky was I to spend some of the best years of my life travelling around, showing people the beautiful sights of Europe and ensuring they all had a fantastic time!' MT

'I met my husband in the Rome camp in July 1969. He was a South African and I was from New Zealand. Forty years later we have three children who have all travelled with Contiki ... and we are still good to go!!' KS

'I went from being a naïve 19 year old whose mother would hardly let her daughter catch a Sydney suburban train, to being a well travelled, experienced and mature woman before my 21st birthday. I loved the camaraderie that accompanied the only time in your life you are free of responsibility, don't have to go to work, have money to spend and have action-packed exciting days and nights meeting new friends and lifelong buddies.' LH

'I will never ever forget my Contiki experience. It totally changed my life as it opened my eyes to another world outside of my hometown of Townsville. The people I met and lived with on tour became my family for six weeks. Those wonderful memories will be with me forever. If only I could do it all over again!' AJ

'My husband of 29 years and I met on tour in 1979. I was engaged to be married to another man at the time, but was taking the trip as a last fling with my best friend, my fiance's sister. Upon introducing ourselves to the rest of the group, my friend told everyone I was engaged to her brother and she was my chaperone. That was a challenge one man couldn't resist and I couldn't resist him. The rest is history.' PY

'I met my husband on tour and our beautiful daughter Catherine was conceived in the Copenhagen camp ground!' CC

'Sometimes I can't believe I lived the life of a supercook for six months. All those early mornings, late nights, living out of a suitcase, constantly thinking about FOOD ... where to buy it, what to cook, did we need more gas, please don't let it rain! I also learnt to be more tolerant, inventive, resourceful and understanding.' MA

'For me, Contiki was the essential "rite of passage". It was my first really big adventure and it has always remained one of my fondest memories in life. I still recommend parents encourage their of-age children to consider a Contiki tour. It also taught many of us the values of working together, resolving conflicts, tolerance, compassion for others and sharing experiences with one another.' SN

'As a staff member, it was the basis for all life experiences that followed. The incredible experience of working 24/7 with people from all over, and having to cope in almost third world conditions, and coming out the other side sane and wanting more. It ruined every subsequent experience because how can you compare? It changed my life!' MM

'A shy girl from Dunedin became a trail-blazer. The first Great Britain trips, then the first 12 weekers, then the first cook in Holland. I became a confident person and a good cook and the four years working for Contiki where the HAPPIEST days of my life. Thank you!' LS

'Whenever I'm having a really bad day I often reflect back on the happy days I enjoyed on my Contiki tour way back in 1988. Such a fun time with such special memories that always seem to lift me. But sometimes nostalgia sets in and I feel worse, as I would love to repeat the whole experience again, but know I can't, but my children have!' AJ

'At the age of 31 I was a late follower of the Contiki magic, but by the time I had done my last tour at the age of 38 I had completed nine memorable tours. Contiki gave me confidence to meet people and challenge myself to explore new places and accept different cultures. It's a pity that the Contiki concept does not extend to tours beyond the age of 35. John if you do start tours for this age group I would be one of the first to join.' PM

'There were so many first experiences on my tour. The first time I'd been out of my comfort zone living with a group of strangers – 48 of them – the first time I'd met a South African who told me all about apartheid, the first time I'd learnt European history, the first time I'd drunk a stein of beer (in fact two), the first time I laughed so much I peed my pants, the first time I'd fallen in love. Thank you Contiki.' AD

'As a young Contiki tour guide in 1972 I took a bunch of happy campers on my first nine-weeker around 16 European countries. I had to lie a little to get the job in the first place (being a tad young) but that's another story! Some 36 years later, every three years the majority of those passengers gather for a reunion. For each of them, and myself, that trip had a profound and long lasting effect ... we're still great friends and relive the humour and the stories from that trip all too frequently! It's only a matter of time before their grand kids are doing their OE!' PC

'The summer of 1981 was the most amazing time. I was working as a chef at the Chateau de Cruix in France with a mixed staff of Aussie, Kiwi, Canadian and English people. We built such a close bond. It sounds clichéd to say we were like a family but it felt just like that. The laughs and antics we got up to are still so clear now. I remember that time with extreme fondness.' LS

'In 1980, Aussie girl Shayne Keating organised the trip of a lifetime for herself and four others. Feeling very ill after the Grand European, Shayne had to pull out of the Russia/Scandi tour. She was diagnosed with advanced breast cancer and died six months after her tour, aged 23. As her younger sister, I went through all this with her and later become a Contiki Tour Leader and Operations Manager of Contiki Australia. Shayne spent a lot of her remission finishing her Contiki photo albums and I like to think that she left this world with joyous memories of the wonderful time she had with Contiki.' DM

'I believe Contiki has become a "rite of passage" for so many young people. On my 36th birthday I received a card wishing me all the best with an added comment "There is now one thing in life you will never be able to do – go Contiki again!"' DA

As you can see, Contiki has had such an impact on so many people's lives. I'm sure it will continue to do so for many more years to come.

29. A WORLDWIDE OPERATION

Towards the end of 1988 I reflected back over the past incredible 27 years I had just travelled through. It had all started with a need – a need for me to see Europe. It then developed into me wanting to show other young people 'my Europe' to give them a similar experience to the one I had originally enjoyed. Then, over the ensuing years the establishment of a recognised international tour operator with the iconic brand name – Contiki.

It has been the most amazing journey, a journey I have wanted to share with you. Nothing just happened, we had to make it happen. We had the courage to give things a go because we believed in the product we were creating, believed in the brand, but above all believed in ourselves. On so many occasions we fell over and failed, but had the courage to get up and try again, but these were more than compensated for by so many of our brilliant successes.

Throughout Europe we had developed and established a major tour operation carrying our young passengers through a staggering 32 countries including the United Kingdom, Ireland, France, Spain, Italy, Morocco, Algeria, Portugal, Greece, Turkey, Yugoslavia, Austria, Switzerland, Andorra, Monaco, Gibraltar, Liechtenstein, Germany, Holland, Belgium, Finland, Sweden, Denmark, Norway, Russia, Poland, Czechoslovakia and extended into Egypt, Jordan, Syria, Lebanon and Israel.

We leased a fleet of around 120 Mercedes-Benz coaches and had a small fleet of European service vehicles. We had an operations base and owned a house in Hellevoetsluis and the Groothuis in Noordgouwe, Holland. We owned a French chateau and had a part-ownership of a 58-berth schooner in Greece. We leased a number of properties including a 13th century Italian villa in Florence, Italy, and a 100-bed chalet in Hopfgarten, Austria, hotels in Devon, Torquay and Caernarvon in the United Kingdom and even a boat on the Rhine River in Germany. We had 15 tent villages scattered throughout Europe, which were being turned into cabins.

In London we had our own retail store in the heart of the West End and a worldwide administration, marketing and operations centre in Bromley, south of London. We had several large hotels in the heart of London with a capacity of 2000 beds contracted to accommodate our passengers.

We had operated the Indian Overland tour through Europe, Iraq, Iran, Pakistan, India and Nepal. And, through Peter Blake, we had operated the African Overland through Kenya, Uganda, Tanzania, Rhodesia (Zimbabwe), Namibia through to South Africa.

We had developed and established a tour operation in the United States with a fleet of 20 coaches travelling through 39 states, plus Canada and Mexico. We had an operations base and sales offices in Los Angeles, a sales office in Toronto and we leased a mansion in New Orleans, Florida.

We ran tours throughout Australia with a fleet of 15 coaches and an operations base and a sales office in Sydney. We built and owned a 150-room resort hotel in the Whitsunday Islands off the Queensland coast. We were running a series of cruises around the South Pacific with *Fairstar* and the *Alexandr Pushkin* and even a local Fijian cruise on *Tua Tai*. We had owned a 30 per cent interest in the company that built the paddle steamer *Showboat* which still plies Sydney harbour.

We established a tour operation the length and breadth of New Zealand, leasing a dozen coaches, with an operations base and sales office in Auckland. We built, owned and operated a 120-bed lodge in Queenstown, owned chalets in Methven near the Mount Hutt ski field and a 65-room hotel in downtown Auckland. We built and owned a 150-room resort hotel in Queenstown.

Under the JAGWAR subsidiary Worldmark, we owned and operated tourism assets. We owned a major camp ground in Rotorua plus land on the outskirts of Auckland. We owned a white water river rafting operation in Queenstown and had part ownership of one in the North Island. We had a part ownership in a jet boat operation, a photography company and owned a T-shirt manufacturing business in Queenstown. We owned a thermal reserve and a float plane company in Rotorua. We had set up tourist information centres in both Rotorua and Queenstown. We owned a 30 per cent interest in a major Auckland Harbour Cruise Company.

In addition to our own sales offices we had appointed General Sales Agents to represent us in other parts of the world including Singapore, Malaysia, Hong Kong, Mexico, Holland, Italy, France, Germany and Scandinavia.

We had divided our worldwide operations into four geographical regions, each with its own company and board of directors who had total autonomy. We had moved the residency of the group to Hong Kong.

We had taken onboard a financially strong new partner, Omnicorp, as a shareholder who had bought 50 per cent of the company with a massive injection of development capital. In addition we had gained new expertise on our board to assist us to take Contiki into what we all knew would be an even more successful future. In 1988 we would carry 50,000 passengers with a turnover approaching US$65 million.

We had constantly reinvested Contiki's profits back into the business to ensure we built a strong base and a viable company for the future.

Together we had created a company that would give other young people the opportunity to see other parts of the world they may not normally have been able to see and experience on their own.

At this point I want to acknowledge all those people who, over the years, contributed to making Contiki what it was then and what it has gone on to be today. To those staff and suppliers for their total dedication and commitment creating such a special company, I say thank you. You can be justly proud of your achievements. And finally to those Contiki passengers – without you, there would not have been a business.

30. THE WHEELS FALL OFF

On Monday, 19 October 1987 the world sharemarkets collapsed and crashed. The clock had begun to tick.

When news of the crash flashed through, it was a Tuesday, Australian time, and I was visiting Sydney. I was not too concerned as I'd seen downward drops in the market before. Everyone was astounded by how heavily the market dropped but the general feeling was that it would correct itself within a few days, though perhaps not back to the level previously enjoyed. The next day the market dropped further and some panic selling began. Since I owned a significant share portfolio in publicly listed companies, equivalent to around US$4 million dollars, I contacted the two sharebrokers who acted on my behalf asking them for advice.

'John, just stay calm and ride the situation out,' was their advice, though my intuition was that they were just as confused as I was.

On the third day the market fell even further and I received a telephone call from Lloyd Morrison, the chief executive of Omnicorp, our new shareholder. He knew I had an extensive share portfolio, although he didn't know I was geared 50 per cent with my own money and 50 per cent with a personal loan from the Bank of New Zealand. Lloyd was blunt.

'John, I'm very serious, this fall is no blip,' he said. 'We think the market will continue to fall with little likelihood of a turnaround. It has all the signs of staying at depressed levels for a considerable period of time and I recommend you immediately sell the majority, if not all of your shares and, if you have any debt, pay it off!' He then abruptly hung up on me.

The Black Monday (US time) stock market decline turned out to be the biggest one-day percentage decline in stock market history and, to this day, eludes easy explanation. At the time, I was not at all enthusiastic to act on Lloyd's recommendation. My sharebrokers had told me to hang in there and there was no way I was going to sell at such low, fire sale prices. I decided to sit on the fence and wait awhile.

The following day Lloyd called again. On discovering I hadn't heeded his advice he made me promise to sell 50 per cent of my portfolio that very day. I placed an order with my brokers to sell just 30 per cent. They were reluctant to carry out my instructions but, on my insistence, they did it. Over the next ten days, with Lloyd constantly badgering me, I sold out in total. The catastrophic loss I had sustained wiped out my paper profits completely and a large percentage of my own investment cash. The sale proceeds were insufficient to pay off the total loan related to the shares. However, Lloyd's insistence to sell did prevent me from suffering far greater losses if I had held on longer.

Fortunately, the crash had little to no effect on Contiki's trading. Passenger numbers kept rising and the company continued to prosper. However, the world property market was also starting to crash. As a result, over the following year the value of the Whitsunday and Queenstown resorts we were building started to plummet. On the personal front, the value of my family home in Auckland also started to fall. I had mortgaged it as security to raise funds to buy the new shares in Contiki that had been issued when Omnicorp bought 50 per cent of the company.

By Christmas 1988 the value of our now completed resorts had fallen like a stone, halving in value. What's more, the ratio of equity to borrowings had broken the strict lending covenants of our lender, the

Bank of New Zealand (BNZ). At the outset we were geared conservatively at around 50 per cent of the cost of building the resorts. With loans on both resorts BNZ suddenly moved on us, instructing us to correct the ratio with a request for an immediate injection of funds, the equivalent of around US$8 million! There was no way the Contiki group could lay its hands on that amount of cash.

When the bank realised we did not have the funds it became extremely aggressive. It wanted its money and was not interested in any arrangement to resolve the situation. None of our reasoning was even considered.

'Pay up or we will sell you up!' was the only response when we tried.

The bank 'terriers' that were set upon us to extract the cash showed no respect at meetings, often referring to me as Anderson, not Mr Anderson. It was a frightening and terrifying personal experience, as I'd never before been treated with such disdain.

Unbeknown to us, at the same time the BNZ had a major financial crisis of its own. You may recall, when we were looking for funds to build the resorts the bank had offered us a deal so attractive that no other bank could match it. I suspect at the time they had been out buying business. They appeared to be lending to anybody and everybody – anything to improve their market share. With so many of their customers in similar situations as us they were in deep strife. I understand an instruction from on high was given to all branch managers to rake in the cash as quickly as possible. Any customer who had broken their covenants, no matter how small or large, was to be vigorously pursued. The bank was quite within its rights to do this, of course, especially since it had its own survival to worry about.

In the meantime, we were desperately trying to resolve the situation while continuing to run the Contiki group of companies (under the JAGWAR umbrella) without our predicament becoming public knowledge. If a rumour started that we were financially strapped our business could collapse overnight. Business is so often about confidence the market has in a business and we couldn't afford to lose that.

We knew our shareholder Omnicorp couldn't assist us as they too had been affected by the Black Monday crash, even more severely than us. The value of Omnicorp's other investments had tanked to the point where it had to sell its company to a Swiss company, Omni Holdings, headquartered in Zurich, Switzerland. This news was shattering as the company had lost what I thought was a strong financial partner, and I'd lost the opportunity to sell the remaining shares I owned in Contiki to the other 50 per cent shareholder – Omnicorp. The two Omnicorp directors on the Contiki board were replaced by two Swiss financial gnomes from Zurich.

We then turned to our other shareholder in the Whitsunday Resort, BLE Capital, which still had a significant loan advanced on the property. BLE's Chairman, with whom I had an excellent relationship, came to New Zealand to assist us with the impasse we had with the BNZ. He endeavoured to negotiate a deal with them but again, they were not the slightest bit interested and he was sent packing. He was staggered at the way he was treated. BLE, however, wanted to safeguard its interest in the Whitsunday Resort so appointed its top executive Peter Blizzard to take over the account and a find a solution.

Peter Blizzard was not your normal sort of banker. He had the ability to think outside the square to solve these kind of matters, rather than on 'tram rails' like some other blinkered bankers. After inspecting the Queenstown Holiday Inn and the Whitsunday Resort, he made his decision. He believed there was an excellent opportunity, given time, that together with BLE's support we could trade the resorts out of the situation. What a refreshing approach compared to BNZ's intransient stance. The pressure for full repayment of our entire loan had become almost intolerable and the BNZ were threatening to 'fire sale' the resorts. BLE Capital decided to take over the entire BNZ loan. A major fire was extinguished. The relief we felt when some of this weight lifted from our shoulders was enormous.

Incidentally, the BNZ was eventually bailed out by the New Zealand Government to the tune of $NZ 800 million! Its reckless lending policies had come back to bite it and, as a result, many of the established and profitable businesses belonging to its so-called 'valued clients' were totally destroyed.

We didn't have time to relax as no sooner had one fire been put out, another one started. This one was threatening to envelop us completely. Our new Swiss shareholder, Omni Holdings, had decided it had no interest in its newly acquired shareholding in JAGWAR. Over the last couple of years JAGWAR had started to borrow to fund the group's expansion and, with the lower valuation of the two resorts, our substantial investment in these had been lost. Without the support of Omni we were faced with the stark reality that the jewel in the JAGWAR crown – Contiki – would need to be sold.

There appeared to be no other option. For over 27 years, the directors and key personnel had worked tirelessly, putting their heart and soul into creating a unique and profitable business. We had reinvested the profits back into the company as we wanted to build a strong Contiki for the future, when our real payback would eventuate. The thought of someone else buying Contiki and receiving those future benefits was utterly devastating. Contiki was our lifeblood and we were about to lose it – it was heartbreaking.

I was summoned from New Zealand to the head office of Omni Holdings in Zurich. It took me two days to get there. My appointment to see their CEO was for 10 am the following morning. I was kept waiting some three hours before being ushered into a very large and plush office to discuss a resolution to the situation. The meeting lasted 10 humiliating minutes.

'We're not interested in being a part owner of a tourist operation and there will be no financial support,' I was told, or words to that effect. The sale of Contiki would be undertaken with the assistance of two Omni Holdings executives. I left feeling completely lifeless for the long, sad flight home to New Zealand.

A prominent London merchant bank, Bankers Trust, was appointed to assist with the sale and a sales memorandum was prepared and sent to likely candidates. I was personally keen to sell to Newman's, one of New Zealand's most respected tourism companies. However, my meeting with its CEO proved fruitless. After two months of discussions with a number of other interested parties, two companies became serious contenders – Insight and Trafalgar, both well-established and successful open age European tour operators. I personally knew their respective Managing Directors very well. Trafalgar emerged as the company who was the keenest and most able to do a deal.

Trafalgar could see the enormous synergies Contiki could bring to its existing business. With Contiki under its wing it could access a different market segment to its current mainstream business and rationalise its operations. For example, both companies had international sales offices in the same cities, but with the two brands under the one owner, only one office in each city would be required. The extra volume of passengers would bring enormous cost savings when negotiating prices with suppliers providing services such as accommodation, coaches, and even ferry tickets.

Trafalgar knew we had become a stressed seller, having no option but to sell. They were so keen to buy the Contiki business they were prepared to pay a fair and reasonable price. This was encouraging as it gave me a degree of confidence. I was also comfortable the company was going to be sold to a well-respected and well-run tour operator who knew the tour business inside out. The sale negotiating team was made up of two representatives from Omni Holdings, one from Bankers Trust and me on behalf of Contiki. Trafalgar commenced its due diligence of the company. We were all keen to complete the sale as quickly as possible to ensure as little disruption to the staff and business.

The first inkling of trouble emerged when information requested by Trafalgar from the other Contiki directors (the management team) started to stall, with the bare minimum of information being provided.

Unbeknown to me, some of the directors had been secretly plotting behind my back to launch their own 'management buyout' for Contiki, cutting me out and aiming to take over the company for themselves.

A week into negotiations with Trafalgar, the sales negotiating team received a request from the other Contiki directors for a meeting. A few days later the Managing Director Garry Draffin and the Finance Director Andrew Fleming were in London, accompanied by their high-powered banking advisor, who had flown in from Sydney especially for the occasion. Ironically the banker was from none other than the Australian branch of the Bank of New Zealand! On behalf of the management team they made an offer to buy Contiki, assuring the sales team they had the finance required in place.

I was speechless, incredulous, mortified. My anger at their move knew no bounds. How could they do this to me after so many years working and developing the business together, through thick and thin? Suddenly I was isolated, standing outside of the management group and unbelievably upset. I felt very much alone.

Despite my feelings of devastation, I could understand their move as they were keen to safeguard their own positions and their investment. They also knew full well the enormous potential the company would grow to in the years ahead. In addition, my close relationship with them had deteriorated over the preceding year due to a number of factors. Primarily, I had become stressed with the situation of the poorly trading resorts and the amount of debt they were carrying that still needed to be serviced. I was also stressed with my own personal situation as the value of my share portfolio had been hammered by the sharemarket crash and the bank pressuring me to repay my personal loan.

There was also another reason. As the company grew, the directors insisted I step even further away from day-to-day management. They wanted me to delegate more and more responsibility to them and their very capable teams, but to their constant frustration I would not let go to the extent they wanted. I was a classic entrepreneur who wanted to be in the action all the time. I kept meddling, became dictatorial and this annoyed them intensely. They also blamed me for some of the poor investments which had been made through my insistence.

The smooth pathway to the sale gave way to a difficult and rocky road. Naturally, the Contiki directors now had no interest in selling to Trafalgar. As due diligence progressed they had a large conflict of interest but still had a duty to provide the information requested by Trafalgar. They carried our their duties, but pointed out as many of the negative aspects of the company as they could, arguing it was information a new owner would want to know. The due diligence and sales process started to become acrimonious. The flow of information slowed even more due to the unenthusiastic attitude of the directors.

As the negotiations became further protracted, Trafalgar became extremely frustrated and started to talk down the amount it was prepared to pay for Contiki. This was to the benefit of the management buyout group (MBO) as it became clear it could only raise a limited amount for the purchase. Omni Holdings had control of the Contiki sale and, in the interests of selling promptly, started to strongly favour the MBO team.

At this point negotiations had been going on for around six weeks and Trafalgar realised the deal might be slipping from its grasp. Its New York-based Chairman and owner Stanley Tollman flew across the Atlantic to see if a deal could be finalised. The sales negotiating team was called to the Trafalgar offices to meet their Chairman after lunch the next day. He strode into the board room, paced the floor in front of us all, smoking a large Churchillian cigar and talked through what his company was prepared to offer. At the end of his speech he placed a US$ cheque on the table.

'This is Trafalgar's full and final offer,' he said. 'It will stand open until lunchtime tomorrow.' He made it clear that if it was not accepted he would withdraw it, further negotiations would be terminated and he would return to New York that afternoon.

The MBO team had to either match the offer or beat it. They were unable to do so. The worldwide Contiki tour operation was sold to Trafalgar

Tours on 15 July 1989. From the sales proceeds a sum was paid to the MBO team to help them defray some of the enormous advisor fees they had incurred. The balance was used to pay down debt.

The Whitsunday and Queenstown resorts, the Queenstown Lodge and a number of other assets not directly related to the Contiki tour operation were retained (with their accompanying debt) by the JAGWAR group. But the jewel in the crown was finally gone, resulting in the JAGWAR shares being worthless. The long friendship I had enjoyed for so many years with my fellow directors was also gone. Three directors are godparents to three of our children – our friendship had been that close.

I was, however, facing another personal catastrophe. The BNZ was demanding I repay the balance of the personal loan I had taken out with them to invest in Contiki at the time Omnicorp had made theirs. I had used my freehold family home as security and Ali and I had signed personal guarantees. Again BNZ was ruthless with its demand for total repayment, but alas, I had no other assets or cash. The bank threatened to bankrupt me and, as a first stage, served me with a notice to sell our home. I had no option. An estate agent was appointed and the house was put on the market.

I had bought this house in 1979, soon after Ali and I returned from the United Kingdom. This was going to be the family home our children would grow up in. It was a magnificent two-storey house with five bedrooms and a swimming pool, situated on two private acres of park-like grounds overlooking beautiful Auckland Harbour. Over the years I had invested extensively in the home by building a conservatory, pool house and tennis court. It was my pride and joy.

The word soon escaped that I was being forced to sell my house and the gossips had a field day. I will never be able to fully explain what a difficult period ensued as I battled fires on all fronts. Worst of all, my family was being dragged through it all too.

It had turned into an emotional nightmare. How could I have put Ali and my family into such a disastrous situation? We were about to lose our family home. The reality of the situation and the unbelievable embarrassment was very hard to endure. Ali stood stoically by me as we tried to support each other. So many nights the two of us sat together, trying to work out a way forward that would minimise the upheaval and disruption to our children. So many tears, so many regrets, but always constant was our devotion to each other and our family. We did, in fact, grow stronger in the face of such adversity. Although we were about to lose our home it was only a material asset which could one day be replaced. What was much more important was that the family still had each other.

At times such as this, you really find out who your true friends are. Yet Ali and I soon discovered how few we had.

Ali had good support from a couple of close and caring female friends but I had none, although I knew hundreds of people. It was only my Wellington stockbroker friend who kept in regular contact. I'm sure there were others who would liked to have given support, but simply didn't know how. That experience taught me how important it is to support those going through difficult times as, like me, they are often very much alone.

We had in the past detected on numerous occasions that many people had been extremely jealous and envious of our situation. We had an exceptionally successful business, a strong and happy marriage, four beautiful children (even two of each gender), and a family home others would die for. In New Zealand and Australia they call it the 'tall poppy syndrome' to explain how people resent others for their successes and relish seeing them fall from their high perch. It's quite unlike the United States where entrepreneurs are admired and respected for their achievements.

Many prospective buyers traipsed through the house until it was finally sold. The bank took all the sale proceeds and left us with the furniture and our two cars. I had lost our home but we had avoided bankruptcy. The day we had to vacate our house is indelibly printed on my mind. Ali and I with our four children, (Sarah 10, James 12, Peter

17, Susie 18), sadly walked down the driveway of the house, holding hands. Ali and I had tears streaming down our cheeks as our lovely home disappeared behind us, but we didn't look back until, at the end of the driveway, we all turned for a last look, and hugged each other. We were now alone and homeless.

Fortunately our next-door neighbour took pity on us and kindly allowed us to stay in a lovely old house he owned on a paddock out in the country not far from Auckland. From that day on we have rented all the houses we have lived in.

BLE Capital who was our sole banker had taken a charge over all the group's remaining assets. They engaged me to continue overseeing the trading of the two resorts and other tourism assets with a mandate to sell them. At least I still had a job! The prime objective was to pay off all the remaining debt of the group. To help ends meet, Ali also took a job becoming a receptionist at a physiotherapist and, later, a similar role at a university.

BLE continued to fund any shortfall in operating costs of the remaining businesses. Peter Blizzard (the bank's executive) was a very personable guy, with a positive attitude and confident that given time, together we could trade our way out of the situation. We worked so well together and became good friends. Within a couple of years all the smaller businesses were sold. The Queenstown Holiday Inn and the Whitsunday Resort were, however, considerably harder to sell as they were high value properties, both of which were continuing to trade at a loss.

After the sale of the Contiki tour operation, the Whitsunday Resort was permitted to use the Contiki name for a period of two years. It was then re-named 'The Island' and subsequently became a 'Radisson' resort. And in December 1993 it was sold to an Australian tourism company, Club Crocodile, and is now called Long Island Resort. The sale price was almost double what the BNZ had wanted to sell for.

A year later in 1994 the Holiday Inn was sold to a Singaporean company for $NZ21.5 million. This was almost double what the BNZ would have achieved at the fire sale price of $NZ11 million it had planned to sell it for. With time, patience and support from our new bankers, the result was outstanding. Soon after, the property was re-launched as a Novotel and today it is a Mercure. So often when a company runs into a temporarily adverse financial position, a bit of patience and time can give it the opportunity to trade its way out of the situation.

The eventual outcome from the two sales was amazing, as it paid off the entire outstanding BLE debt, plus all the accrued interest. BLE stated it was the best outcome it had ever experienced in trading a company out of its difficulties. The Queenstown Lodge was the very last asset to be sold. The prime objective had been fulfilled, with nothing remaining but the worthless shell of the JAGWAR Holdings.

Over the next few years Ali and I managed to survive with Ali working full time. BLE were so pleased with the sale of the remaining JAGWAR assets, in appreciation they assisted me in establishing a new business setting up a chain of retail stores in Auckland selling pre-packaged fresh food. However, an unsuccessful store operating in the America's Cup village in 2000 put an end that venture.

*

Early in 2002, after the last of our children left the nest, Ali and I decided on a change of lifestyle. We moved away from Auckland to a country town in the South Island of New Zealand. We had little money but fortunately through an ex-Contiki staff member we were able to rent an amazing homestead situated on a deer farm.

I wanted to start another business but had limited confidence and no start-up money. Sound familiar? Yes, I was right back at square one in the same position I'd been in exactly 40 years before! I took on a number of management consulting jobs and even ended up pruning and wrapping grape vines for a local wine company. With our entrepreneurial flair still alive, Ali produced copious bottles of quince and crabapple jelly, which she sold at the local farmers' market. Later, I bought 2000 olive trees from a nursery that was closing down and joined Ali to sell them at the local markets. We both loved the experience and the local country people we met. Living in a country town turned out to be a wonderful new life for us.

One morning I received a call that was to change our lives. A local resident, Malcolm Taylor, who knew a little about Contiki asked if I would like to speak at the National Sheep and Beef Farmer's Conference he was organising in Napier, New Zealand. They wanted a speaker with a truly inspirational business success story. I duly accepted and delivered the talk, receiving an extremely enthusiastic ovation. A professional speaker at the same conference heard me and told her speaking agency about me and my story. The owner of 'Celebrity Speakers' in Auckland contacted me soon after, suggesting the next time I was in town she would like to meet with me to explore the possibility of becoming a professionally paid speaker.

An opportunity had crossed my path – and I grabbed it! I promptly replied saying I just happened to be coming to Auckland the following week and may just be able to squeeze in a meeting with her. Of course, I had no such plans but why delay? This was an opportunity I had to explore. I promptly booked my flight, met the owner Debbie Tawes, and two days later I was given my first well-paid speaking assignment. I carefully crafted a presentation to suit the client's brief and again presented to a very responsive and enthusiastic audience.

I have now been on the professional speaking circuit for four years. I'm represented by a number of the top speaking agencies and travel extensively throughout Australia, New Zealand, the South Pacific and South East Asia.

I love telling and sharing my story with others in the hope it will help and inspire them to achieve. It may be taking that first step into starting up their own business, or having the courage to give something a go in an existing business. I don't talk about the catastrophic events Ali and I endured after that 1987 sharemarket crash; I've saved those for this book.

It has taken considerable courage for Ali and me to expose the full details relating to our demise. Naturally, it has left us feeling a little vulnerable, but we believe it does not take away, even one iota, from what we achieved over a period of 28 years, in creating an international business and brand that has and will continue to change the lives of so many young people in the future.

EPILOGUE: CONTIKI INTO THE NEW MILLENNIUM

Now you've read my story. I hope you have found it entertaining, amusing, occasionally sad, but overall inspiring and thought provoking. I parted ways with Contiki in 1989 but the company went on to grow and prosper under its new ownership over the next 20 years.

The registered headquarters of Contiki moved from Hong Kong to Bermuda. Dave Hosking – the whiz kid from the early days who had so many hunks of meat thrown at him – was appointed as the new Managing Director of Contiki. In 1996 he moved from London to Geneva in Switzerland, where he has resided ever since, still with the overall responsibility of running the company.

Over the next year the other directors resigned from the company for a variety of reasons. Of the original JAGWAR directors, Garry Draffin and Wayne Page had already moved to Australia, with Andrew Fleming following soon after. All moved to Australia with the wives they had met while working for Contiki. They preferred the good life in Australia to bring up their families just as I had chosen New Zealand. Richard Lewis returned to live back in New Zealand. Alison Lloyd moved from her director role at Contiki, to a marketing role at Trafalgar Tours where she remained for several years, but has since moved on.

Contiki became much more commercial in the way it was run. This was inevitable, as it had become a large international organisation requiring a very sophisticated management structure. With the combined tour companies (Contiki, Trafalgar, Insight and AAT Kings) now owned by a holding company, The Travel Corp., considerable rationalisation was carried out such as the overseas sales offices of the four companies being combined at each location. The brand names, however, were kept strictly apart from one another. This is especially pleasing to me as the Contiki brand has remained synonymous with quality and the youth market and I still feel a part of that brand.

To safeguard the reliability and supply of coaches in Europe, The Travel Corp. purchased the entire Vermaat coaching operation in Holland. When left-hand coaches were permitted to operate in the United Kingdom, the Contiki operation base was moved back to the United Kingdom on the outskirts of London.

Many of the special stopovers were deleted from the European tour programme. The Villa Torre de Gattia in Florence was required by the local authorities to implement very strict new building regulations, which proved to be commercially unrealistic, so the lease was terminated. The Artemis boat in Greece became too small for the increased volume of passengers and, owing to its size, was often unable to sail in certain weather conditions. The Groothuis in Holland, with the operations base moved, became surplus to requirements and was sold. The boat on the Rhine was sacrificed owing to irreconcilable differences with the owner and skipper. However, Chateau du Cruix in France remains and I estimate over 350,000 people have had the experience of staying there and partying down in The Cave.

Contiki operations in Australia, New Zealand and America have continually been improved with even more innovations and over the years have all grown in size. Contiki worldwide now carries over 100,000 passengers every year, with a turnover of several hundred million dollars!

A few years ago I was speaking with Dave Hosking about the worldwide Contiki operation.

'JD, we haven't changed much from the original concept,' he told me. 'All we have done is tighten things up a bit and offer a few more options. The basics are still the same.'

Contiki re-introduced tours around South Africa starting in 1997 but they were withdrawn after four years due to a lack of sales. In 2009, Contiki introduced a range of tours to South East Asia.

In Europe the areas of operation have been extended considerably. There is now a choice of options and departure dates on offer to suit virtually everybody. Our youngest daughter Sarah recently took a Contiki eight-day cruise along the Croatian Coast. Initially, she was reluctant to go (so like her mother 42 years ago!), but on return she raved on and on about the experience. Interesting too, is that our son Peter chose to drive coaches for the opposition, Eurobus around Europe and also for Kiwi Experience in New Zealand for a year. He felt more comfortable driving for the competition, so he could never be outed as the Contiki founder's son! Our oldest daughter Susie worked on the Whitsunday Resort for a period. Now working as a graphic designer, Susie also had input into the cover design of this book. Our other son, James, works in the film industry and is hoping to make a documentary of the Contiki story at some stage in the future – all he needs is the funding. It's a real family affair!

My children will all vouch for the fact that I have always said to them: 'Achieve something worthwhile with your life.'

I repeat 'Achieve – something – worthwhile – with – your – life!' I'm so proud of what that original group of young people achieved with Contiki, and the subsequent generations who have progressed the company to what it is today. To date Contiki has given just over two million young people the opportunity to see other parts of the world. But what's more important to me is the fact that they have seen them in the company of other young people of different nationalities, ethnic backgrounds, religious beliefs, opinions and values.

I started Contiki with a simple idea, just £25 and a belief in myself and those around me. Today I'm proud to leave a legacy.

Whenever I see a Contiki coach on the street or on the highway anywhere around the world, packed full of young people having fun, I always look up and wave. They don't know who I am, but I know what we have given them.

And what of John Anderson now?

'I simply have the memories.'

'TAKE THE CHALLENGE'

Thank you for reading my story. I would like to invite you to participate in this challenge. If you are in business, why not encourage your staff to do the same?

Throughout *Only Two Seats Left* there are a number of *personal and business messages* I have shared with you. I hope you have found some of these are of benefit to you personally, or perhaps how they could relate to your own vocation or business. Many of these messages contain advice on what to do when building your own project or business, but more importantly, some provide an insight into what not to do!

To enter go to: **www.onlytwoseatsleft.com/challenge**. You must identify, list and prioritise what you believe are the most important messages, both personal and business. A short written paragraph about the book *Only Two Seats Left* is also required to complete your entry. The challenge will be open until 31 January 2011. All entries from around the globe will be collated and compiled to find out what readers believe are the top priorities. These results will be made available on the website on 10th February 2011. This will give everyone who has taken the challenge a chance to compare individual lists with what the rest of the world thinks.

The winner aged under 35 will receive a **Contiki** 21 day hotel tour of Europe. The winner aged over 35 will receive a **Contours** 21 day tour of South America.

GO ON – 'TAKE THE CHALLENGE!'

SOUTH AMERICA – HERE WE COME!

Have you ever dreamed of travelling to South America to explore and experience the wonders of this great continent? Ali and I had, so we decided to do just that!

We contacted Ted Dziadkiewicz who, after his time as one of Contiki's early minibus drivers, went on to visit South America. He enjoyed the experience so much he set up his own tour operation. (Sound familiar?) Ted and 'Contours' recently celebrated an impressive 35 years of successfully operating tours to Latin America.

With an extensive itinerary prepared by Ted and his team, Ali and I visited Chile, Peru, Bolivia, Argentina and Brazil, accompanied by personal guides. We were amazed by what we saw and experienced. On completion I had the same feeling I'd had after my first year in Europe. I had to show others this unique and exciting continent.

Two years ago, Ted and I teamed up to create a new and exclusive series of tours to South America, designed specifically for the 'Baby Boomer' generation. We have named it the 'Contours Collection'.

We took all the key elements that had made Contiki so successful and adapted them to suit the different age group (45–65). The tour series includes the main sights, with many off-the-beaten-track tours, and some sensational inclusions. Small groups (a maximum of 18 people), a wide range of transport (flights, buses, trains and boats), more comfort (4–5 star accommodation), unique sights and experiences (such as local community projects) and each tour accompanied throughout by an experienced tour leader.

For further details go to **www.contourstravel.com.au/thecollection**

Corporate Incentives
Contours also specialise in group tours to South America specifically designed for the incentive market. If you are in business and are looking for a unique opportunity to reward your high achievers, why not consider something different – a specially tailored tour of South America.
Contact: **tedD@contourstravel.com.au**

SPEAKING ENGAGEMENTS

Over the last four years I have enjoyed speaking to an extensive range of audiences. These have included the staff of the major Australian banks, corporates such as McDonalds, Shell, Canon, Westfield, Ericsson, Jetstar, Telstra, and a wide variety of franchise groups. I have also been asked to speak to graduates at their graduation ceremonies.

I am an an inspirational speaker able to adapt my presentations to suit any type of audience or occasion, be it a keynote address, the opening or closing of a conference or as an after-dinner speaker.

My aim is to inspire, engage, entertain and provide the audience with valuable personal and business messages. These include reference to taking calculated risks, branding, sales and marketing, innovation, teamwork, training, quality, competition and change, to mention just a few.

Here are a few comments from some of my clients:

'Extremely well received, did his research and fine tuned his address which had tremendous relevance, delivered powerful messages to a diverse mix of professionals and academics, he has a great sense of humour – outstanding!' **CPA Australia**

'Heartfelt, emotional, touched people, connected with the audience, received standing ovation, people swarmed him afterwards, genuine, passionate, loved him.' **Tourism New Zealand**

'Blew everyone away, gave it everything, his presentation was spot on, he understood the brief perfectly.' **Coca-Cola Australia**

'John's presentation was not only outstanding, but was considered by many to be the highlight of the entire event. John's story was informative, entertaining and moving leaving us inspired and emotional. John more than exceeded all our expectations. 10/10.' **RACV Australia**

If you would like to consider me for a speaking engagement, please contact me at **John_Anderson@ihug.co.nz**